Paediatric minor emergencies

Paediatric minor emergencies

James Bethel

Paediatric Minor Emergencies
James Bethel

ISBN: 978-1-905539-35-2

First published 2008

British Library Catalogue in Publication Data
A catalogue record for this book is available from the British Library

Notice
Clinical practice and medical knowledge constantly evolve. Standard safety precautions must be followed, but, as knowledge is broadened by research, changes in practice, treatment and drug therapy may become necessary or appropriate. Readers must check the most current product information provided by the manufacturer of each drug to be administered and verify the dosages and correct administration, as well as contraindications. It is the responsibility of the practitioner, utilising the experience and knowledge of the patient, to determine dosages and the best treatment for each individual patient. Any brands mentioned in this book are as examples only and are not endorsed by the Publisher. Neither the publisher nor the author assume any liability for any injury and/or damage to persons or property arising from this publication.

The Publisher

The publishers have endeavoured to obtain permission for every image in this book prior to publication, however the formal requests for permission for images below were still pending at the time of printing. The full sources and copyright holders have been acknowledged in this text.

Page 134 - Table 15.2
A comparison of burns dressings
Source: British Medical Journal 2007

Page 191 - Figure 21.1
The herpes simplex virus
University of South Carolina, United States
(www.paediatrics.wisc.edu/education)

To contact M&K Publishing write to:
M&K Update Ltd · The Old Bakery · St. John's Street
Keswick · Cumbria CA12 5AS

Tel: 01768 773030 · Fax: 01768 781099
publishing@mkupdate.co.uk
www.mkupdate.co.uk

Designed & typeset by Mary Blood
Printed in England by Ferguson Print, Keswick

Contents

About the author   vi
Acknowledgements   vii
Introduction   1

Part I Caring for children and adolescents
Chapter 1   A word about anatomical terminology   9
Chapter 2   A child's view of emergency care   13
Chapter 3   Pre-hospital care of children   17
Chapter 4   Communication, consent and advocacy   21
Chapter 5   Pain relief in children   29
Chapter 6   Child protection   37
Chapter 7   Care of the adolescent and young adult   45
Chapter 8   Safe discharge of children   59

Part II Minor injury
Chapter 9   Defining minor injury in the child   65
Chapter 10   Clinical examination   69
Chapter 11   Minor head injury   81
Chapter 12   Injuries of the upper limb   91
Chapter 13   Injuries of the lower limb   109
Chapter 14   X-ray requesting and interpretation   117
Chapter 15   Burns and scalds   123

Part III Minor illness
Chapter 16   Assessment of illness in the child   139
Chapter 17   Recognition of the unwell child   145
Chapter 18   Febrile convulsion   151
Chapter 19   ENT and respiratory illness   155
Chapter 20   Abdominal and genito-urinary illness   175
Chapter 21   Dermatological illness   189
Chapter 22   Musculo-skeletal illness   199
Chapter 23   Ophthalmic complaints   209

References   215
Index   229

Paediatric minor emergencies

About the author

James Bethel FFEN, RGN, BSc (Hons) Clinical Practice, ENB Higher Award, Post Graduate Certificate in Learning and Teaching in Higher Education, Post Graduate Award Emergency Care, Emergency Nurse Practitioner, is a Senior Lecturer in Emergency Care at the University of Wolverhampton and Honorary Nurse Practitioner in the emergency departments of Walsall Hospitals NHS Trust and Dudley Group of Hospitals. Prior to this he worked in various roles as a nurse manager and lead nurse in emergency services. He has worked in emergency care since 1986 in emergency departments in Birmingham, the Black Country, Shropshire and Staffordshire.

James developed a particular interest in the emergency care of children when working as a lead nurse in Birmingham. During this time he developed a paediatric-specific, academically accredited training course for nurse practitioners. This was marketed, as part of a training module, to staff from emergency departments, minor injury units and NHS walk-in-centres in Birmingham, the Black Country, Shropshire, Staffordshire, Herefordshire, Leicestershire, Worcestershire and Warwickshire.

He is now module leader for emergency care courses at Wolverhampton University, including modules concerning the emergency practitioner care of minor injury and illness. He has also developed work pertinent to the emergency care needs of children. He is a Fellow of the Faculty of Emergency Nursing, chair of the Midlands Emergency Care Group, sits on the editorial board of the Emergency Nurse journal and is a member of the steering committee of the Royal College of Nursing Emergency Care Association. He also holds honorary status as a nurse practitioner in the emergency departments of Walsall Hospitals NHS Trust and Dudley Group of Hospitals where he works on a regular basis to support emergency care students and maintain clinical competence.

Acknowledgements

Acknowledgements

The inspiration for writing this book came from all the children I have dealt with in emergency care settings during the 21 years of my career so far. Their humour, vulnerability, courage and honesty provide a never-ending challenge in the workplace and truly help me to enjoy my work. I would also like to thank my employer, the University of Wolverhampton, for providing me with support and encouragement during the writing of this book. Most of all I thank my wife, Rachael, and my children, Georgia and Patrick, for tolerating my behaviour over the years and supporting me in developing my work.

Paediatric minor emergencies

'Play is the work of the child'

Friedrich Froebel (1782-1852)

Introduction

There is a dearth of written work relating specifically to the emergency care of the child. Why this should be the case is perhaps not as perplexing as it may initially appear: although children make up between 25% and 30% of the attendance of many emergency departments, constituting approximately 3.5 million attendances a year (Royal College of Paediatrics and Child Health (RCPCH) 1999, 2007), there has until recently been little specific provision made for them. (The figure of 3.5 million does not include attendance by children at minor injury units or NHS walk-in centres.) The Healthcare Commission, an inspectorate body tasked with the monitoring of quality standards within the National Health Service of the United Kingdom (UK), has recently reported that although 1.8 million children attended mixed adult and paediatric emergency departments in 2006 almost one in five of these departments still failed to provide adequate life support resources for children at night. It also found that many nursing and medical staff had not undertaken child protection training, a recommendation of Lord Laming subsequent to the Victoria Climbié abuse enquiry (Department of Health 2003). Staff were not always able to detail effective communication strategies when caring for children (Healthcare Commission 2007).

The Healthcare Commission, and various bodies concerned with the provision of healthcare to children in the UK, have concluded that a lack of resources makes current aspirations for service provision unattainable. It advocates the reconfiguration of paediatric services such that those children requiring specialist care may access regional centres of excellence rather than the local district general hospital. It is envisaged that these centres would have all the necessary resources to manage the care of severely ill or injured children. Children requiring care for minor injury or illness would continue to be treated more locally in units that would not now be required, or expected, to provide specialist care for children as this would now be the task of the regional centre. Thus the available paediatric expert resources would be utilised in a more effective manner (Healthcare Commission 2007, RCPCH 2007). This recommendation broadly mirrors those recently made for the reconfiguration of all emergency services by the Department of Health (2006a). Thus in the future it may be that children with minor injuries and illnesses will be cared for in environments that are predominantly led by staff other than doctors, or where paediatric specific medical expertise and support is not available. Under these circumstances the Royal College of Paediatrics and Child Health recommends the enhancement of paediatric knowledge and skills for staff working in such areas and in particular those relevant to the recognition of abuse in children and the differentiation of the well from the unwell child (RCPCH 2007). The College additionally recommends that all non-medical practitioners independently managing the care of children, such as those caring for children with minor injury and illness, should have education specific to the anatomical, physiological and psychological differences of children, in addition to training concerning history taking, clinical examination and diagnostic decision making in children (RCPCH 2007). The provision of training to address these service changes is therefore imperative in order that the care of children with minor complaints is not compromised.

The Royal College of Paediatrics and Child Health has also defined which categories of paediatric attenders it would expect to be treated within the environment of a minor injury unit or NHS walk-in centre. These included children with mild pyrexial illnesses, mild respiratory or gastrointestinal disorders and superficial soft tissue injuries (RCPCH 2002). Children who have more severe illness or injury, because of their potential need for specialist in-patient services, should be seen within a secondary care centre. Although the guidelines produced by the RCPCH seem laudable in terms of risk management, they call upon parents and carers, and pre-hospital service providers, to make an accurate differentiation between mild, moderate and severe symptomatology. This may not always be a realistic expectation and many minor injury units and NHS walk-in centres may still find themselves stabilising unwell children prior to transfer to secondary care facilities because they were the nearest care facility or because parents, carers and pre-hospital staff did not have the necessary skills to know that the child concerned was more unwell than they thought. In view of this, other recommendations in the RCPCH document appear more pertinent (RCPCH 2002):

- Staff within minor injury units and NHS walk-in centres should take part in clinical rotations through an emergency department in order to develop or refresh their skills and experience in managing the care of unwell children.
- The same group of staff should also be trained in paediatric life support.
- There should be a designated liaison paediatric nurse, working between the minor injury unit/NHS walk-in centre and the emergency department, to co-ordinate staff development in the emergency care of children.

Recommendations about the provision of separate facilities for children attending emergency departments (RCPCH 1999) have not always been acted upon in many acute trusts. A minority have developed separate emergency departments and completely isolate children from adults in emergency care. Many more have attempted to cordon off particular areas within existing emergency departments and reserve their use for children. This strategy is of some value but does not always address the need to geographically and visually separate certain categories of adult attender from children. It also sometimes fails at times of high activity when there is pressure on space in the department. A significant minority of departments have made no separate provision for the emergency care of children. This may be due to financial constraints or other more pressing imperatives in emergency care service provision. The ability and feasibility of minor injury units and walk-in centres to provide a separate service for children is open to question. These emergency care settings may be less well resourced and may not have a significant enough paediatric workload to justify separate service provision. Although minor injury units and walk-in centres were not subject to the 1999 recommendations of the Royal College of Paediatrics and Child Health they are subject to recommendations made in their 2002 document *Children's attendance at a minor injury/illness service* (RCPCH 2002) in which the provision of facilities such as play areas was one of the recommendations made. Many have made attempts to provide specific, if not separate, facilities for children. This is usually in the form of play areas and facilities for carers to be able to attend to the hygiene needs of infants.

Paediatric minor emergencies

Again subsequent to the recommendations of the RCPCH many departments have employed registered sick children's nurses or child branch trained nurses in an effort to enhance the care of children in emergency departments. Many of these nurses were recruited from in-patient paediatric wards or directly from university upon qualification as a child branch nurse. Their experience of emergency care, whether of children or adults, was therefore limited and the extent to which the registered sick children's nursing course prepares students for the emergency care of children has been questioned (Bethel 2006). Thus although this initiative was undertaken with the laudable intention of enhancing the emergency care of children, the reality of the situation was that these staff would take some time to acquire the necessary emergency care skills required to do this, and that during this time their training needs were not identified and therefore went unmet.

The *Reforming Emergency Care* document (Department of Health 2001) makes little specific mention of children and their care was presumably thought to be subsumed within the streaming system that the initiative advocates. The more widespread proliferation of emergency nurse practitioners and emergency care practitioners subsequent to this initiative also threw up challenges concerning the emergency care of children. Few nurse practitioner training programmes had paediatric specific content despite the fact that nurse practitioners were generally expected to manage the care of children with minor injuries and in some cases minor illness as well. Even now there are very few paediatric specific programmes of training aimed at nurse practitioners. Some programmes of training now include paediatric content, which has been 'bolted on' to the original programme in many cases.

These circumstances perhaps therefore make it less surprising that there is little written specifically about the emergency care of children: lack of recognition of training needs of children's nurses working in emergency care settings, a lack of paediatric specific input to nurse practitioner programmes and no separate recognition in the most influential document concerning UK-based emergency care in the new century probably all mitigate against the generation of great volumes of work in this area.

Whilst not addressing all of the challenges outlined here, it is hoped that this work will provide some of the necessary knowledge for emergency nurses and nurse practitioners, emergency care practitioners, medical care practitioners, physio-therapy practitioners, radiographer practitioners, pre-hospital staff and medical staff working in emergency departments, minor injury units and walk-in centres and other emergency care settings, that will enable them to enhance the care of the child with minor injury or illness.

Part I

Caring for children and adolescents

Chapter 1
A word about anatomical terminology

In taking on expanded roles in emergency care, nurses and allied health professionals have to learn a new language as well as develop new knowledge and skills. To communicate effectively with colleagues in medicine, when discussing patient case history or referring to specialty teams, practitioners need to be able to converse in the same language in order to achieve optimal outcomes for the patient and to enhance the credibility of the practitioner service. Patients may be put at risk if practitioners from different professional backgrounds are not able to communicate effectively with each other. False assumptions may be made about meaning and inference that lead to mistakes being made. In taking on some of the historical roles of the medical profession such as history taking and physical examination, practitioners will be better supported by medical staff if they are seen to have made the effort to master the language associated with performing these skills.

Table 1.1
Terms of location

Terms of location

Anterior/Posterior	Towards the front/Towards the back
Superior/Inferior	Towards the top/Towards the bottom
Central/Peripheral	Towards the centre/Towards the edges
Proximal/Distal	Nearest to/Furthest away
Lateral/Medial	Away from the midline/Towards the midline
Plantar/Dorsal	Of the foot: sole of the foot/Top of the foot
Ventral/Dorsal	Towards the front/Towards the back
Palmar/Volar	Of the hand and wrist: Flexor surface/Extensor surface

Paediatric minor emergencies

As can be seen from Table 1.1, some different terms can apply to broadly the same locations. Sometimes the term depends upon the part of the body being talked about such as the specific terms for the hand and foot.

Movement

Movement happens in three planes:
- Longitudinal (up and down)
- Transverse (across or side-to-side)
- Anterior-posterior (front to back)

An example of longitudinal movement is raising the arm straight above the head. Transverse movement may be exemplified by lifting the leg up sideways and an example of anterior-posterior movement is to rotate the arms in an arc from the front to the back of the body.

Table 1.2

Terms associated with movement

Terms associated with movement

Movement	Example
Flexion/ Extension	Flexing the elbow brings the hand to the shoulder. Extension takes the hand in the opposite direction and straightens the arm.
Inversion/ Eversion	Inversion of the ankle is when the ankle is 'turned over' or bent away from the midline as in simple ankle sprains. Eversion takes the ankle in the opposite direction (towards the midline).
Pronation/ Supination	Pronation of the forearm involves rotating the forearm so that the palm of the hand faces downwards. Supination is the opposite – the forearm is rotated so that the palm of the hand faces upwards.
Abduction/ Adduction	Abduction of the hip or shoulder involves lifting the straight leg or arm sideways away from the midline. Adduction is the opposite, with the shoulder or hip moved sideways towards the midline.

A word about anatomical terminology

Ulnar deviation/
Radial deviation

Ulnar deviation is sideways movement of the wrist joint towards the midline (towards the ulna) with the palm facing upwards. Radial deviation is the opposite, with the wrist being moved away from the midline (towards the radius) with the palm upwards.

Dorsiflexion/
Plantarflexion

Dorsiflexion of the ankle involves moving the ankle upwards so that the toes of the foot point upwards. Plantarflexion is the opposite, where the toes are pointing down to the ground.

Rotation and
circumduction

Some joints have a greater degree of flexibility and can move in more planes. Examples are the thumb and shoulder. These joints can also rotate in a 360-degree arc and this is called circumduction.

Chapter 2
A child's view of emergency care

Whether it is a large emergency department or a smaller minor injury unit or walk-in centre, the child's experience of emergency care will be shaped by the preconceptions they have already gained about emergency care and illness and by the manner in which staff treat them during their current episode of care.

Depending upon their age and developmental level, children will form ideas about hospital settings, emergency care settings and the people working within them, from the media and from their peers. Fictional or non-fictional television programmes concerning healthcare and emergency care have proliferated over the last several years in line with the proliferation of TV channels and access to them. Children may passively receive this information because of the viewing habits of family members or carers, or may actively seek out such programmes. Internet access enables children to actively seek out information relating to healthcare and digital technology enables them to store information and retrieve this information more readily than before. Children will also form ideas about healthcare based upon their interactions with peers: the good or bad experience of a friend going to the hospital or the emergency department may therefore shape the perceptions of healthcare that children have. Obviously if a child has personal experience of emergency care then this will shape their current perceptions and expectations of it, and this is probably true of many adults as well.

Children's experience of illness, injury and death within their circle of family or carers will also shape current experience. Perceptions of the worth and the nature of healthcare, and the attributes of the people working within it, may have been moulded by injury, illness or even the death of a family member or carer and their recollections of the event.

Paediatric minor emergencies

Children have fantastical ideas about what will happen to them in emergency care settings and are anxious about such things as loss of limbs, loss of life and separation from parents and carers (Bentley. 2004). Addressing these anxieties early in the consultation, by giving the child an honest account of their likely path through care and by telling them what will and will not be happening, will facilitate co-operation and enhance care.

The current experience of the child is also important; children, like many adults, will recollect perhaps most vividly the first person they encountered during their episode of care, when they were feeling most vulnerable and anxious and were perhaps also in pain. If this experience has been a negative one then it is all the more difficult to overcome the negative perceptions formed later on in the episode of care. This may detrimentally affect the quality of care given and, particularly in the case of children, may mitigate against co-operation and trust which are vital in the formation of a therapeutic relationship. This emphasises how it is everyone's responsibility, from pre-hospital services, receptionists and triage nurses to emergency practitioners and doctors, to attempt to enhance the child's experience of emergency care in order to facilitate best possible care for them.

All of these factors contribute to the manner in which the child will present. Assessment of the child may be enhanced by the child presenting in a state of co-operative and eager excitement, tinged only slightly with anxiety, or may be hampered by pain and an overwhelming fear of the environment and people within it. The first set of circumstances is easier to work with and the child's co-operation is yours to lose. The second set of circumstances presents more challenges. In placing the child in the unfamiliar environment of an emergency care setting, parents or carers have imparted to the child that they can no longer care for them and manage their current problem. Parents or carers, who may prior to this have seemed all seeing, all caring and all knowing omnipotent figures to the child, are suddenly not able to help and may, by virtue of their own behaviour and anxiety related to the child and their injury or illness, actually compound fear and anxiety in the child. In choosing strategies to address these challenges it is therefore useful to consider some measures that will encourage the child to believe that they have a degree of control in the situation and just as importantly that their parents or carers are perceived to have a degree of control also. Simple, effective strategies include:

- Introducing yourself to the child and their parents or carers and smiling in an attempt to make the environment less formal and intimidating for the child.

- Assuring the child that their parents will be able to stay with them throughout their emergency care experience.

- Where appropriate, gaining implied consent or otherwise advising parents/carers and the child before initiating any assessment procedures such as observations or physical examination.

- Making some enquiries about previous experience of healthcare settings in order to inform your approach to the child.

- Getting down and talking at the level of the child: again this will make you appear less intimidating.

- Remembering to offer pain relief.

- Explaining in as much detail as possible the child's probable trajectory through the emergency care setting. If, for instance they have a potential bony injury explain that they will go to x-ray after you have seen them. Explain what will happen in the x-ray department and then explain that they will have their x-ray looked at and what is likely to happen if the x-ray is either normal or abnormal. This will also help to allay the anxiety of the parents and carers.

- Where possible offering the child choice in terms of treatment options or comfort measures. Would they for instance like a sling or are they more comfortable as they are? How would they like to be transported to the x-ray department? Conferring a degree of control in an otherwise unfamiliar environment may reduce child and parental anxieties.

Assuring children that parents/carers will be able to stay with them is an important measure: separation from parents/carers is one of the anxiety-provoking fears that children have when attending for emergency care (Bentley 2004). Make this assurance explicit rather than assuming the child and parents/carers are aware of this. Consult with colleagues in the radiography department if necessary and ensure that this is also the case there. In difficult assessment it may be worth considering enlisting the assistance of other members of the team. For instance, a child may not co-operate with a male member of the team whereas they will with a female member or vice versa. Where available you may want to enlist the help of a registered sick children's nurse as a source of expert advice. In providing play and distraction therapy for children, a nursery nurse with a hospital play specialist qualification is a rare though invaluable commodity in emergency care. Simple measures that any practitioner may employ might include reading a book to a child, playing simple games or blowing bubbles as a means of distracting the child's attention. What is essential is a degree of personal and professional insight and to know when you have either reached the limits of your expertise in attempting to gain the co-operation and trust of a child or where, because of personal attributes, you are not the best person to attempt to do this. This should be seen as a positive not negative attribute of your work: it may do more harm to continue attempting to coerce a child into co-operation where expertise is lacking and confidence is low than to accept that other members of the team may be more qualified or better able to do this with better outcomes for the child. Obviously you may want to address this learning need in the future.

A large-scale study of children's concepts of illness in nine European countries undertaken between 1990 and 1993, known as the COMAC childhood and medicines project (Trakas & Sanz 1996), discovered that children, far from being passive recipients of healthcare had a very active view of what illness entailed. Sometimes this involved speculation about why illness had happened to them. Aside from attaching negative attributes to illness such as fever and headache, children also ascribed some positive attributes to being ill such as having lots of visitors and receiving a lot of attention (Trakas & Sanz 1996). Children also varied markedly in their attitude towards prescribed medication, with some seeing the medicine as an omnipotent curer of illness and others seeing it as a necessary evil, with its own side effects (Trakas & Sanz 1996). Awareness of such factors will therefore enhance the assessment process and will also benefit the management of children's complaints in terms of their compliance with treatment and drug therapies.

Chapter 3
Pre-hospital care of the child

Little is written about the pre-hospital emergency care of children other than in purely clinical terms describing the management of illness or injury. Children with minor injury will, for various reasons, sometimes still find themselves transported to minor injury units and emergency departments in an ambulance, though the more widespread utilisation of emergency care practitioners may reduce the incidence of this. Although much emphasis is placed upon the environment in which children find themselves being cared for once in a hospital or minor injury unit, little attention has been given by bodies such as the Royal College of Paediatrics and Child Health to the pre-hospital environment children may find themselves in. Little attention is also given to the expertise and qualifications of pre-hospital practitioners in terms of their ability to care for children, whilst much is given to the provision of adequately trained and experienced practitioners within emergency departments and minor injury units. In urban areas transport times to emergency departments or minor injury units are measured in times of less than ten minutes and the separate provision of paediatric expertise might be thought by some to be less than critical, or superseded by other more important factors. In rural areas transport times to hospital may be up to one hour. In these circumstances the availability of particular expertise may be thought to be more important.

The pre-hospital environment may provoke as much anxiety and fear in the child as the emergency care settings within hospitals or minor injury units. The pre-hospital practitioner has fewer resources available to deal with the physical and psychological needs of the child:

Paediatric minor emergencies

- Their formulary of medications and ability to administer them will generally be more limited.

- They are not able to enlist the help of colleagues such as nursery nurses or paediatric trained staff in caring for the child.

- They have fewer means of distraction within the ambulance than within an emergency department or minor injury unit.

Pre-hospital practitioners therefore have to be more independently resourceful in providing care that addresses both the physical and psychological needs of the child. Pre-hospital practitioners may more readily employ some methods that may reduce fear and anxiety in the child such as the following:

- Provide children with first name details and promote an informal atmosphere that also reassures parents and carers.

- If possible, encourage the child, parents or carers to bring a favourite toy or game with them on the journey. This will provide familiarity for the child and may be useful on longer journeys and as a distraction technique.

- If appropriate, praise the child, parents or carers for any first aid measures that have been undertaken and reinforce their effectiveness.

- Get down and talk at the level of the child in order to appear less intimidating. Involve parents and carers in your enquiries about the child's medical history.

- Attempt to give the child, parents or carers some control over the situation: give choices in care when appropriate, show the anxious child what the array of on-board equipment is for and demonstrate this with the child if necessary.

- Where possible, attempt to give the child, parents or carers some idea of their likely trajectory through emergency care and how long this might take. Tell children that their parents/carers are able to stay with them throughout the episode where this is known to be the case.

- Where possible, give the child, parents or carers an idea of what to expect when they reach the emergency department or minor injury unit in terms of the geography of the department, and what facilities may be available for children. Reassure parents or carers and the child, where possible, that the department or unit has specially trained staff to care for children.

Pre-hospital care of the child

Pre-hospital practitioners are in a unique position to influence the whole of the emergency care experience for children. As a point of first contact for many children they may enhance this experience or have the opposite effect and make co-operation with the child a difficult challenge for emergency department or minor injury unit staff. They may allay fear and anxiety at an earlier stage than would otherwise be possible by employing some of the measures outlined above. Strategies to be avoided by the pre-hospital practitioner, like any other practitioner, include lying to children in order to gain short-term co-operation. This will lead to difficulties in regaining the confidence of the child later in their journey through emergency care. Do not forget to ask permission of the child, or advise them of what you are doing, before attempting any sort of procedure: this helps to instil a sense of control within the child.

In being considered a part of the emergency care team, pre-hospital practitioners should be offered similar training opportunities to their emergency care colleagues working within hospitals or minor injury units. Emergency care practitioners should have the same paediatric specific input to their training as is advocated for nurse practitioners by the Royal College of Paediatrics and Child Health (2007). The ability of all pre-hospital staff to positively influence the child's experience of emergency care, and thus to potentially positively affect clinical outcomes, should encourage a more collaborative approach to emergency care provision that acknowledges this unique set of circumstances.

Figure 3.1

Pre-hospital emergency care providers are in a unique position to positively influence the care of the child.

(Photo courtesy Brilliant TV and www.timmymallett.co.uk)

Chapter 4
Communication, consent and advocacy

Seminal work undertaken by Resnick and Hergenroeder in 1975 at the Johns Hopkins Hospital in the United States gave expression to the fears that children have when attending emergency departments (Resnick & Hergenroeder 1975):

- fear of needles
- fear of pain and painful procedures
- fear of loss of control
- fear of loss of limbs
- fear of scarring
- fear of loss of parental support (separation from parents)
- fear of being hospitalised
- fear of death.

Knowledge of this kind is invaluable in shaping the consultation with the child. By addressing such fears early on in the process the co-operation of the child will be more readily gained and the child's experience of emergency care enhanced. It is therefore essential to make explicit to the child that parents/carers will be able to stay with them throughout their journey in emergency care and that they should not therefore fear being separated from parents or carers.

Not lying to children is essential in developing and maintaining trust: if by examining the probable trajectory that the child's journey through emergency care will take it is likely that some form of injection may be involved, if any sort of procedure may be undertaken, if in-patient care is likely to be a consequence of attendance or if scarring is a likely consequence of injury then this should be made clear at as early a stage as possible. Too often this discussion never takes place, or takes place too close to the event for any meaningful discussion or reassurance to happen (Bentley 2004). In providing time for the child to think about and discuss these issues before they occur, their co-operation during procedures is more likely. Conversely, if the child's journey will not involve certain interventions then make this clear at the start of the consultation. Do not assume that the child, or their parents or carers, have a similar understanding of the apparently minor nature of their injury as the practitioner and that they therefore also understand that loss of a limb or even death are not possibilities during this episode of care.

Fragmentation of care has also been demonstrated to have a potentially negative impact on the child's experience of emergency care (Bentley 2004). The emergency practitioner is in a good position to minimise the number of different people involved with the emergency care of the child. Many emergency practitioners have a holistic approach to their care and undertake the treatment that they themselves prescribe subsequent to clinical examination. Others will work flexibly, moving between this model of working and delegating treatment to others as a changing workload demands. An awareness of the value of holistic care in children may raise the threshold for such delegation, particularly if a therapeutic relationship has been established during initial consultation.

An awareness of the developmental stages of children in terms of their communication skills is obviously important in pitching consultation at an appropriate level for the child. Developmental milestones in children's communication level are discussed in Chapter 10 dealing with clinical examination. Allow parents/carers to offer advice about normal patterns of interaction for the child and be guided by these as well.

Be wary of patronising children during the consultation: older children in particular may resent what they interpret as a patronising attitude on the part of the practitioner. Such children, or young adults, may value being consulted directly about their care needs rather than via a parent or carer. Knowing when to make the transition from involving parents as a means of reassuring the child that control is still within the nucleus of the family and addressing the child directly to avoid being perceived as patronising is difficult and mistakes may be made. The age at which this may become appropriate differs from child to child and is also dependent upon the perceived severity of injury and previous experience of healthcare settings. A little ground work in these areas at the start of the consultation, along with some observation of the family dynamic, may give more insight into the nature of the individual and help to avoid errors in judgement.

Discussions of this nature allude also to the issue of consent in children attending for emergency care. Consent in children is a complex area, and may be more so in the field of emergency care. Although when dealing with minor injury and illness formal consent for treatment is not usually required and gaining co-operation is a greater issue, there may be times where knowledge of the guidelines pertinent to paediatric consent may help the practitioner make certain decisions. This may be the case, for instance, where emergency contraception is being prescribed or administered, or where the child may be refusing certain interventions such as intramuscular injections.

The law concerning consent in children is governed by two Acts of Parliament. Between birth and the age of 16 the Children Act (Department of Health 1989) is pertinent; between the ages of 16 and 18 years the Family Law Reform Act of 1969 (Department for Constitutional Affairs 2006) governs consent procedures. At the age of 18 therefore children, as set out in the Children Act of 1989, become adults and are then empowered to take decisions regarding consent to treatment independently. The Family Law Reform Act of 1969, which sets out the principles pertinent to consent in 16- and 17-year-olds, asserts the following principles:

- The child may give consent to treatment of a medical, surgical or dental nature but cannot consent to take part in research trials.
- Children's decision to refuse emergency treatment can be overruled by those who hold formal consent for the child.
- A court can also overrule the decision of the child.

This presents a somewhat confusing picture in stating that a 16- or 17-year-old child may consent, but any refusal of consent may be overruled. Below the age of 16 years the principles of Fraser competence (formerly known as Gillick competence) apply:

- Parental rights are not absolute.
- Parental responsibility is only needed until the child is capable of making independent decisions.

A crucial part of this concept is the child's capacity to make independent decisions. How might this capacity be measured? The principle of capacity is explained as being the child's ability to understand and retain information relevant to their decision, and that they are able to understand the consequences of undergoing or refusing certain treatment and can use this information to come to an informed decision. Obviously in the emergency care environment, where the practitioner will only have known the child for a matter of minutes, it is difficult to make this sort of assessment. The sort of judgements that the practitioner is being asked to make are:

- Is the child of a sufficient level of maturity to make the decision?
- Do they have a reasonable level of understanding of the pertinent issues?
- Are they of at least average intelligence for their age?

In the 1985 case that gave rise to the concept of Fraser competence the court appeared to uphold the right of the child who fulfilled the above criteria to make independent decisions regarding consent to healthcare irrespective of age. Since that time other decisions have contradicted this view. It is recommended that where practitioners are faced with dilemmas of this nature, in the first instance discussion take place with a senior colleague and where necessary advice is sought from the organisation's legal representatives. Meticulous note taking should also be ensured during such consultations.

As a final point on the issue of consent it is worth remembering who holds the responsibility of providing consent for the child and who does not. Those who do have parental responsibility include:

- the mother of the child
- the father of the child provided he is married to the mother, or has registered the birth jointly with her (if the child was born after 1 December 2003), or has right of consent with the agreement of the mother, or has obtained a court order granting right to consent, or has acquired the right as stated in

the will of the mother on death

- those appointed guardians of the child
- those who have adopted a child.

Those who do not hold responsibility for providing consent and cannot therefore give consent for a child include:

- the father of the child if he is not married to the mother or has not taken any of the steps detailed above
- the father of the child if not married to the mother and the child was born before 1 December 2003 (unless the birth has been jointly re-registered since this time)
- grandparents or other relatives unless they have been appointed guardians of the child.

However the Children Act of 1989 does point out that a person who does not have parental responsibility for providing consent for the child but has care of the child may do what is reasonable to provide for the safeguarding of the child's health. Thus there are no clear and unequivocal guidelines for the practitioner. Each case has to be assessed separately and advice from colleagues and legal representatives taken where necessary. In practice it is advisable to establish who has attended the department or unit with the child and document this. If necessary it should be ascertained who has parental responsibility for the child and is therefore capable of giving consent on their behalf. In the case of children who attend the department or unit on their own, it is advisable to make an attempt to contact the people who have parental responsibility for the child unless the child states that they do not wish this and are of sufficient age and maturity to make this decision. Under such circumstances, advice should be sought to support decisions made and documentation of all relevant details ensured. If those who have parental responsibility are contacted then an outline of the reason for attendance and proposed treatment should be given and their verbal consent or refusal to this sought and documented. Under some circumstances it may be advisable to wait until those people with parental responsibility are in attendance before providing treatment for the child.

Whilst most cases currently being managed by the practitioner in emergency care are of a minor nature and may not require formal consent, good practice in ensuring adequate knowledge is provided to make informed decisions should be encouraged. There are circumstances when relying on the implied consent of children attending for emergency care may lead to conflict and misunderstanding. Providing children with the information they need when attending for emergency care, whether they are in a position to provide consent or not, may overcome some of these problems. As the caseload of the emergency practitioner becomes more complex, the issue of consent will undoubtedly become more pertinent.

An advocate for the child

An advocate for the child

Children are in a uniquely vulnerable position when attending for emergency care. There are several reasons for this:

- Children may not be able to verbalise in a way that is readily understood by adults. This is obvious in pre-verbal infants but may also be the case in children who have communication, sensory or cognitive problems for whatever reason and it may also be a function of fear and anxiety. Thus whereas adults are generally able to tell emergency care staff exactly what hurts and how much it hurts, children may not be able to do this. They may also be unable to tell staff about whether analgesia has been effective or not.

- Fear and anxiety may make the child less able to communicate effectively and may also affect the assessment of their complaint. Some staff may assume that certain symptoms in the child may be entirely attributable to fear and anxiety and pathology may be missed or may be delayed in its diagnosis.

- Some emergency care staff have a poor understanding of the needs of children attending for emergency care. This results in a lack of confidence on the part of these staff which may make assessment and management of the child more problematic than would otherwise be the case.

- Children may have fantastical notions of illness or injury and their consequences which may have been developed and reinforced within their peer groups. These notions will affect the child's perception of their illness or injury and the likely outcome.

- Children form a disproportionate part of the emergency department workload. This is because they are more likely to be ill or injured than most adults. They are not always able to protect themselves from injury in the way that adults can, they have poorly developed immune systems in comparison to adults, they lose heat more readily than adults, their gait and co-ordination are less well developed as infants, they are more likely to suffer multi-system trauma than adults because of the close proximity of neighbouring structures in their smaller bodies, they may have to rely on adults for their wellbeing for instance in providing a smoke-free environment or adequately restraining them in motor vehicles and this reliance may be poorly founded.

- The very reason that the child is attending for emergency care may be secondary to their vulnerability in that it may be a consequence of abuse by an adult.

The nurse has a duty to 'promote the interests of patients and clients' (Nursing and Midwifery Council 2004) and this is perhaps imperative where, as in the case of the child, the patient or client is unable to do this on their own behalf. Promoting the interests of children within emergency care settings is a very broad agenda and will include facilitating the learning of others, leading by example in the care of children and being aware of presenting complaints that may indicate that a child has been abused. On another level, promoting the interests of the child will mean involving them in the planning of their care and where possible giving them choice in this. It will involve ensuring that pain is effectively measured and that pain relief is both provided and evaluated for effectiveness. It will entail suggesting to other staff that they cannot cannulate the child yet because the anaesthetic cream has not been in place long enough and that they should refer to the photograph taken of the child's deformed limb in preference to manipulating the arm again and inflicting pain. Promotion of the interests of children and acting as an advocate for them will also involve deferring care to other members of the team when you have reached the limits of your professional or personal competence.

Chapter 5
Pain relief in children

Historically and nowadays pain relief in children in emergency care environments has been and remains sub-optimal (Maurice *et al.* 2002). Pain relief is not given in effective doses, inappropriate analgesia for the level of pain is used, inappropriate routes of administration are used, or administration is delayed. This has been largely caused by a lack of paediatric-focused expertise in emergency care and an inability to recognise and acknowledge manifestations of pain in children. Many departments are still failing to benchmark against recommendations made by the British Association for Emergency Medicine in 2004. The association made recommendations for the relief of pain in adults and children in emergency care environments. Recommendations for children are shown in Figure 5.1.

Pain relief in children

Figure 5.1

Pain relief in children
(Source: British Association for Emergency Medicine 2004)

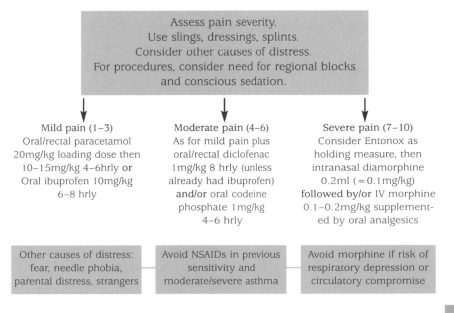

Assess pain severity.
Use slings, dressings, splints.
Consider other causes of distress.
For procedures, consider need for regional blocks and conscious sedation.

Mild pain (1–3)
Oral/rectal paracetamol 20mg/kg loading dose then 10–15mg/kg 4–6hrly **or** Oral ibuprofen 10mg/kg 6–8 hrly

Moderate pain (4–6)
As for mild pain plus oral/rectal diclofenac 1mg/kg 8 hrly (unless already had ibuprofen) **and/or** oral codeine phosphate 1mg/kg 4–6 hrly

Severe pain (7–10)
Consider Entonox as holding measure, then intranasal diamorphine 0.2ml (= 0.1mg/kg) **followed by/or** IV morphine 0.1–0.2mg/kg supplemented by oral analgesics

Other causes of distress: fear, needle phobia, parental distress, strangers

Avoid NSAIDs in previous sensitivity and moderate/severe asthma

Avoid morphine if risk of respiratory depression or circulatory compromise

Note that intra-muscular (IM) medication in children is not recommended and should be avoided where alternate routes are available.

The assessment of pain in children

Assessment of pain

Several clinical tools have been devised for the assessment of pain in children. The most universally recognised, and perhaps the one most widely utilised, is the Wong-Baker smiley faces scale (Wong & Baker 1988). This tool is suitable for use in children aged approximately 3 years and above. Numerical rating scales are not suitable for use in children below the age of approximately 7 years because of their reliance upon the child's numeric skills.

The faces scale (based on the Wong-Baker scale)

Figure 5.2

The faces scale (based on the Wong-Baker scale)

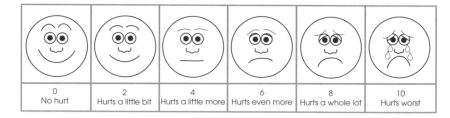

| 0 No hurt | 2 Hurts a little bit | 4 Hurts a little more | 6 Hurts even more | 8 Hurts a whole lot | 10 Hurts worst |

Pain scoring in pre-verbal children relies more upon behavioural interpretation than patient self-reporting as such children are not able to report pain in a way that is understood by emergency care staff. One such tool is the FLACC assessment tool which has been validated in infants as young as 2 months (see Table 5.1, p.31).

The Royal College of Nursing (RCN) in its document The *Recognition and Assessment of Acute Pain in Children* (Royal College of Nursing 1999) emphasised the importance of children being believed when their pain is being assessed. Evidence had been found that, although healthcare professionals tended to believe children when they reported having no pain, many still found children's reporting of pain unreliable and such reports had been ignored or disbelieved (Royal College of Nursing 1999). The document again also emphasises the importance of involving parents or carers in the episode of care: parents or carers will be able to inform the emergency care practitioner of the child's normal pain behaviour and their pain history. Thus the assessment of pain in children should involve a tripartite approach (Royal College of Nursing 1999):

- the use of a rating scale for a child to report their level of pain or the use of a behavioural assessment tool in infants and pre-verbal children
- the use of the child's own account of the location and quality of the pain
- the use of parental or carer advice about previous pain behaviour.

Table 5.1

FLACC assessment tool

(Source: Merkel *et al.* 1997)

FLACC assessment tool

	Scoring		
	0	**1**	**2**
Face	No particular expression or smile	Occasional grimace or frown, withdrawn, disinterested	Frequent to constant quivering chin, clenched jaw
Legs	Normal position or relaxed	Uneasy, restless, tense	Kicking or legs drawn up
Activity	Lying quietly, normal position, moves easily	Squirming, shifting back and forth, tense	Arched, rigid or jerking
Cry	No cry (awake or asleep)	Moans or whimpers, occasional complaint	Crying steadily, screams or sobs, frequent complaints
Consolability	Content, relaxed	Reassured by occasional touching, hugging, or being talked to. Distractible	Difficult to console or comfort

Pain management

Pain management

Pharmacological approaches to pain relief have been outlined above (on p.29) in the British Association for Emergency Medicine's 2004 recommendations for pain relief in children. Wherever possible pain management should be benchmarked against these guidelines and periodic audit should take place to identify any reasons for non-adherence such as resource or training issues. In providing pharmacological pain relief, the importance of re-assessment of pain should not be forgotten. Re-assessment should take place after administration of medication and should be performed in the same manner as the initial assessment of pain, i.e. using the same assessment tool and incorporating parental/carer and patient accounts where possible.

Pharmacology is just one aspect of pain management in children. Non-pharmacological strategies for the relief of pain will provide intrinsic benefit to patients but will also enhance the effectiveness of any pharmacological agents used. Such strategies include:

Comfort and positioning

Comfort and positioning

Consider the most appropriate position for the child being cared for. This may be recumbent on a trolley or sitting upright in a chair or wheelchair. Restrict movement from this position of comfort as much as possible. If for instance you can predict that a child will be going to the x-ray department once you have addressed their need for pain relief then consider caring for them on a trolley or wheelchair rather than having to ask them to move from a couch or chair in order to be transported to the x-ray department later. Consider also the use of elevation in pain relief. When positioning the patient consider elevating upper or lower limb injuries on pillows which will also confer a degree of positional comfort. Consider the use of a high arm sling to elevate the upper limb in more mobile children. Appropriate splinting of limbs may also be considered.

Distraction therapy

Distraction therapy

Distraction therapy, in the form of play or other child-centred activity, is a useful adjunct to pharmacology in pain relief. Not only will the child's attention not be primarily focused on their injury or illness but the successful inclusion of distraction therapy in treatment will also be invaluable as a means of facilitating co-operation and trust in the child. Distraction therapy, and the other non-pharmacological approaches to pain, should not however be thought of as a substitute for adequate pharmacological relief of pain. In most circumstances non-pharmacological strategies will be an adjunct to medication and will enhance its effectiveness. For distraction therapy and play therapy to be employed successfully, the emergency care worker will need to be familiar with the developmental stage that the child has reached and what sort of attributes and behaviour may reasonably be expected of the child at different ages. They will also need to be able to confidently employ their communication skills with children whose attention is focused on their injury or illness and who may also be fearful and anxious in the emergency care environment. Nursery nurses, particularly those with a hospital play specialist qualification, are an invaluable source of expertise in this area of practice and can be a very effective aide in the episode of care.

Promoting relaxation

Certain strategies to allay fear and anxiety in the child, such as empowerment in decision making where possible, involvement of parents and carers in planning care and the giving of adequate information, have already been discussed. Additional means of promoting relaxation include an explanation of what the child might expect to encounter in the x-ray department, information about the analgesic medication you may be considering dispensing and how it may make them feel, reassurance that the emergency practitioner with whom they may have become familiar, and invested trust in, will be able to care for them until they are discharged or admitted, praising co-operation and the provision of bravery badges and certificates when appropriate. The emergency practitioner responsible for the care of the child should also provide the child with their first name in order that they have a point of reference for care in the department and are able to communicate with staff members more effectively.

Manipulating the environment

Changes in the physical environment can contribute to effective pain relief: the use of blankets for warmth and comfort, the dimming of lights to facilitate a less harsh and clinical environment, the use of ice or heat locally as an adjunct to medication, attempting to keep extraneous noise to a minimum and the provision of food and drink when appropriate are all means by which the environment may be manipulated to the

Promoting relaxation

Manipulating the environment

benefit of the child. Certain paediatric and emergency departments have also relinquished the requirement for staff to wear formal uniforms. In dealing with children, formal uniforms may appear intimidating and may provoke anxiety. More child-friendly attire, using vivid colours and familiar childhood characters from television and other media are successful in mitigating these effects.

Culturally sensitive care

Blenner categorised healthcare providers' attitudes towards the cultural influences on health and illness into three broad types (Blenner 1991):

- **Culturally unaware**: staff do not recognise different cultural needs and treat all patients in the same manner.
- **Culturally non-tolerant**: staff recognise diverse cultural needs but do not modify care given.
- **Culturally sensitive**: staff obtain information on cultural beliefs and work within that belief system to adapt healthcare to meet the needs of patients.

That culture influences health and illness is incontrovertible. In adopting a culturally unaware or non-tolerant approach to care, practitioners are failing to provide best care for patients. In terms of minor illness and injury, pertinent factors may be pain behaviour, and culture and pharmacology.

Pain behaviour

Helman (2007) divides pain into 'private pain' and 'public pain'. He defines private pain as the perception of pain within the individual. Public pain involves the decision to make others aware of this pain, and the manner in which this is done. The way that people behave when in pain, or the way in which they make pain public, is learned during childhood and is influenced by the cultural norms prevalent within the family and larger societal groups. Young children are still learning to behave in an appropriate manner when in pain which is why they sometimes behave in a manner that differs from the expectations that their parents or carers have of them. Older children will have internalised, through repeated encounters and feedback, the manner in which they are expected to behave when in pain.

Western societies tend to value a stoical approach to pain whereby the public expression of pain is minimised, or pain is not made public at all. This attitude may be reinforced by aspects of religion which influence whether people feel that pain may be deserved, or visited upon them by a higher being over which they have little control (Helman 2007). Other societies value a very demonstrative way of presenting public pain, which is thought to be an attempt to cope with the anxiety that pain engenders (Zola 1966). If the manner in which pain is expressed publicly matches the expectations of the practitioner who is responsible for alleviating pain then it is more likely that pain will be dealt with effectively (Todd *et al.* 1993, 2000, Zoucha 1998).

Culture and pharmacology

Culture also has an influence on the way that children perceive the benefit of pharmaceutical agents. In Western societies, where pharmaceutical agents have become one of the foundations of modern healthcare, drugs are seen as a means of alleviating symptoms and curing illness. Children from different cultural backgrounds may see drugs as either just one (and by no means the most important) means of getting better, or may see them as a necessary evil on the road to recovery, or may see them as being of little value at all. For instance, children living in cultures where life events such as illness are attributed to an external control (i.e. to God or some form of higher being) may not believe that it is within their power (or that of the healthcare provider) to provide the means to recovery and that this is only possible if the external controller (i.e. God) wills it (Royal College of Nursing 2006). Certain modern secular societies in the West are now becoming sceptical of the benefits of traditional medicine and associated pharmacology and children from such backgrounds may be reluctant to take medicines, or may refuse to take them at all (Helman 2007).

In providing care for a culturally diverse society, practitioners should be aware of the cultural profile of the population they serve and have some understanding of the influences culture has on health and illness. Most importantly, they should be aware of their own assumptions and beliefs about health and illness and not allow these to detrimentally affect the care they are providing.

Chapter 6
Child protection

You are personally accountable for your practice. This means that you are answerable for your actions and omissions, regardless of advice or directions from another professional.

You must promote the interests of patients and clients. This includes helping individuals and groups gain access to health and social care, information and support relevant to their needs.

(Nursing and Midwifery Council 2004)

In child protection cases, a doctor's chief responsibility is to the well being of the child or children concerned, therefore where a child is at risk of serious harm, the interests of the child override those of parents or carers.

All doctors working with children, parents and other adults in contact with children should be able to recognise, and know how to act upon, signs that a child may be at risk of any form of abuse or neglect, not only in a home environment, but also in residential and other institutions.

All doctors working with children, parents and other adults in contact with children must be aware of, and have access at their place of work to, their local Area Child Protection Committee's Child Protection Procedure manual.

(British Medical Association 2004)

Child protection is the responsibility of everyone working in emergency care. It is a vital part of each practitioner's role. Child advocacy is integral to child protection and some of the themes of advocacy are developed in this chapter. The job of the emergency practitioner with reference to child protection is simple and twofold: to recognise child abuse when it happens and to do something about it. Thus familiarity with patterns of presentation in child abuse and with the referral guidelines that pertain locally will fulfil these duties in protecting vulnerable children.

Presentational factors that should raise the index of suspicion for a non-accidental injury include the following (Joughin 2003, National Society for the Prevention of Cruelty to Children 2006):

- a delay in presentation and seeking help for the child
- where there is associated domestic violence between parents/carers
- a history concerning mechanism of injury that does not correspond with the actual injury
- poor detail concerning how the injury was sustained
- strange atypical interaction between parents/carers and the child
- an overt declaration of abuse by the child
- parents/carers attempting to silence children by providing the history and denying the child an opportunity to contribute
- previous attendance/multiple attendance at different facilities.

These presentational factors should raise the index of suspicion for child abuse. None of them provide incontrovertible evidence that abuse has taken place but they should alert the emergency practitioner to the possibility of abuse and prompt them to take steps to exclude or confirm this.

Child abuse was classified into four areas by the National Society for the Prevention of Cruelty to Children in 2006. These classifications help to explain the variety of abuse that children may suffer, the mechanism of injury associated with each and the sort of injuries that may be expected (see Table 6.1).

Table 6.1

Forms of child abuse

Forms of child abuse

(adapted from National Society for the Prevention of Cruelty to Children 2006)

Physical abuse	Hitting, shaking or throwing children. Burning or scalding them. Drowning or suffocating children. Deliberately causing or feigning symptoms of ill health in a child, as in Munchausen's disease by proxy.

Emotional abuse   Persistent emotional mistreatment of children. Engendering feelings of worthless-ness, stupidity or inadequacy. Frightening children. Emotional abuse is involved with other forms of abuse like physical and sexual abuse but can occur in isolation.

Sexual abuse   Forcing or enticing a child to take part in sexual activity whether or not the child is aware of what is happening. This may involve penetrative or non-penetrative contact but also includes encouraging children to view pornography or watch the sexual activities of others.

Neglect   Persistent failure to meet a child's basic physical and/or psychological needs, resulting in damage to health or development. Failing to provide food, shelter, or access to medical care.

Risk factors

Risk factors

Certain circumstances may act as risk factors for the abuse of children, and the identification of such factors, in association with suspicious injury, during history taking and physical examination should raise the suspicion of abuse. As with presentational charac-teristics, these do not provide proof of abuse but should alert the emergency practitioner to this possibility.

Risk factors for child abuse (adapted from Labbe 2003)

In the parents

- Previous abuse of another child
- Lack of knowledge of normal child development and behaviour
- Poor impulse control and aggressiveness
- Young age/single parent without support
- Social isolation

- Criminal record
- Poverty
- Mental illness and/or mental retardation
- Conjugal violence
- History of substance abuse

In the child

- Result of an unwanted pregnancy
- Different from parental expectations
- Born prematurely or born handicapped
- Difficult or perceived as being so
- Hyperactive
- Developmental delay

Presentation, signs and symptoms of physical abuse

Signs of physical abuse

Presentation of physical abuse depends upon the type of abuse inflicted. Typically children may suffer bony injuries, burns and scalds, bruising, lacerations and biting. In general children who suffer physical abuse will be fearful of intervention by healthcare workers in case the perpetrator is identified and this leads to further abuse. They may wear inappropriate clothing to cover injury and may be reluctant to undress because of obvious injury. They may fear physical contact and appear frightened and withdraw when this happens. Children may be aggressive towards others and older children may think of harming themselves or may actually do this (National Society for the Prevention of Cruelty to Children 2006). A more detailed discussion of self-harm in children appears in Chapter 7.

In assessing physical injury, it is advantageous to be aware of developmental milestones relating to motor activity in the child. This may be of assistance for instance in deciding upon whether an injury is incongruent with the stated mechanism of injury, or in deciding whether a child of a certain age is capable of sustaining such an injury accidentally. Not until a child is age six or seven months old for instance are they able to roll side to side independently. Not until approximately 12 months of age can a child pull itself to a standing position and walk holding on to furniture and not until around two years of age can children walk fully independently and be capable of pulling a toy around behind them, walk up stairs with the aid of a support or climb up and down from furniture (Barnes 2003, Hockenberry 2004). See Table 6.3 for a summary of injuries giving cause for concern.

Table 6.3

Specific injuries that should give cause for concern

Specific injuries that should give cause for concern
(adapted from Labbe 2003, National Society for the Prevention of Cruelty to Children 2006)

Injury	Rationale for suspicion of physical abuse
Torn frenulum	May be a consequence of a fall on to the face but may also be a result of a punch to the mouth or from having a dummy or feeding instrument forced into the mouth. May also occur as a consequence of forced fellatio in sexual abuse by males.
Metaphyseal and diaphyseal fractures	The diaphysis and metaphysis are the strongest parts of a child's bone. Injury requires a degree of force not usually associated with simple falls. Spiral fractures are rarely sustained during simple falls and they are more commonly associated with a twisting injury during a fall (e.g. the Toddler's fracture) or from having the limb forcibly pulled and twisted whilst the child is resisting this in an attempt to escape an abuser.
Fractured ribs	All bones in children are relatively plastic and compliant compared to adults. The chest wall is similarly compliant and it takes a great deal of force to fracture a rib in a child. Underlying injury should be excluded, as children's chest walls have the capacity to 'give' during injury because of their greater elasticity, causing damage to underlying organs.

Paediatric minor emergencies

Injury	Rationale for suspicion of physical abuse
Any fracture in child not yet walking	It is difficult to envisage how a child who is not yet walking might sustain a fracture of its own volition.
Bite marks	Unexplained bite marks should give cause for concern. They are not a normal part of interaction with the child.
Cigarette burns	These may mimic dermatological lesions; there may be more than one lesion, however, and the child will not have any associated features of dermatological illness such as fever or pruritis.
Sharply delineated burns or scalds	Sharply delineated scalds imply immersion injury where a child has been restrained in a hot liquid rather than falling into it. There will be no splash marks and there may be associated fingertip bruising where the child has been restrained.
Fingertip bruising	May appear anywhere, e.g. pinch marks on the cheeks of the face or the side of the head.
Skull fractures	Skull fractures may be indicative of abuse or may be a result of an accident.
Fractures of differing ages	Fractures of differing ages that show up during the same consultation are of concern. Ascertain whether medical help was sought for previous injury.
Hand slap marks	Evidence of hand slap marks provide evidence of significant force used during injury.

Emotional abuse may obviously be a factor that exists in conjunction with other sorts of abuse or may happen in isolation. Children experiencing emotional abuse will typically be hyper-critical of themselves, stating that they are worthless or stupid. They may react disproportionately to criticism, may be extremely passive or conversely aggressive and may exhibit neurotic behaviour such as self-mutilation or repeated habitual movements (National Society for the Prevention of Cruelty to Children 2006).

Sexual abuse may manifest with a variety of signs, symptoms and behaviours (National Society for the Prevention of Cruelty to Children 2006):

- having sexual knowledge beyond what is appropriate for age
- being overly familiar with others
- depression, self-harm, leaving home, anorexia
- regression to younger behaviour – thumb sucking is an example
- not wanting to be alone with certain people
- nocturnal enuresis and nightmares
- using sexually explicit language or behaviour.

Physical signs and symptoms may include recurrent complaints of abdominal pain, evidence of sexually transmitted disease, bleeding from, or trauma to the vagina, penis and/or rectum, torn frenulum secondary to forced fellatio and oral sexually transmitted diseases.

Neglect of the child may manifest as constant hunger and scavenging for food, emaciation and dehydration, parasite infestation, poor clothing or clothing inappropriate for environmental circumstances, poor hygiene, untreated medical problems and evidence of few friends or other contacts (National Society for the Prevention of Cruelty to Children 2006).

Some children may be subject to more than one form of abuse and this may complicate presentation. Where non-accidental injury is suspected, the practitioner should document their concerns and follow local guidelines for the reporting of such suspicion. In all cases it is advisable for the practitioner to discuss their concerns with another colleague; this may help to put the situation into perspective or may focus the concerns raised. If, however, a colleague does not agree with the concerns and the practitioner remains concerned then it is the practitioner's responsibility to report this.

Practitioners should become familiar with local arrangements for the reporting of child abuse and their role within these arrangements. Each acute trust will have a named nurse for child protection as a source of expert advice. The area child protection committee (ACPC) co-ordinates the multi-agency response to abuse and often provides training programmes. Duty social workers take referrals from emergency practitioners and where patients are to be admitted or this is thought advisable then the advice of paediatric specialists, working at registrar level or above, should be sought. General guidelines for assessment and referral emphasise the following points (British Medical Association 2004, National Society for the Prevention of Cruelty to Children 2006):

- If you suspect abuse then report it.

- Document your concerns and document meticulously any consultation process you undertook with the child and parents/carers.

- Do not attempt to investigate the matter beyond your scope of expertise – do not for instance begin a systematic examination of the child if they have already been referred for further assessment. Repeated assessment may lose the co-operation of the child and may incline the child to think that they are not being believed.

- If a child alleges abuse then they are to be believed.

- The prime concern of the practitioner is the child, not parents or carers.

- If necessary, inform parents/carers of your actions in asking other professionals for an opinion about their child's injuries. Remember, however, that the prime focus of care is the child and if by informing parents or carers of your action the child is likely to be removed from care then parents or carers should not be advised of your actions.

- If parents/carers attempt to leave the emergency care setting with the child then do not attempt to restrain them. Inform the police of the situation and circumstances surrounding it.

Children, along with certain adults, are in uniquely vulnerable positions in society and may need to rely on the skills and knowledge of emergency practitioners to ensure that this vulnerability is not exploited. Each practitioner has a responsibility to be aware of child protection procedures and to maintain and update their knowledge about clinical aspects of child abuse and the measures taken to address this.

Chapter 7
Care of the adolescent and young adult

The United Nations Children's Fund (UNICEF) recently identified the United Kingdom as the worst of 21 industrialised countries in which to grow up. The UK finished bottom overall in categories relating to (UNICEF 2007):

- material well-being
- health and safety
- educational well-being
- relationships
- behaviours and risks
- subjective well-being.

A year earlier, the BBC reported that youths in the UK were among the worst in Europe in terms of bad behaviour and this specifically related to (BBC 2006):

- the use of drugs and alcohol
- underage sexual intercourse and rate of teenage pregnancy
- violent behaviour.

Correlation of these two groups of phenomena has not been attempted. The UNICEF report painted a picture of neglect and 'poverty of aspiration' amongst teenagers in the UK. The report found that the proportion of UK teenagers who trusted their friends was less than half that in comparable countries in Europe and that almost 35% aspired only to menial, unskilled work (UNICEF 2007). The Institute for Public Policy Research work (Margo *et al.* 2006), reported by the BBC, found that teenagers in the UK spent less time with their parents than any of their European counterparts and pointed to a growing disconnection between parents and children. It also highlighted the fact that

38% of UK teenagers had used cannabis, compared to 7% in Sweden and 27% in Germany. British teenagers were also found to be the third worst binge drinkers in Europe, lagging behind only the Danes and the Irish (BBC 2006).

This outline of British teenagers is of course a very broad one and it would be unfair to assume that all teenagers behave in the ways described or feel quite as disempowered and neglected as the UNICEF report implies. It is reasonable to assume, however, that where adolescents and young adults attend for emergency care they have their own particular needs and have a propensity to certain sorts of behaviour that may lead to health risks. These include deliberate self-harm, drug and alcohol ingestion and early encounters with opposite or same sex sexual partners. The Royal College of Paediatrics and Child Health advocates the provision of quieter, more private, waiting areas for teenagers in emergency departments, with the provision of appropriate CDs and DVDs in addition to material promoting sexual health and drug and alcohol advice (Royal College of Paediatrics and Child Health 2007).

The Society for Adolescent Medicine, working in the USA, has identified that the provision of school-based health-promoting, prevention-oriented care for adolescents and young adults reduced attendance at the emergency department by more than 50% (Key *et al.* 2002). In the absence of these sorts of facilities in the UK, at least on a widespread basis, the responsibility for care will continue to fall upon emergency departments and their staff. It has however been identified, in a UK-based study, that staff responsible, for instance, for the assessment and management of self-harm in adolescents often have little knowledge of the particular needs of this patient group and often display a negative attitude towards them (Crawford *et al.* 2003). It would therefore appear imperative that the knowledge base of emergency care staff be enhanced with reference to the care of adolescents and young adults.

There is evidence that although male children and young adolescents use health-care with the same frequency as their female counterparts, older male adolescents show a marked reduction in such use which continues into male adulthood. Opportunities to address some of the risk-taking behaviours, that are more prevalent amongst males anyway, are therefore reduced and the morbidity and mortality associated with these behaviours continues (Marcell *et al.* 2002). Homosexual males are at greater risk of emotional problems and more often attempt to harm or kill themselves than their heterosexual or bisexual peers, yet homosexual females do not tend to have such problems and it is females in heterosexual relationships that engage more in risk taking and self-harm (Udry & Chantala 2002, Crawford *et al.* 2003).

Much risk-taking behaviour amongst teenagers has been attributed to the development of low self-esteem in childhood (McGee & Williams 2000). This, together with the fact that many adolescents have a heightened sense of invulnerability, even when they are aware of the risks associated with certain behaviour (Greene *et al.* 2000), makes the appropriate care of adolescents and young adults particularly challenging.

Deliberate self-harm

Deliberate self-harm

Deliberate self-harm and suicide have an intertwined relationship, with between 0.5% and 2% of all those who harm themselves subsequently committing suicide (Owens *et al.* 2002). Factors that are thought to be particularly influential in deliberate self-harm and suicide in the adolescent and young adult include:

- a history of sexual abuse in childhood
- bullying and physical abuse at school and/or home
- use of drugs and/or alcohol
- where there has been the suicide of another family member
- depressive illness in the family
- significant life events such as death of a family member
- the lack of a confidant to talk to.

(See Garber *et al.* 1998, Garnefski & Arends 1998, Garnefski & DeWilde 1998, Sandin *et al.* 1998, Baldry & Winkel 2003, McNairn *et al.* 2004, Bywaters & Rolfe 2005, Cerel & Roberts 2005, Basile *et al.* 2006.)

A London-based study (Crawford *et al.* 2003) found that many staff responsible for the assessment and management of self-harm in adolescence (in emergency departments and elsewhere) held a negative attitude towards these adolescents. It was also found that many staff lacked knowledge about caring for such patients: more than 75% of staff were unaware that a history of sexual abuse or homosexuality made deliberate self-harm more likely. One-third of staff were unaware that adolescents who have self-harmed are at increased risk of suicide (Crawford *et al.* 2003). Others have found that where adolescents have asked for help from healthcare staff, and from ambulance staff, they have been faced with ridicule and hostility (Mental Health Foundation 2006). Emergency care staff and others responsible for the care of adolescents who have self-harmed should familiarise themselves with the risk factors associated with this and not allow attitudes towards self-injurious behaviour to compromise care. In disclosing self-harm, adolescents are acting with a degree of courage. The fostering of a therapeutic relationship is important in order to gain the trust of the adolescent, enquiry should take place at a pace dictated by them and should not focus exclusively on physical manifestations of self-harm. In delivering a multidisciplinary response to the adolescent who has self-harmed, all of the parties involved need to deliver a similar message in a similar way for care to be most effective.

All adolescents who have harmed themselves or attempted suicide should be referred to specialist in-patient services for further assessment and treatment. Once medical problems have been dealt with (e.g. any toxic effects of an overdose of medication or the management of self-inflicted wounds), a psychiatric assessment should also take place in order to identify what has made the adolescent behave in this way. Given the risk factors associated with self-harm in the adolescent, this may be a precious opportunity to identify such phenomena as sexual abuse, addiction, or bullying and physical abuse and should not be squandered.

Paracetamol poisoning

Paracetamol poisoning

In the UK the most common group taking an overdose of medication are female adolescents aged 15–19 years, though the rate of suicide is highest in young males (Samaritans 2005). Paracetamol is by far the most common agent used in overdose in the UK (Prince 2000).

Care of the adolescent and young adult

As plasma concentrations of the drug peak four hours after ingestion, blood is taken at this point where possible in order to establish plasma concentration. Treatment for the overdose is based upon this: patients with low levels of paracetamol may not need antidotal treatment. However, this pattern of treatment makes two assumptions:

- that all of the medication taken in overdose was taken at the same time
- that patients will present for care within four hours of overdose.

Unfortunately many patients do take staggered overdoses over a number of hours or days and may also not present for care until many hours or days after the overdose, when the physical manifestations of toxicity have become apparent. Patients who present in these ways are at greater risk of morbidity and mortality than those who take an overdose in a single episode and present for care within four hours. Where plasma concentration is expected to exceed 150 mg/kg then antidotal therapy should be commenced (Hartley 2002). It is of vital importance therefore to establish the circumstances of overdose when assessing the patient.

Plasma concentration of 150 mg/kg may cause liver damage, a common side effect of ingestion, and concentrations exceeding 350 mg/kg are very likely to cause such damage. Other side effects of overdose may be related to liver damage and include prolonged clotting times. Abdominal pain, nausea and vomiting may not become apparent for approximately 24 hours after ingestion. Some patients, perhaps being unaware of the liver damage associated with overdose, will only present at this stage when feeling physically unwell and this has obvious implications for the management of the patient, as liver damage becomes far more likely.

Giving activated charcoal to decontaminate the GI tract may be of value in patients who present within one hour of ingestion. Specific antidotal treatment is the intravenous administration of n-acetylcysteine (Parvolex) and this is most effective in reducing liver damage when given within eight hours of ingestion. Where patients present more than eight hours after ingestion, this treatment should be started immediately without waiting for plasma concentration to be measured.

Patients should be weighed before giving n-acetylcysteine as the dose is dependent upon this. Some patients experience allergic or anaphylactic reactions to the drug and where this is the case the treatment should be stopped and the reaction treated. Only in anaphylaxis is treatment stopped permanently. Other reactions are treated with anti-histamine and cortisone drugs and the antidotal treatment re-started (Hartley 2002). Methionine is an alternative antidotal treatment to n-acetylcysteine and may be used where there is a known history of anaphylactic reaction to n-acetylcysteine or where this happens while giving the drug. However if liver damage has already occurred methionine may make this worse and it should not be given more than 12 hours after ingestion (Hartley 2002).

Treatment of paracetamol poisoning

Treatment with n-acetylcysteine & methionine

n-acetylcysteine

Children > 20kg:

- 150 mg/kg body weight in 100ml 5% dextrose slow IV infusion over 15 minutes *then*
- 50mg/kg IV in 250ml 5% dextrose over 4 hours *and then*
- 100mg/kg IV in 500ml 5% dextrose over 16 hours

Children < 20kg:

- 150 mg/kg in 3 ml/kg 5% dextrose slow IV infusion over 15 minutes *then*
- 50 mg/kg by IV infusion in 7ml/kg 5% dextrose over 4 hours *and then*
- 100 mg/kg in 14ml/kg of 5% dextrose over 16 hours

Methionine

- Child > 6yrs: 2.5g orally every 4 hours for 4 doses (10g in total)
- Child < 6yrs: 1g orally every 4 hours for 4 doses (40g in total)

The potential for liver and kidney damage mean the monitoring of their function in toxic patients is mandatory. These problems generally develop within about two to four days of ingestion. The extent to which PT and INR times are lengthened has been found to be indicative of the severity of liver damage and therefore prognosis (Prescott 1983).

Care of the adolescent and young adult

In pregnant patients paracetamol does cross the placenta but it is thought that the fetus is less prone to toxic side effects of the drug than the mother (McElhatton 1990). Neither methionine nor n-acetylcysteine are contraindicated in pregnancy.

Encephalopathy, identified by a deteriorating level of consciousness not attributable to other causes, is a sign of impending liver failure and the patient will need referral to a specialist liver unit. Referral to such a unit should also occur under the following conditions (Hartley 2002):

- INR > 2 at 24 hours, > 4 at 48 hours or > 6 at 72 hours OR
- PT greater in seconds than number of hours since ingestion
- elevated plasma creatinine
- hypoglycaemia
- persistent acidosis
- hypotension.

Alcohol and drug use

Alcohol and drug use

Alcohol and drug use in adolescence has been associated with childhood abuse and familial instability, in that such adolescents will begin drinking alcohol and/or taking illicit drugs at an earlier age, and consume more alcohol and drugs than their peers (Dube *et al.* 2006, Kliewer & Murrelle 2007). Adolescents who use alcohol and/or drugs themselves tend to express dissatisfaction with their lives (Zullig *et al.* 2001). Other studies have found that alcohol use in adolescence is also related to whether or not there is approval of this by parents or carers and also found that alcohol use was more common in adolescents who also practised other risky behaviours such as illicit drug use (Donovan 2004, Kokkevi *et al.* 2006). In the UK alcohol and illicit drug use has been reported as being higher in boys than girls, though girls reported a greater incidence of smoking. Alcohol and drug use was generally higher in the white population than black or British Asian adolescents. The most common drug used was marijuana (Rodham *et al.* 2005). A relationship has also been found between peers in groups, with individuals far more likely to use alcohol or drugs if members of their peer group also do (Sieving *et al.* 2000).

In addition, when under the influence of alcohol adolescents participate in other risky behaviour such as driving under the influence of alcohol (Van Beurden *et al.* 2005). Information of this kind is of obvious value in the prevention of alcohol-related injury and illness but is also of benefit when treating the adolescent in emergency care settings. Practitioners should look beyond the 'apparently drunk' adolescent and make some attempt to establish what has caused the individual to consume as much alcohol and/or illicit drugs as they have.

The ability to resist peer pressure to use drugs and/or alcohol during adolescence is seen as crucial to the prevention of injuries and illness associated with these (Barkin *et al.* 2002) and, as if this is not enough, adolescents are also exposed to pressure from popular culture, in the form of music videos for instance, to use alcohol and/or drugs (Gruber *et al.* 2005).

Given the relationship between alcohol and drug taking and other risky behaviours such as unsafe sexual activity and driving under the influence of alcohol (Tapert *et al.* 2001, Van Beurden *et al.* 2005) it is recommended that any interventions to reduce drug or alcohol intake should also take into account the prevalence of these other behaviours as well (Tapert *et al.* 2001, Van Beurden *et al.* 2005).

Alcohol poisoning

Alcohol poisoning

In overdose, alcohol is just as toxic as many other drugs and it also has a tendency to enhance the toxic effects of any other drugs that may have been taken (Warner-Smith *et al.* 2001, Karbakhsh & Zandi 2007). Symptoms of mild poisoning include nausea and vomiting. Those who continue to take alcohol at this point are prone to more severe alcohol poisoning which may feature:

- a decreasing level of consciousness and coma
- respiratory depression.

Alcohol is widely available and comparatively inexpensive. Binge drinking is sub-culturally approved of. These factors combined account for an increasing level of short-term and long-term health problems associated with alcohol poisoning (BBC 2002).

Rapid absorption of alcohol renders activated charcoal of little value in alcohol poisoning. And as there is no antidote for alcohol, treatment is aimed at supporting vital functions. The airway may have to be secured as the patient's level of consciousness decreases and the risk of aspiration of stomach contents grows (Brick 2005). Assisted breathing may become necessary. Alcohol reduces the liver's store of glycogen and this makes the patient prone to hypoglycaemia. An estimation of blood sugar level is mandatory in all patients who present with alcohol poisoning.

Decreasing level of consciousness and poor cognitive abilities, in conjunction with the difficulty in speaking clearly when under the influence of alcohol, mean that the patient is far more vulnerable than usual. Alcohol may effectively hide the symptoms of other illness or injury. It will minimise pain from injuries that may then be unrecognised. Symptoms such as amnesia, decreasing levels of consciousness, and vomiting associated with a complicated head injury, for instance, may be very difficult to distinguish from those caused by alcohol poisoning. Extra care should be taken in the assessment and management of such patients to avoid making assumptions that will compromise care. It may not be possible for patients with alcohol poisoning to give a medical history and this can obviously also be detrimental to their care. Every effort should be made to contact next-of-kin where necessary and to attempt to gain more information about the patient from these sources.

Opiate poisoning

Opiate poisoning

Heroin addicts are the most likely victims of opiate poisoning when they take a particularly potent source of the drug or take alcohol at the same time (Warner-Smith *et al*. 2001, Karbakhsh & Zandi 2007). Opiate poisoning is characterised by pinpoint pupils, respiratory depression and decreased level of consciousness or coma. Such symptoms in combination (alcohol poisoning for instance dilates the pupils) in patients who present in this way should be assumed to be opiate poisoning and treated accordingly, whatever the history given (or lack of it when a patient is unconscious).

Naloxone is a specific antidote for opiate poisoning and may be administered intravenously or intramuscularly where venous access cannot be secured. Intranasal naloxone has also been found to be of clinical value and has the added benefit of not exposing emergency care staff to potential needlestick injuries (Barton *et al*. 2005). Naloxone needs to be given frequently or as an infusion because its action is short-lived. Whilst awaiting response to naloxone, patients may need airway and breathing support.

Opiate and alcohol poisoning poses an increasing health problem in the developed world. The use of alcohol and drugs in combination is associated with increased morbidity and mortality (Warner-Smith *et al*. 2001) and given the tendency of some adolescents to indulge in multiple risk behaviours this may dispro-portionately affect them.

Sexual activity

Sexual activity

The UK has the highest teenage pregnancy rate, defined as conceptions per 1000 females who are under 18 years of age, in Europe. It is five times higher than that in the Netherlands and three times that in France (Department for Education and Skills 2005). A government-funded body, the Social Exclusion Unit, published a teenage pregnancy report in 1999. It acknowledged that teenage pregnancy was a multi-faceted and complex health challenge but identified the following relevant factors associated with it (adapted from Social Exclusion Unit 1999):

- Many adolescents and young people have low expectations and expect to live their lives on benefits. Thus they can see no reason not to become pregnant.

- Knowledge of contraception and parenting skills were limited amongst adolescents and young people.

- Popular culture promotes sexual activity amongst adolescents and young people. They feel under pressure to be sexually active but feel that they cannot discuss this with their parents or teachers.

Most recent data appears to indicate that overall the rate of teenage pregnancy has declined slightly from 42.8 per 1000 in 2002 to 42.3 in 2005 but the rate amongst 13–15-year-old girls actually rose in this period (Office for National Statistics 2005).

Care of the adolescent and young adult

The implications of teenage pregnancy for both the mother and the child are (Department for Education and Skills 2005):

- that the mother is unlikely to complete her education and is likely to secure only a menial job or live with the support of benefits
- that teenage mothers are more likely to be lone parents and to live in poverty
- the child faces more health risks than other children and, if a girl, is more likely to become pregnant during adolescence herself.

Emergency contraception

Emergency contraception

Emergency contraception is now available as a single dose treatment and can be purchased over the counter (OTC). However, as it is priced at approximately £25.00, adolescents in particular may still access emergency care settings where the treatment is provided free of charge. It is also only available OTC to those over 16 years of age unless the pharmacy has a patient group directive that enables administration below this age..

As in disclosing self-harm, it takes a degree of courage on the part of the adolescent to present for emergency contraception, particularly if they are younger than the legal age for intercourse, which in the UK is 16. Unfortunately adolescents presenting for emergency contraception sometimes encounter the sort of staff response that is also associated with the presentation of self-harm. Reactions such as judgementalism and scorn are documented (Bell & Millward 1999, Fallon 2003). Other patients, having mustered the courage to present for care, have found themselves referred backwards and forwards between one service provider and another as they are viewed as 'inappropriate' attenders in, for instance, emergency departments (Bell & Millward 1999). Interestingly, some staff responsible for prescribing emergency contraception admitted making an evaluation of the patient's deservedness for treatment first: if patients were in a stable relationship and had what was deemed a responsible attitude to birth control then the treatment would be provided, whereas if the patient was not in a stable relationship and was deemed to be having intercourse on a casual and therefore, in their view, irresponsible manner the treatment was less likely to be provided (Cannell 1990). That the provision of emergency contraception to any patients should depend upon the attitude and moral outlook of the prescriber is obviously unacceptable and should be reflected upon within the context of the professional codes of conduct for all groups of staff.

It has also been found that staff lack confidence in prescribing emergency contraception because of a lack of knowledge about the treatment itself (Fallon 2003, Strozuk *et al.* 2005). A nine-point questionnaire has been developed for pharmacists since the treatment became available for OTC purchase (Schering 2007):

- The patient is asked to verify their age and if less than 16 years is referred to medical or nursing staff for treatment.
- The patient is asked to confirm that the treatment is for their own use.
- The patient confirms that they have had unprotected sex within the last 72 hours.
- The patient should report any unusual symptoms during her last period as the treatment will not be effective if the patient is pregnant already.
- The patient is asked to confirm that this occasion is the first occasion of unprotected sex within their current menstrual cycle.
- The patient is asked to confirm that they have not already taken emergency contraception during the current menstrual cycle.
- The patient is asked to detail any medications that they are taking.
- The patient is asked to confirm that they do not have inflammatory bowel disease or liver pathology as emergency contraception may then be contraindicated.
- The patient is asked to detail any previous emergency contraceptive treatment and whether any symptoms of allergy were evident at that time.

This questionnaire is easy to administer and should form the basis of initial assessment.

A supportive attitude toward adolescents who present for emergency contraception is more likely to achieve the desired results of such activity, this being the reduction of the teenage pregnancy rate, and all of its attendant social problems. When, in particular, dealing with adolescents and young adults under the age of 16, it may be necessary to verify that intercourse was consensual and that there is no indication of sexual abuse. Although in strictly legal terms such adolescents are breaking the law, the responsibility of the healthcare provider is to ensure that abuse is not a factor in presentation and that the opportunity to promote sexual health is taken (Faculty of Family Planning and Reproductive Health Care 2004). Any disclosure of information to third parties such as parents, social services or the police, particularly where the adolescent is deemed Fraser competent, would need to be justified in terms of serving the best interests of the patient.

Adolescents under the age of 16 are able to consent to emergency contraception without the need for parental involvement if (Prodigy 2006k):

- the young person can understand the advice that is being given
- the young person cannot be persuaded to permit parental involvement
- the young person is likely to be sexually active with or without intervention
- the young person's physical or mental health may suffer if treatment is not given
- it is in their best interests.

The patient should be reassured with the advice that there is a very low failure rate if the treatment is taken within 24 hours (0.4%) and remains largely successful up to 72 hours after unprotected intercourse. They should be advised to return for treatment if they vomit within two hours of taking the medication, and be advised that the treatment may cause nausea. If their subsequent menstrual period is late they should be advised to obtain a pregnancy test and should avoid unprotected sex at least until their next period. The opportunity should be taken to discuss longer-term birth control strategies or identify where the patient may find this information.

The provision of sexual health clinics, offering advice upon contraception and sexually transmitted disease, has been shown to be an effective way of linking with an adolescent population and reducing unwanted pregnancy (Brindis *et al.* 2003). The consistent and widespread provision of such services is not evident in the UK where they are provided by a mix of primary care, secondary care and private facilities. In the absence of such a 'one stop' facility adolescents may be unsure of where to access services or may access different services at different times. A lack of effective communication between service providers may therefore lead to no sexual health profile being developed and no one service taking responsibility for co-ordinating this. Attendance in emergency care settings is an opportunity to begin the development of a coordinated service for adolescents and young people.

Chapter 8
Safe discharge of children

For the child, discharge is the most satisfying part of their emergency care journey: they are now back in the control of their parents or carers and will shortly be in a familiar environment. Their fears about admission to the hospital, loss of limbs or even death have been proven unfounded. Their fears about pain and needles have either also proven unfounded or have been put into rational perspective by a practitioner who is sensitive to their needs. In order to maintain this perception on the part of the child, discharge should be as safe and effective as possible so as to avoid unscheduled re-attendance or sub-optimal aftercare in the home environment.

As soon as it is clear that the child being cared for is appropriate for discharge, as the vast majority of children with minor injuries and illness will be, attention should begin to be focused on the discharge process. Depending upon the injury sustained, parents, carers and where appropriate the child themselves need to be provided with enough information, in language that they understand, to be able to care for their injury or illness during recuperation at home and avoid unscheduled re-attendance. In general the sort of information required will be:

- Advice about how long the child may expect to experience pain as a consequence of injury or illness: soft tissue injuries will take several weeks to become pain free but pain should diminish during that period; viral respiratory tract infections should subside in 7–10 days.

- Advice about physical activity: children with soft tissue injuries should be encouraged to gradually begin mobilisation of the affected part but participation in contact sports, which may exacerbate injury, should be avoided for the period during which the injury is healing.

Paediatric minor emergencies

- Advice about analgesia: what is the best sort of painkiller to take for a particular injury or illness? How often should it be taken?

- Advice about scarring: parents and children will need reassurance about scarring as a result of burn injury or head injury for instance. Realistic advice about the length of time it will take for skin to re-model should be given.

- Is there anything the child or parents/carers can do to accelerate or promote healing? Give advice about exercises in soft tissue injury and wound care advice following burn injury or lacerations and abrasions that may have been subject to wound closure techniques. Encourage the appropriate use of anti-pyretic medication in febrile illness.

- What happens if things go wrong? Identify under what conditions parents or carers need to bring the child back to the department or unit, depending upon the nature of the injury. Head injury advice should be given in written form but should also be discussed to ensure comprehension. Provide parents and carers with the telephone number for the department or unit and also for NHS Direct in England and Wales and NHS 24 in Scotland.

- Do I need to come back? Provide parents and carers with clinic and follow-up appointment information and ensure it is convenient for them in order to avoid non-attendance and consequent poor clinical outcomes.

Some parents or carers may be particularly anxious about caring for their children at home, particularly for instance after a minor head injury or a febrile convulsion. It is worth spending some time ensuring that such parents or carers understand what is expected of them and have some confidence in their ability to fulfil these roles. Encourage parents to voice any concerns that they have, however irrational they may appear to the healthcare provider. As the safety of the child is of paramount importance, it may sometimes be safer to admit children to hospital, or observe them for a period of time, where such parental anxiety exists and seems insurmountable.

Although emergency departments, minor injury units and walk-in centres usually have health visitor liaison staff who actively screen attendance of children for emergency care, this is sometimes limited to children under the age of five years. Where children are being followed up in a different care setting then it is good practice to correspond directly with other healthcare providers in the community for instance, in order that continuity of care is maintained and the child's best interests are served.

Parents and carers will need specific advice about wound care if their child has, for instance, had a wound closed. Advice specific to the method of closure should be given and written down if necessary. If the wound has been sutured then information about when and where sutures need to be removed should also be provided. In very young children, where a therapeutic relationship has been established, parents should be given the choice of returning to see the same practitioner for removal of the sutures where this is feasible.

Some parents and carers may also be reluctant to administer analgesia to their children and again this may be the case after head injury. There is a fear amongst some parents and carers that analgesia may mask the symptoms of serious head injury. They will need reassurance that this is not the case and the need for analgesia to accelerate recovery should be emphasised.

If any medication such as antibiotics has been prescribed, ensure that the parents or carers, and the child if necessary, understand when to take the medicine and how often. If penicillin-based medication is being prescribed, ensure that parents or carers are familiar with symptoms of allergy and know what action to take under such circumstances. Do not forget to enquire about penicillin allergy prior to administration.

If children are being discharged in the evening or at night time, ensure that a safe means of transport is available to take them home. Also make sure that they have enough analgesia for short-term requirements.

Do not forget to give the child praise for co-operation in their episode of care. Providing them with bravery certificates and badges will reinforce this and make any future attendance less anxiety-provoking for the child.

Ultimately, children, parents and carers should always be given the option of returning to the place of care if they feel it necessary and this should be made explicit.

Part II

Minor injury

Chapter 9
Defining minor injury in the child

A definition of minor injury is elusive. From the perspective of the child, a minor injury may take on more gravity because of associated pain, fear, anxiety and concern about outcome. From a professional perspective, it may be necessary to develop a definition in order to frame the working parameters of minor injury practitioners in emergency care. From an organisational perspective, it may be important to define which categories of attenders may be treated within a minor injury unit or walk-in centre and those that will need to attend the emergency department for care.

Young, Barnett and Oakley, writing in Australia, attempt to define minor injury in the child as one that 'can be reasonably expected to heal with minimal medical intervention' (Young *et al.* 2005a). Such a definition seems limited in its application because, as the authors acknowledge, injury is a continuum from minor to major rather than separate and discrete levels of injury and the assessment of all injury will need to distinguish moderate or major injury from minor injury. Thus the assessment will need to take into account more than just the presenting complaint: factors such as the mechanism of injury, past medical history of the child and physical examination findings also have the potential to convert an apparently minor injury into a more serious event. The Royal College of Paediatrics and Child Health (RCPCH) considers that attendance at minor injury units or walk-in centres should be limited to children with 'mild pyrexial illnesses, minor respiratory or gastrointestinal disorders, or superficial soft tissue injuries' (Royal College of Paediatrics and Child Health 2002). Although this guideline appears to make sound clinical sense in terms of avoiding the risks associated with not having resuscitation and paediatric specialist facilities available for children when needed, it still requires that parents or carers make a reasonably accurate assessment of the severity of injury or illness in the child. Owing to lack of knowledge, overwhelming anxiety or the closer proximity of certain services, this may not always be feasible.

Thus although minor injury and illness seem to have been defined by professionals, it is still accepted that this definition may sometimes have to take place at the point of first contact with emergency practitioners rather than beforehand, and that this may sometimes lead to risk for the child. The RCPCH makes several recommendations to minimise this risk and these should be considered by practitioners where appropriate (adapted from RCPCH 2002):

- Education of local populations where necessary to advise them of the appropriate use of minor injury/illness and emergency department services.

- Ensuring that NHS Direct in England and Wales and NHS 24 in Scotland are referring children to appropriate resources.

- Ensuring that minor injury service staff have requisite training in the resuscitation of children and undertake clinical rotations through the emergency department to maintain and improve these skills.

- The establishment of clinical networks involving emergency care staff from different provider areas and the establishment of a paediatric clinical link nurse to promote best practice and monitor this.

- Common triage nomenclature between minor injury services and the emergency department.

Triage nomenclature that is shared by minor injury services, primary care services, pre-hospital providers and emergency departments may overcome some of the risks associated with children being placed at risk in an inappropriate healthcare environment. Although this would still not overcome the problem of parental referral to inappropriate services, it may make their identification more speedy and because of a common language and understanding may also facilitate more timely transfer of the child to an appropriate environment. The triage nomenclature would obviously need to take into account the presenting complaint of the child but to be an effective tool for directing children to appropriate resources would also need to take into account past medical history, mechanism of injury, and examination findings such as temperature and obvious deformity. The paediatric algorithms of the Manchester Triage System (Manchester Triage Group 2005) would appear to fulfil these criteria and could perhaps be employed beyond the confines of its historical home in the emergency department.

Chapter 10
Clinical examination

There are three components to the clinical examination: history taking, physical examination and documentation. Each will be dealt with in turn. The specific skills that facilitate the effective consultation and communication with children are also discussed in the chapters dealing with communication with children, acting as an advocate for children and a child's view of emergency care.

History taking

History taking

History taking is a two-way process in which information is shared between the patient and the practitioner to inform diagnosis. Obviously information needs to be given to the practitioner by the patient but in order to make this information more relevant, and to facilitate best outcomes for the patient, information also needs to travel in the opposite direction from the practitioner to the patient. Patients need to receive feedback on the information they are giving to the practitioner in terms of its relevance and importance in the diagnostic process. They will need reassurance on certain points, will need to have anxieties addressed and where appropriate in older children may want to contribute to the plan of care being formulated. Involving the patient in this way, and addressing concerns, will increase co-operation and trust and enhance the consultation process.

The consultation process with children will be additionally enhanced by involving the parents or carers in the process and this is particularly true with more dependent, younger children. In pre-verbal children the entire history taking process will rely on the testimony of other people, generally parents or carers. Their co-operation will be more effectively gained if the practitioner is seen to be addressing their concerns and attending to the physical needs of the child. Ways of facilitating this include:

- Attending to the possible need for analgesia for the child whilst taking a history from parents or carers.

- Addressing the immediate concerns of parents or carers rather than deferring or ignoring them. These concerns may be verbalised by the parents or carers or they may be implicit in their body language and demeanour. The parents of a child with a skin rash for instance may not feel confident enough to verbalise their concern about meningitis but their obvious anxiety and manner make this clear. If this is made explicit by the practitioner and the probability and prognosis explored then the co-operation and trust of parents and carers is more effectively secured. If the practitioner does not address these concerns in a timely manner parents or carers are left to feel either that the practitioner is inexperienced and has not identified obvious signs of illness, in which case they will continue to be anxious, or that in not identifying their concern the practitioner may be supercilious or belittling. Either outcome does not facilitate co-operation and trust.

- If appropriate ask parents or carers what they think may be wrong with the child. Acknowledge their superior expertise in knowing what is normal and abnormal for the child. If information is volunteered do not treat it dismissively; build upon the information given to inform diagnosis. Outline choices in investigation and treatment and give parents the opportunity to express preferences about these.

- Provide first aid and comfort measures for the child whilst taking a history from parents or carers; provide a sling in upper limb injury and give praise for co-operation on the part of the child.

- Give parents or carers some idea of the likely outcome for the child. It may be possible, in obvious injury, to give a reasonably specific picture of outcome. If this is not possible then give as accurate a picture as possible of likely outcomes, emphasising that these may change as they progress through the journey but that they will be kept informed about such changes. Try to give some indication of how long they are likely to be in the department or unit. Arrangements may have to be made for the feeding of children or the care of siblings.

History taking in the older child may rely more often on the testimony of the child themselves. The injury is less likely to have been witnessed by parents or carers, as the child, being more independent, may not have been under their direct supervision. They may have been playing with friends or may have been at school. The injury may therefore have been unwitnessed or witnessed only by other children of a similar age to the child. Skills in communicating with children therefore take on greater importance. An awareness of the developmental stages of children and therefore the sort of language that they will comprehend and utilise, is of obvious importance in this process, as is a knowledge of other cognitive and motor developmental milestones when, for instance, attempting to match mechanism of injury with the presenting complaint of the child (see Table 10.1).

Use knowledge of the developmental milestones pertinent to cognitive development and communication to shape the sort of questions being asked of children of different ages. Complex open-ended question structures requiring similarly complex responses are obviously not appropriate in a child under four years of age where closed type questions may yield more information both in terms of the child's comprehension of the question and their response to it.

Older children will be able to provide an adequate history providing that they feel that the practitioner is someone they can confide and place their trust in. It is important not to be seen to patronise older children, particularly adolescents, during the consultation process. Such children, being more independent, may resent too much emphasis being placed on the testimony of parents or carers and it may be advisable to consult the child first. Adolescents may also appreciate having their concerns addressed directly rather than the practitioner asking the permission of parents or carers to do this. Where appropriate, this should be undertaken.

An awareness of self in terms of the verbal and non-verbal cues being employed is essential during history taking. Practitioners may unwittingly lose the co-operation and trust of children if they display body language or use language that appears to imply disapproval or lack of interest. Being aware of personal prejudice and beliefs and not allowing them to impinge upon professional duties to patients will help in avoiding these situations. Always give the patient enough attention during the consultation process. Patients, including children, appreciate being treated like (and feeling like) individuals when speaking to practitioners and not being made to feel like just another mundane part of the daily workload. If the practitioner is going to document findings during the consultation process, rather than retrospectively after the consultation has concluded, they should ensure that their focus upon note-taking is not interpreted as a lack of interest by the patient. Some practitioners find their work enhanced by note-taking during consultation, as they may forget certain details of consultation when documentation is attempted retrospectively, or note-taking during consultation may prompt a more systematic approach to consultation. If this is the case then an explanation of this at the start of the consultation will avoid any misinterpretation on the part of the patient. Allow the patient time to express fears and concerns, allow them to describe in their words what has prompted them to attend for emergency care. The initial part of the consultation should be an attempt to gain as much information as possible about the attendance. It is the job of the practitioner to sort and refine this and the consultation may subsequently become more focused, using more closed questions, when suspected diagnosis is being refuted or confirmed. If this process is not allowed to develop then the patient, parents or carers, will leave feeling that their problems and concerns have not been addressed. This may result in poor compliance with treatment regimes that have been prescribed and repeat attendance in an attempt to have concerns addressed.

In taking a history from the patient, a systematic approach to the gathering of information may assist in prompting the practitioner to ask relevant questions and enhance the ability of the practitioner to interpret the relevance of signs and symptoms. In taking on historically medical roles of history taking, physical examination and subsequent documentation, emergency practitioners need to become familiar with the medical model applied to these processes (see Table 10.2).

Table 10.1 Developmental stages

(adapted from Barnes 2003, Hockenberry 2004, Child Development Institute 2006)

Age	Cognitive development	Motor development	Emotional/moral development
0–6 months	Recognises familiar persons at 3 months May imitate sounds/actions at 6 months Localises to sound	Nose breathes Rolls back to side at 4 months Rolls abdomen to back at 5 months	
6–12 months	Responds to own name Understands simple verbal commands	Parachute reflex develops – limbs outstretched during falls. Manipulates small objects, stands holding furniture	Stranger anxiety and separation anxiety begin to develop
12–18 months	Vocabulary of 10 or more words Mimics parents	Walks unaided at about 13 months Anterior fontanelle closed	May endure brief separation from parents or carers
18 months –3 years	Can use 2 or 3 word phrases and words like 'me', 'you', 'him' Answers yes/no to simple questions Attention span is longer	Climbs stairs – 2 feet on each step Can turn a knob or remove a lid Toilet training may start and develop	Separates more readily May be jealous of younger siblings at around 3 years
3–4 years	Uses sentences of 4–5 words States personal ideas and feelings Vocabulary of 1500 words or more	Climbs stairs – alternates footing	Selfish, impatient, shows off Obeys because of rules, not a sense of right and wrong
4–5 years	Understands more complex questions Vocabulary of 2100 words or more Language more understood by strangers	Enjoys sport and activity with parent of same gender Balances on one foot – eyes closed	Less quarrelsome Less fearful: knows rules are for protection
6–9 years	Sentences more complex Uses imagination and can listen appropriately	Likes to compete – play may be rough Vision reaches maturity	Can share and co-operate May be modest/self-critical
10–12 years	Uses the telephone, writes letters, surfs the internet	Slow growth in boys – may gain weight	Interest in opposite gender Sense of diplomacy begins
Adolescence	Cognitive independence, greater sense of the self as independent from parents	Fully independent – secondary sex characteristics appear	Looks for new norms/values Narcissistic, wide mood swings, fear of rejection

Paediatric minor emergencies

Table 10.2 History taking: Medical model

Introduction	Greet the child and smile. Tell the child your name and title. Give the child an overview of the consultation process.
PC: Presenting complaint	What is the child complaining of? Use their words if necessary, e.g. painful right knee – do not attempt to over-interpret this and document a presenting complaint of 'right supra-patellar tenderness' as over-interpretation at an early stage in the consultation may lead the practitioner to an incorrect diagnosis based on assumptions made about the presenting complaint. Pain in the knee may indicate anything from a minor contusion to joint pain indicative of systemic illness. Where the patient thinks the knee begins and ends may be different to the practitioner's understanding. Do not assume children or parents have the same understanding of anatomy as the practitioner.
HPC: History of presenting complaint	How did the child sustain the injury? Attempt to ascertain mechanism of injury: this may give valuable clues about likely injury.
	When did the child sustain the injury? If presentation is delayed, why is it delayed?
	Where did the child sustain the injury: at home? school? At play?
	Who was involved? Did anyone witness the injury?
	Why did the child sustain the injury? Could it have been avoided? Is there opportunity for health promotion or accident prevention strategies? Is there any suspicion of non-accidental injury?
O/E: On examination	Physically examine the injured part. Visually inspect the area – is there any obvious deformity, swelling or bruising? Palpate the injured part. In children start at an area away from the injury and work towards it in order to gain co-operation. Identify areas of tenderness. Assess sensation, motor function and blood supply distal to injury. A comparison with the unaffected side may be beneficial.
PMH: Past medical history	Patients may not understand what 'medical history' means; ask in terms that they understand. Has the medical history contributed to the accident? Will the medical history be exacerbated by the injury?
DH: Drug history	Ask about drug history. Will regular medications complicate or alter management? Will they interact with analgesia being considered?
SH : Social history	Who does the child live with? Are aftercare arrangements satisfactory?
Allergies	Does the child have any known allergies? Will these affect the management plan?
Imp: Impression	Using information from history taking and physical examination, establish an impression, or provisional diagnosis, to base subsequent investigation on. There may be more than one impression at this stage. Where further investigation is not required this may be the final diagnosis and the next two stages of the process may be omitted.
Investigations	The impression should guide investigations ordered. Any investigations requested should be justified. Provide the child and parents/carers with an explanation of investigations requested.
Interpret investigations	Once the results are available, combine this information with that already gained from history taking and physical examination. Is the impression refuted or proven? Has the number of potential diagnoses been narrowed down? Is there now enough information to establish diagnosis? Is consultation with a colleague warranted?
Diagnosis	Establish a final diagnosis and inform the child and parents of this.
Plan	Discuss the plan of care with the child and parents. Are options in care available? What is the likelihood of compliance? Does the child need to be reviewed? Provide the child and parents with adequate discharge advice if they are going home. If referral to specialist teams is warranted then provide the child and parents with an explanation of this and what it is likely to entail.

Physical examination

Physical examination

Physical examination skills in the child differ from those in the adult: look at the injured part of the child first and identify obvious deformity, swelling and bruising. Make some estimation of likely injury and subsequent pain before beginning to palpate the area. It is advisable to administer analgesia, and wait for it to become effective, prior to physical examination. Begin palpation away from the injury; this will familiarise the child with the process the practitioner wants to employ in a pain-free area and will promote trust. Identify areas of tenderness in anatomical terms and provide the child with positive feedback for co-operation. Assess sensory innervation, vascular status and motor function distal to injury. Where possible, compare the injured side with an unaffected side, e.g. in limb injuries. Emergency practitioners may be taught to assess sensory innervation with a hypodermic needle. This is not appropriate in young children and a less threatening object (such as a cotton bud) should be utilised. Remember to assess sensory innervation prior to administering local anaesthesia such as a digital block. Vascular supply may be assessed by palpation of a pulse distal to the injury, e.g. the radial pulse distal to a forearm injury, or by estimating capillary refill time if the injury is to the periphery of the upper or lower limb. Motor function should be assessed by asking the child to move the joint that is distal to the injury, or directly involved in the injury, through its normal range of movement. The elbow should be assessed therefore by asking the child to flex, extend, supinate and pronate the joint. Limitation or absence of movement should be noted and a differentiation should be made between limitation of movement secondary to pain and limitation of movement secondary to damage to motor structures such as tendons. One way of making this differentiation is to provide the child with effective analgesia in order to exclude pain as a factor in limitation of movement. Direct visualisation of a wound under local anaesthetic may also lead to identification of partial or complete damage to tendons. In very anxious or fearful children adequate examination may not be possible without sedation or even general anaesthesia. Remember to be honest and not lie to children: if an examination or investigation or administration of analgesia is going to hurt then tell the child that it will hurt and outline the benefits thereafter. Lying to the child will lead to losing their co-operation later.

Documentation

Documentation

Careless or incomplete record keeping often highlights wider problems with the individual's practice.

(Nursing and Midwifery Council 2005)

If it's not written down it wasn't done.

(Guly 1996, p. 5)

Documentation is not an adjunct to the clinical examination process that may be completed in a careless or indifferent manner if for instance the practitioner is particularly busy, if the case is seen as trivial or if documentation is thought less important than the history taking or physical examination processes. Documentation is an integral part of the clinical examination process and should be deemed as important as history taking and physical examination. As Henry Guly stated in his influential 1996 book on history taking, examination and record keeping in emergency medicine 'if it's not written down it wasn't done' and 'poor records = poor medicine' (Guly 1996 p. 5). The Nursing and Midwifery Council (NMC) expands upon this last point in asserting that problems with the practice of certain individuals may be exemplified by poor documentation (Nursing and Midwifery Council 2005). Thus poor documentation may not just reflect a busy practitioner who, though clinically competent, undervalues the need for comprehensive and accurate documentation, but may also reflect an incompetent practitioner whose clinical faults are highlighted by their poor documentation. The most able practitioner will not be able to provide evidence of assiduous history taking and physical examination techniques if they have failed to document how they went about this and what their findings were. The need for good documentation skills is more obvious than ever in the more litigation-conscious environment that prevails in emergency care now and with nurses and AHPs taking on expanded responsibilities in emergency care to prove their added value in these roles. It is good practice to individually audit documentation skills and to reflect on changes in documentation skills during the transition to new roles in emergency care. It is also advantageous when maintaining and improving documentation standards for departments and units to periodically audit documentation and review and benchmark it against professional guidelines.

Documentation should always be written legibly and in black ink to facilitate photocopying of records where necessary. All documentation should begin with insertion of the time and date and the name (not just the initials) of the practitioner undertaking the clinical examination of the patient (Nursing and Midwifery Council 2005). The documentation will follow the medical model in its layout as outlined earlier (see p.74). If the documentation is not undertaken during the physical examination and history taking processes it should be written up as soon as possible afterwards. Do not be tempted, for the sake of speed and productivity, to see a number of patients and dispatch them to the x-ray department, to the treatment area or home and decide to write the batch of notes up retrospectively during a break or at the end of the shift. By this time many of the patients may have gone home and details that were thought to be easily recollected have been forgotten. This can lead to speculative, inaccurate and therefore potentially dangerous documentation or can result in an embarrassing phone call to parents or carers of the child at home, asking them to remind the practitioner of which arm it was they had injured.

All documentation should be sequential and consecutive; do not be tempted to try and insert notes in between other passages of documentation in a retrospective attempt for instance to appear more diagnostically accurate in first impression than perhaps was the case. This may lead to at the least embarrassing repercussions when called upon to explain this apparent discrepancy in the structure of the notes, and at worst litigation if the motive for insertion is thought to be, or is, an attempt to hide misdiagnosis or falsify assessment methods retrospectively. Any additions to notes made after the initial examination should be dated, timed and signed even if made by the same practitioner as undertook the original examination (Nursing and Midwifery Council 2005). Notes should not include meaningless jargon, and subjective or offensive statements about the patient or their parents/carers, which again can lead to embarrassing explanations at a later date, particularly if care may be seen to be compromised by a value judgement on the part of the practitioner.

Patients, and their parents or carers, now have access to their medical records subsequent to the Access to Health Records Act of 1990 (Department of Health 1990) and the Data Protection Act of 1998 (Home Office 1998). Notes should be written in terms that the patient may be expected to understand and it may be advisable, where appropriate, to construct the notes with the involvement of the patient or to make them aware of what is being documented. This may be pertinent, for example, in cases of alleged assault or child abuse where the notes will be examined subsequently. All care planned and discharge advice given should be documented and where treatment has been delegated to others, for instance healthcare assistants, their actions should be countersigned by the responsible practitioner.

Electronic documentation is becoming more prevalent as information technology develops and many providers of patient care are moving towards the electronic patient record (EPR). Guidelines for documentation are also applicable to electronic documentation and in some ways electronic documentation may dispense with some of the problems sometimes associated with written notes: electronic means of record keeping can for instance be set up so that it is impossible to enter jargon or to retrospectively alter documentation. Rules concerning the confidentiality of patient records are also applicable to computer-held records and the practitioner should be assured that guidelines concerning access to electronic patient records exist within the workplace.

Contact details for the child and carer, the details of the general practitioner and the name of the child's school should be verified for accuracy and to facilitate follow-up care by staff such as health visitors and school nurses.

AWAJ (A word about jargon)

Jargon

The difference between jargon and acceptable abbreviation is a fine one and is commonly misunderstood. As a general guideline, acceptable jargon is that which would be readily understandable by any other similar practitioner. Thus abbreviations associated with the medical model of history taking such as PC (presenting complaint) or O/E (on examination) are acceptable abbreviations. The abbreviation FOOSH (fell onto outstretched hand), though commonly employed to describe a certain mechanism of injury, would not be universally understood and is not therefore an acceptable abbreviation. If there is any doubt about the appropriateness of an abbreviation being used then do not use it. See Table 10.3.

Table 10.3

Acceptable and unacceptable abbreviations

Acceptable and unacceptable abbreviations

Acceptable abbreviations/jargon		Unacceptable abbreviations/jargon	
PC	Presenting Complaint	FOOSH	Fell Onto Outstretched Hand
HPC	History of Presenting Complaint	RIE	Rest, Ice, Elevation
O/E	On Examination	DNW	Did Not Wait
IMP	Impression	SBT	Snuff Box Tenderness
Rx	Treatment	NKO	Not Knocked Out
PRN	As Necessary	CMS	Colour, Movement, Sensation
♂♀	Male/Female	LWBS	Left Without Being Seen
#	Fracture	PD	Provisional Diagnosis
PIP	Proximal InterPhalangeal	AD	Anterior Dislocation
DIP	Distal InterPhalangeal	PD	Posterior Dislocation

It can be tempting to jargonise work and abbreviate aspects of practice not readily understood by others. It shows that not only has the language of medicine been learned but that it has been mastered to the extent of adding new vocabulary. Too much jargon isolates certain levels of practitioner from others and from the patients they serve. Its indiscriminate use to deliberately obfuscate practice displays poor documentation skills which, as the Nursing and Midwifery Council states, may be an indication of general poor practice. It is wise to bear in mind when documenting patient records that each piece of work written may be later examined by the patient, other professionals and professional bodies or within the framework of the legal system.

Chapter 11
Minor head injury

Head injury is the biggest traumatic cause of death in children aged 1–15 years and the most common way of children sustaining such a head injury is when as a pedestrian they are struck by a motor vehicle (Advanced Life Support Group 2005).

Children's heads are disproportionately large compared to the head of an adult. They form up to a 2.5 times larger area of the body compared to that of an adult. As the head is disproportionately large, injury is more likely. This phenomenon is compounded by the fact that the cervical spine of the child is relatively flexible compared to that of the adult, and cord injury may occur even without radiological evidence of a bony injury to the cervical spine (Advanced Life Support Group 2005), by the fact that infants' gait and co-ordination is not fully developed and that below the age of eight to nine months the defensive reflex of putting out an outstretched hand to prevent injury (parachute reflex) to other areas has not yet developed.

The assessment of the child with a head injury may be complicated by the fact that the injury was unwitnessed or was witnessed only by peers of the child. If the child is at a pre-verbal stage of development then information concerning the mechanism of injury and consequent symptoms, some of the foundations on which assessment of head injury is based, will not be forthcoming or may not be couched in terms that are clinically reliable. The National Institute for Health and Clinical Excellence (NICE) guidelines for the assessment of head injury in adults and children, with associated decision making criteria for CT scanning (National Institute for Health and Clinical Excellence 2003, 2007c), are a mix of clinical findings and findings from history taking. Without a reliable history these guidelines become more difficult to utilise.

Under these circumstances the physical examination of the child takes on more importance, as does the testimony of parents or carers concerning the condition of the child.

History taking

History taking

History taking will concentrate on trying to establish the mechanism of injury, which will give the practitioner clues to the potential severity of the injury, and an analysis of symptoms surrounding the event. The challenges sometimes associated with this process when applied to children have already been outlined.

The testimony of others may have to be given more weight when assessing the child with a head injury. If the child has injured themselves at play, at school for instance, then this may amount to the testimony of the child's peers who will probably be of a similar age and developmental stage as the patient. This sort of testimony is obviously of mixed value depending on the age of the witnesses and their ability to recount the details to you effectively. If however the injury was witnessed by an adult then more reliable information may be forthcoming. The injury may have been witnessed for instance by a teacher or playtime supervisor who, if they have not accompanied the child to the emergency care facility, should be contacted to gather details about the injury. Sometimes schools and nurseries will provide a brief written account of the event for emergency care staff, that has been compiled by a witness to the injury. This sort of practice should be encouraged as the account is written soon after the event, when recollection is still fresh in the mind, rather than at a later stage when certain details may have been forgotten or rationalised as being insignificant.

The role of parents and carers in providing information to enhance the assessment of their child should not be overlooked. Recommendations for early recognition of meningococcal disease in children have emphasised the importance of such input: 'The knowledge of parents and their help-seeking behaviour were important in making management decisions' (Granier *et al.* 1998). Similarly in children with head injury, parents or carers with a more intimate and detailed knowledge of the child are in a better position to recognise subtle changes in behaviour and interaction with others on the part of the child than emergency care staff. This sort of information if not volunteered should be sought, as such symptoms may be indicative of early increase in intra-cerebral pressure in the child (National Institute of Health and Clinical Excellence 2007c).

Significant mechanisms of injury that will necessitate comput-erised tomography (CT) scanning include any child that as a pedestrian or cyclist has been hit at greater than 30km/h by a vehicle, any child that has fallen more than 3 metres and any child that may have sustained a high velocity injury (Royal Children's Hospital of Melbourne 2006, National Institute of Health and Clinical Excellence 2007c).

It is not uncommon for young children to have an episode of vomiting after head injury. NICE originally published guidelines for the assessment of head injury in children in 2003 and these have recently been partially updated (National Institute for Health and Clinical Excellence 2003, 2007c). These state that children that have more than three separate episodes of vomiting after head injury should be considered for CT scanning of the brain. However the guidelines also state that clinical judgement should be used to attempt to ascertain the cause of the vomiting prior to any decision about CT imaging in children aged 12 years or less. Significance of vomiting after head injury in children will therefore depend upon when and for how long it happens; vomiting of repeated or prolonged duration or vomiting that began some time after the head injury is of greater clinical significance than one or two episodes of vomiting that happened immediately after the head injury, and has stopped, in an otherwise well child.

Other signs and symptoms, elicited during history taking, that will require the child to undergo a CT scan include witnessed loss of consciousness of more than five minutes duration, amnesia of more than five minutes duration either prior or subsequent to injury, abnormal drowsiness, a reduced Glasgow Coma Score, any sign of a basal or depressed skull fracture and any infant (less than one year old) with a bruise, swelling or laceration more than 5cm in size on the head (National Institute of Health and Clinical Excellence 2007c).

The clinical examination

The clinical examination

Examination of a child with a head injury will entail gaining the trust and co-operation of the child as described in earlier chapters. It may also involve giving the child adequate analgesia to facilitate examination. After these conditions have been fulfilled the examination can proceed.

Palpation of the head to elicit the presence of scalp lacerations, haematomas or boggy swellings is an important first step. Large scalp lacerations may be a consequence of significant force in the mechanism of injury and should raise the index of suspicion for underlying brain injury. Remember that injuries to the parietal or temporal bones of the skull are more likely to subsequently provoke cerebral bleeding because the meningeal arteries traverse these bones. Boggy swellings may also represent the surface appearance of an underlying skull fracture with the consequent twelve-fold increased risk of brain injury (National Institute for Health and Clinical Excellence 2003). This finding will necessitate referral to in-patient teams for further assessment and observation.

Where there is suspicion of an associated injury the cervical spine the neck should be immobilised in a hard collar, providing the cooperation of the child can be gained. Where co-operation cannot be gained then strapping the child's head to a trolley should be avoided, as a distressed child moving uncontrollably in such circumstances may exacerbate injury: an attempt should be made to apply a hard collar without further restraint (Royal Children's Hospital of Melbourne 2006). Children less than three years old may be best managed by having parents or staff hold the head and body or by immobilising the neck with sandbags or towels (Royal Children's Hospital of Melbourne 2006). It should be remembered that children may have cord injury, because of the comparative flexibility of the cervical spine, without any evidence of bony injury on a plain x-ray of the cervical spine. This phenomenon is known as SCIWORA (significant cervical spine injury without radiological abnormality). If SCIWORA or a bony injury to the cervical spine is suspected from information concerning the mechanism of injury or clinical findings then the neck should be immobilised and arrangements made for the child to have a CT scan of the cervical spine.

Rhinorrhoea or otorrhoea, cerebrospinal fluid (CSF) leak from the nose or the ears respectively, is another factor that needs to be excluded on physical examination. Knowledge that CSF leakage from the nose or ears is symptomatic of a basal skull fracture will prompt the practitioner to look for other clues, from history taking and examination that confirm or refute this.

Table 11.1

Basal skull fracture: clinical signs

Basal skull fracture: clinical signs

Rhinorrhoea or otorrhoea	Cerebrospinal fluid leak from the nose or ears
Panda's eyes	Also known as 'raccoon eyes' this clinical feature of fracture of the base of the skull involves bilateral peri-orbital bruising
Battle's sign	Bruising over the mastoid area is known as battle's sign and is a clinical feature of fracture of the base of the skull

Apart from the clinical findings already discussed, children with head injury should also be referred to in-patient teams for further assessment and observation if the Glasgow Coma Score (Teasdale & Jennett 1974) is less than 15, or has been less than 15 either at the time of the incident or at any time since then. Has there for instance been any evidence of a period of loss of consciousness? Estimation of the Glasgow Coma Score (GCS) in children may be more challenging than that in adults because the verbal response component will differ, particularly in pre-verbal children. In the adult coma scoring chart the verbal response component is made up of criteria such as 'orientated', 'confused', 'inappropriate words' and 'inappropriate sounds'. Obviously in infants and very young children the use of these criteria in the assessment of conscious level would not yield reliable findings. Motor response criteria are modified but follow a similar pattern to those used in the adult. A paediatric coma scoring tool has been developed and is outlined below (see Table 11.2).

Paediatric minor emergencies

Table 11.2

Paediatric coma scoring tool

Paediatric coma scoring tool

(Adapted from NICE guidelines 2003)

Component	Response	Score	Total
Eye opening response (E)	Spontaneously	4	
	To speech	3	
	To pain	2	
	No eye opening response	1	
			E:
Motor response (M)	Infant moves spontaneously or purposefully	6	
	Infant withdraws from touch	5	
	Infant withdraws from pain	4	
	Abnormal flexion to pain	3	
	Extension to pain	2	
	No motor response	1	
			M:
Verbal response (V)	Infant coos or babbles (normal activity)	5	
	Infant is irritable and continually cries	4	
	Infant cries to pain	3	
	Infant moans to pain	2	
	No verbal response	1	
			V:
Total (E + M + V)		GCS =	

An alternative method of estimating conscious level in both adults and children is to use the AVPU system. AVPU is a simple mnemonic that was developed for its ease of use and the ease with which practitioners were able to recall its component parts without having to refer to a written version of the tool. It thus lends itself to use in rapid initial assessment and may be more useful than the GCS in pre-hospital settings. The component parts of AVPU are:

A: **A**lert

V: responds to **V**oice

P: responds to **P**ain

U: **U**nconscious

The relationship between the AVPU tool and the Glasgow coma scoring system is shown in Table 11.3.

Table 11.3

AVPU and GCS

AVPU and GCS

AVPU score	GCS score
A	15
V	13–14
P	8–12
U	3–7

Summary of pertinent examination and history taking criteria:

- Can you establish mechanism of injury from the child or witnesses to the event?

- When and where did the injury occur?

- Is there any suggestion that the GCS of the child has been less than 15 or is it less than 15 now?

- Is the child otherwise symptomatic: how many episodes of vomiting have they had and when did they begin? Is there evidence of amnesia or loss of consciousness? Is there any evidence from parents or carers that the child is unwell?

- Are there any associated wounds to the face or scalp and is the cervical spine tender? Does the cervical spine need to be immobilised prophylactically because of a significant mechanism of injury?

- Remember to ask about medical history of the child and gauge whether this complicates assessment and management (children with clotting disorders for instance). Enquire about immunisation schedules.

- Is there any evidence that the injury may have occurred as a result of physical abuse of the child?

- Formally calculate a Glasgow Coma Score and remember to offer the child analgesia. Involve the child and parents/carers in decision making and discuss the plan of care, based upon your examination and history taking, with them.

A child with no loss of consciousness after the incident and with only one or no episodes of vomiting, whose condition is currently stable, and who is alert and interactive, and neurologically normal, is extremely unlikely to have sustained any intracranial injury. Such a child may be safely managed at home.

(Young *et al*. 2005b)

The majority of children that attend either the emergency department, minor injury unit or NHS walk-in centre with a minor head injury will fit the patient description outlined above and may be safely assessed and independently managed by the emergency practitioner and cared for at home with appropriate discharge advice.

A minority of children seen in a minor injury unit or NHS walk-in centre will however need to be referred for secondary care to the emergency department or paediatric assessment unit of an acute Trust. NICE has also produced guidelines for the selection of patients with head injury to be transferred to secondary care from a less acute setting. Under any of the following circumstances the patient should be transferred (see NICE clinical practice algorithm number 2: referral of patients with a head injury by community medical services, e.g. General Practice, paramedics, NHS walk-in centres, dental practitioners or NHS minor injury clinics, National Institute for Health and Clinical Excellence 2003):

- if the GCS has been less than 15 at any time since the injury
- if there has been any suggestion of loss of consciousness since the injury
- if there has been any focal neurological deficit since the injury
- if there is any suspicion of a skull fracture or penetrating head injury
- if there is any amnesia related to events before or after the injury
- if there is persistent headache
- where vomiting is prolonged or delayed
- if there has been a seizure since the injury
- if the patient has a history of previous cranial surgery
- if there is a significant mechanism of injury
- where physical abuse is suspected as a cause of the injury.

Discharge

Discharge

Head injury in children can cause disproportionate anxiety in parents and carers based upon previous experiences or perceptions of prognosis in head injury. This anxiety needs to be addressed in concerned individuals in order that they have confidence in the discharge and in their ability to recognise symptoms within their child that will necessitate returning to the hospital. Failure to address this need may result in sub-optimal care for the child where parents may be too anxious to care for the child effectively at home, or may make repeated return visits to the emergency department or other care facility. In cases of extreme parental anxiety, or where parents are unable to comprehend the aftercare advice required for safe discharge, then it is not unprecedented for the child to be admitted for observation.

All parents and carers will require adequate discharge instructions to care for the child safely. Such instructions are generally given in the form of a head injury advice card with a list of symptoms that parents need to be alert for in addition to advice about activity and analgesia. Such advice needs to be given verbally and in written form. It is important therefore that the practitioner explains the instructions to parents and carers and elicits feedback to a level that satisfies them that the parents or carers are able to comprehend the instructions. In addition to always giving the parents or carers the option to return to the hospital and providing the telephone contact number for the emergency department, minor injury unit or walk-in centre, the practitioner should also provide them with the telephone number for NHS Direct in England and Wales or NHS 24 in Scotland.

NICE has developed a head injury advice template for use in children and it advises parents or carers to re-attend if any of the following circumstances arise (adapted from National Institute for Health and Clinical Excellence 2003):

- unconsciousness, or lack of full consciousness (e.g. problems keeping eyes open)
- any confusion (not knowing where they are, getting things muddled up)
- any drowsiness (feeling sleepy) that goes on for longer than

one hour when they would normally be wide awake or any difficulty waking the child up

- any problems understanding or speaking
- any loss of balance or problems walking or any weakness in one or both arms or legs
- any problems with their eyesight
- very painful headache that won't go away or any vomiting – getting sick
- any fits (collapsing or passing out suddenly)
- clear fluid coming out of their ear or nose
- bleeding from one or both ears or new deafness in one or both ears.

Parents and carers are further advised that they may expect their child to suffer mild symptoms such as nausea, dizziness, irritability, fatigue and a loss of appetite for a period of up to two weeks following injury. They are encouraged to promote rest and not to leave the child unsupervised for a period of 48 hours after the injury. The advice sheet is available to download from the website of the National Institute for Health and Clinical Excellence at: http://www.nice.org.uk/guidance/index.jsp?action = byID&o = 11836

Chapter 12

Injuries of the upper limb

Injuries of the upper limb take on characteristic patterns in children just as they do in adults and older people. Similar mechanisms of injury in an adult and a child may result in quite different injuries. A fall onto the outstretched hand for instance will in older patients tend to result in a Colles fracture of the wrist, a fracture of the radial head or a fracture of the neck of the humerus. In the child a Torus fracture of the radius, a supracondylar fracture of the elbow or a fractured clavicle are more likely consequences of a similar accident.

Young children are more likely to fall and injure upper limbs; as novices in the exercise of walking, children make more mistakes whilst developing competence. Unawareness or lack of cognisance of potentially dangerous or accident prone situations and circumstances also contribute to childhood incidence of injury. Young children also rely upon adults to adequately protect them from accidents or injury; sometimes this reliance is, unfortunately, poorly founded. For instance, in circumstances where young children rely upon adults to adequately restrain them in motor vehicles, or to provide them with adequate head and limb protection when using cycles, these obligations on the part of the parent or carer are sometimes not met. More unfortunately some children are maliciously injured by parents or carers.

Fracture of the clavicle

Fracture of the clavicle

This injury may be the result of a fall onto an outstretched hand or may occur as a consequence of direct trauma to the clavicle. Of such injuries, 80 % are to the middle third of the bone where it is at its weakest. The remainder affect the proximal or distal part of the bone (Brilliant 2007). The proximal clavicle is securely fixed within the thoracic cage adjacent to the sternum and greater force is therefore required to sustain a fracture. In fracture of the proximal clavicle, associated injury to local blood vessels, adjacent ribs and the lung on the affected side will need to be excluded, particularly if the mechanism of injury is a significant one. Clavicular injuries may be associated with injury to the brachial plexus and this should also be excluded by assessing sensation in the associated upper limb.

Children will present with perhaps an obvious deformity, most commonly to the mid-clavicle, and will be in obvious pain. Once pain relief measures have been initiated, attention should be given to the degree of deformity. Most injuries will be managed conservatively but where deformity is such that there is 'tenting' of overlying skin then advice concerning management should be sought from orthopaedic medical staff. Such a degree of deformity, confirmed on an x-ray of the shoulder and clavicle, will mitigate against conservative management because of the associated degree of angulation between the fractured bone ends. There is also potential for the fracture to become open when fracture ends protrude through overlying skin. Overlying skin, where there is severe deformity and significant pressure from the underlying bone, may also become avascular as small capillary vessels are, in effect, crushed or obliterated under pressure. Some fractures of the distal clavicle will also involve the acromio-clavicular (AC) joint. Under these circumstances the child should also be referred to orthopaedic staff.

Management of fractured clavicle is dependent on location and severity. Uncomplicated fractures of the middle and proximal bone can be managed in a broad arm sling for approximately three weeks. Fractures of the middle or proximal clavicle that are angulated, distal fractures that also involve the AC joint, and fractures that involve the brachial plexus should be referred to orthopaedic staff for perhaps more aggressive treatment.

Parents or carers of children who are being discharged with a broad arm sling often need reassurance about the prognosis for their child in terms of residual deformity. Many are concerned about the deformity over the fracture site and the fact that it does not appear to be cared for as aggressively as this deformity appears to warrant. They need to be reassured that the deformity and associated lump over the fracture site will last for a period of around 12 months and will gradually become less evident as the bone is re-modelled (Young *et al.* 2005b). They also need to be advised that the prognosis for such healing and re-modelling is particularly good in children and that the treatment regime is based on vast previous experience. Review of the child with uncomplicated clavicle fracture is not necessary and parents and carers should be advised to consult the primary care general practitioner or the emergency care facility if problems arise during the three to four week period that the sling will need to remain in place for. Contact sport should be avoided for a period of approximately six weeks (Young *et al.* 2005b). Parents and carers should be provided with the telephone number for the emergency care facility where they have been treated.

Supracondylar fractures of the elbow

Supracondylar fractures

Again this fracture may result from a fall onto the outstretched hand or from a fall directly onto the elbow. Children will generally present in obvious pain with the affected limb held in a position of maximal comfort, or minimal discomfort. The proximity of neurovascular structures, such as the radial and brachial arteries, and the radial, median and ulnar nerves, to the elbow joint makes assessment of pulses and sensation distal to this injury imperative. Such assessment should take place on presentation and after each occasion on which it is necessary to move the child's arm (i.e. on splinting the arm or placing it in a sling or on moving the arm in the x-ray department). This serial assessment of neurovascular status should be documented in the patient records. It is possible for a child with such an injury to present with intact neurovasculature distal to the injury but for this to be compromised during procedures undertaken to care for them. Children with sensory and/or vascular compromise should be taken to the operating theatre for exploration and decompression or repair of the deficit as soon as possible and certainly within four hours of injury, to avoid the possibility of permanent ischaemic or neurological damage to the limb. Prolonged ischaemia of muscles can lead to the development of Volkmann's ischaemic contracture, where fibrosed and contracted muscle causes deformity of the hand that is difficult to remedy.

Paediatric minor emergencies

The need for analgesia is apparent in such injuries and pain should be assessed and managed with appropriate reference to the age of the child and the guidelines provided by the British Association for Emergency Medicine (see p.29). In addition to medication, other non-pharmacological adjuncts to pain relief should be considered: this may take the form of a sling if its application does not involve too much flexion of the elbow. As already stated, children will have found a position of maximal comfort prior to presenting at the hospital. This may not be with the affected elbow at the approximate 90-degree angle required to apply a sling. If it is not, then rather than flexing the elbow and making the child uncomfortable (and potentially causing a neurovascular deficit), consider the use of other strategies: splinting the arm may be a very effective alternative or even the application of a temporary plaster of Paris. Most children with these injuries will be more comfortably cared for lying on a trolley and elevation of the affected limb on a pillow will also provide comfort under these circumstances. Do not forget to re-assess and document neurovascular status distal to the injury after you have moved the child's arm.

Effective analgesia and comfort measures having been implemented, the child will need to be taken to the x-ray department for lateral and AP views of the elbow. In interpreting these x-rays the practitioner will need some knowledge of the chronology of the development of the bones of the elbow in children. Some bones of the elbow will ossify at different times to others and it is not until the age of approximately 12 years that all of the bones have ossified. This is obviously important in the interpretation of x-rays in young children. The developmental chronology is usually remembered with the aid of the mnemonic CRITOL (see Table 12.1).

Table 12.1

CRITOL

(Source: Raby et al., 1995)

CRITOL

Bone	Age
Capitellum	3 months
Radial head	5 years
Internal epicondyle	7 years
Trochlea	9 years
Olecranon	11 years
Lateral (external) epicondyle	12 years

Knowledge of this chronology of development is particularly important in fractures of the internal epicondyle. The internal or medial epicondyle is the point of insertion for the flexor muscles of the entire forearm. Contraction of these muscles may therefore cause an avulsion fracture of the relatively immature internal epicondyle. This avulsed piece of bone may be mistaken for another ossification centre on the elbow. In older children therefore (approximately nine years and above) where the trochlea can be seen, then if the internal epicondyle cannot be seen it may be avulsed as it always ossifies before the trochlea (Begg 2005).

Supracondylar fractures of the distal humerus in children can have very subtle x-ray appearances and other diagnostic skills are needed when interpreting x-rays of the elbow. The bloody effusion that is the result of a fracture displaces fat pads that normally line and cushion the joint away from their normal position. In the elbow there are an anterior and a posterior fat pad and they are best looked for on the lateral x-ray. They will show as darker lines in the light soft tissue surrounding the bones of the elbow. On the lateral film an anterior pad can generally be seen following the curve of the elbow which is not indicative of a fracture. If however this anterior fat pad has been displaced by an effusion of blood then it no longer follows the curve of the elbow but is displaced further away into the soft tissue. This displacement is called the 'sail sign', as the shape of the fat pad is now thought to resemble the sail of a ship. A positive sail sign is diagnostic of a fracture in the elbow. The posterior fat pad of the elbow normally lies behind the olecranon in the olecranon fossa and is therefore never normally visible on a lateral x-ray. The presence of a posterior fat pad therefore indicates that the pad has been displaced by an effusion of blood and again is diagnostic of a fracture in the elbow (Begg 2005). The identification of a posterior fat pad or displaced anterior fat pad should prompt a re-assessment of the x-ray in another attempt to locate the fracture they are diagnostic of. Fractures associated with positive fat pad signs are supracondylar fractures and fractures of the radial head. If the fracture still remains elusive then treat the child on the assumption that they have a fracture. Conversely, the absence of a fat pad does not exclude fracture and the child should be treated according to symptomatology and clinical findings. See Figure 12.1 (overleaf).

Paediatric minor emergencies

Figure 12.1

A lateral x-ray of the elbow showing a displaced anterior fat pad (sail sign – arrowed) and a posterior fat pad (arrowed). Such findings are always abnormal and are diagnostic of a fracture.

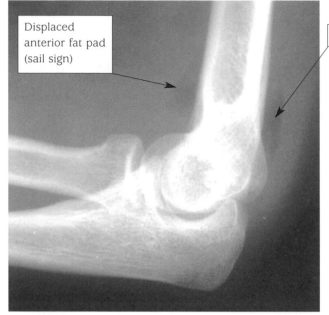

Displaced anterior fat pad (sail sign)

Posterior fat pad

(Source: http://uwmsk.org/residentprojects/pediatricelbow.html used with permission.)

Another diagnostic aid in the interpretation of x-rays of the elbow in children is to follow the path of the anterior humeral line on the lateral view. If an imaginary line is drawn along the anterior humerus on the lateral view, extending down beyond the capitellum, then in patients with a normal elbow at least one-third of the capitellum will lie anterior to, or in front of, this line. Patients who have sustained a supracondylar fracture that is not evident on x-ray may have a lesser proportion of the capitellum anterior to this line because of displacement of the capitellum (Begg 2005).

Figure 12.2

The anterior humeral line: one-third of the capitellum should lie anterior to this imaginary line. In this lateral x-ray of the elbow only around one-tenth lies anterior to the line, suggesting displacement of the capitellum as a result of supracondylar fracture.

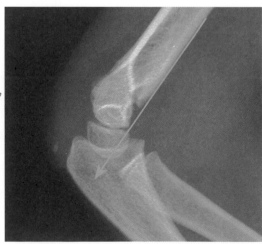

(Source: www.xray2000.co.uk used with permission.)

Supracondylar fractures are treated according to severity. Displaced or comminuted fractures should be referred for operative fixation. Undisplaced fractures may be managed in a collar and cuff and/or backslab plaster and arrangements made for review in an orthopaedic clinic. If the child is going home, parents and carers should be made aware of the potential for neurovascular compromise in such injuries and also be apprised of the signs and symptoms associated with this. If these circumstances do arise then they need to be advised that they should return the child for emergency care again urgently.

The Monteggia fracture-dislocation

Monteggia fracture-dislocation

The Monteggia fracture (see Figure 12.3 overleaf) was first described in 1814 by Giovanni Monteggia. Although not specific to childhood, the management of such fractures in children differs from that in the adult where it is a more serious injury. A Monteggia fracture is defined as a fracture of the proximal one-third of the ulnar shaft with an associated dislocation of the radial head. Fractures of this type are caused either by direct trauma to the area or forced hyperpronation of the forearm. The fracture is classified into four types depending upon the direction of dislocation of the radial head and whether there is an associated fracture of the radius proximally (Wheeless 2007a). About 60% of fractures involve anterior radial head dislocation. After referral to orthopaedic specialists, this fracture in children is treated predominantly by closed reduction unless the radial head cannot be relocated by this means. The ulnar fracture is re-positioned manually and then put into a plaster cast. This procedure is most effectively achieved in younger children under a general anaesthetic and older children will at the least require adequate analgesia and explanation to facilitate reduction. Parents/carers and the child should be reassured that despite the sometimes striking nature of the injury, in terms of clinical presentation and x-ray findings, functional and cosmetic results following conservative treatment with closed reduction in children are particularly good.

Paediatric minor emergencies

Figure 12.3

The Monteggia fracture: note the fracture of the proximal third of the ulna in conjunction with the dislocation of the radial head. Radial head dislocation may be identified by employing the radio-capitellar rule in interpretation of the x-ray and as can be seen from the arrow would have identified this particular lesion.

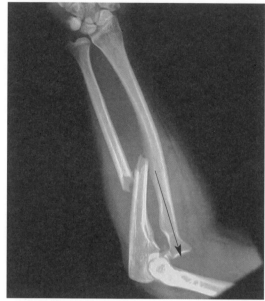

(Source: www.xray2000.co.uk used with permission.)

The radio-capitellar rule (see Figure 12.4) in interpretation of lateral x-rays of the elbow is particularly useful in identifying injury to the radial head. If an imaginary line is drawn through the centre of the shaft of the radius, continuing through the head and into the elbow joint, then this line should pass through the capitellum. If it does not, then dislocation of the radial head is likely. If the rule is routinely applied in proximal fractures of the shaft of the ulna then it is less likely that an associated radial head dislocation (thus constituting a Monteggia fracture) will be missed.

Figure 12.4

The radio-capitellar rule. A straight line drawn through the shaft of the radius on the lateral x-ray should pass through the capitellum.

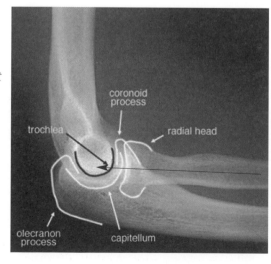

(Source: www.xray2000.co.uk used with permission.)

The Galeazzi fracture-dislocation

Galeazzi fracture-dislocation

Sometimes referred to as a reverse Monteggia fracture, the Galeazzi fracture (see Figure 12.5) is a combination of a fracture of the lower one-third of the shaft of the radius with a dislocation of the distal ulna. Unlike the Monteggia fracture, the Galeazzi fracture in children more often requires open reduction or at least closed reduction under general anaesthesia because of problems associated with achieving optimal radial alignment using other methods (Wheeless 2007b). Children may then need to be prepared for general anaesthesia.

Figure 12.5

The Galeazzi fracture: note the fracture of the radius but also the dislocation of the ulna at the radio-ulnar joint distally. (There is also a fracture of the ulna in this example.)

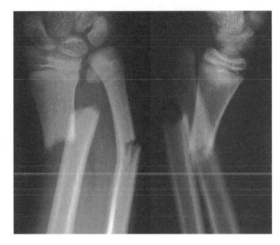

(Source: www.xray2000.co.uk used with permission.)

Other fractures of the forearm in children may predominantly be treated conservatively in plaster without the need for invasive fixation unless there is a degree of angulation that mitigates against this. In a greenstick type fracture, 30 degrees of angulation is acceptable, in older children no more than 10 degrees (Davies 2003). Unacceptably angulated fractures should be referred for specialist care as they may need manipulation under anaesthesia and closed reduction or surgical fixation by open reduction

The Torus fracture

The Torus fracture (see Figure 12.6 overleaf) is the most common fracture of the forearm in early childhood (Solan *et al*. 2002). Usually a history of a fall onto an outstretched hand will be given and as a consequence of this injury to the elbow and clavicle should also be excluded. The child will be reluctant to use the affected limb and there may be some swelling, though little in the way of deformity, over the distal radius. Neurovascular status should be assessed distal to the injury and findings documented.

In view of the tenderness over bone and loss of function in the affected limb x-ray investigation is warranted. It is wise to ask for x-rays of the elbow as well as the forearm to exclude an associated dislocation of the radial head which may be under-reported in children with pain from a forearm fracture (Wheeless 2007a). Prior to sending the child to x-ray, appropriate analgesia should be administered. Remember to ask parents or carers if they have already administered any analgesia to the child to avoid double dosing and toxicity. Consider other comfort measures such as a sling.

X-rays should be inspected carefully for irregularity of the cortex. Many Torus fractures have been missed because of their particularly subtle appearance on x-ray. Often the fracture only manifests as a slight buckling (it is sometimes referred to as a buckle fracture) in the cortex of the bone with no displacement of the fracture site. It should be ascertained that only one cortex is involved in the fracture: if both cortices are involved then the fracture is inherently more unstable and may need a greater degree of immobilisation (e.g. a full plaster that also may cover the elbow). Most Torus fractures occur 2–3cm proximal to the radial epiphysis and this area should be closely inspected on the AP and lateral x-rays to exclude injury, particularly in the symptomatic child where there is a high index of suspicion for fracture.

Figure 12.6

Lateral x-ray of the Torus fracture showing buckling of the cortex of the bone.

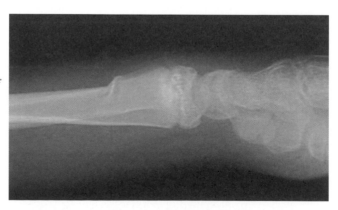

(Source: www.xray2000.co.uk, used with permission.)

Torus fractures are immobilised in plaster of Paris for a period of approximately three weeks and arrangements are made for the child to be reviewed as an outpatient by orthopaedic staff, generally in the orthopaedic or fracture clinic of a hospital. Many centres now find the application of a light fibre glass splint in stable forearm fractures gives as good cosmetic results and similar analgesic benefits as a plaster of Paris. Such measures obviously incapacitate the child to a lesser extent but depend upon the availability of such resources locally.

Be aware in assessing the wrist and forearm of a child who has fallen onto an outstretched hand that scaphoid injury, although most common amongst young adults, is not unheard of in children (Auburn & Bethel 2007). Calcification of the scaphoid bone occurs between the ages of seven and nine years and it may therefore be necessary to consider this as a rare cause of wrist pain. Under such circumstances, assessment for scaphoid tenderness should take place and where appropriate scaphoid views of the wrist should be requested.

Pulled elbow

Pulled elbow

Pulled elbow, also known as nursemaid's elbow or toddler's elbow, describes the process by which the head of the radius subluxates from the annular ligament, which retains it in its normal anatomical position, in the elbows of infants and small children. The annular ligament in infants and small children is a relatively immature structure and is still developing the tensile strength needed to effectively retain the head of the radius in position. Pulled elbow is therefore most commonly seen in children of four years and less but may be considered or excluded as a diagnosis in older children as well. The head of the radius generally subluxates when axial traction is resisted by the child whose forearm is pronated and extended.

Parents or carers will bring the child to the department or unit stating that they are reluctant to use the affected limb which will generally be immobile at the child's side. Common circumstances for sustaining the injury include the child being forcibly pulled from the path of danger, being pulled up and over an obstacle,

Paediatric minor emergencies

having an arm pulled through an item of clothing or at play when swinging a child by its arm. Some of these circumstances being relatively innocuous the parents or carers may not relate the injury to this presentation, being apparently baffled about why the child will not use their arm. Others may recollect specific circumstances since when the child has not used the limb. History taking may therefore facilitate the diagnosis, or may leave this unclear. Physical examination of the limb should aid diagnosis. There will be no obvious deformity or swelling in the limb and only moderate tenderness around the radial head. The elbow may be passively flexed and extended and elicit only minimal distress. Supination and pronation of the forearm is resisted more forcefully. Distal neurovascular function should obviously be intact.

If, from the history taking process and the physical examination, it can be reasonably established that the child has a pulled elbow rather than more serious pathology such as a fracture around the joint then x-ray investigation is not necessary. If the diagnosis remains unclear then x-ray investigation is warranted. X-ray investigation in pulled elbow will show a normal joint with no bony injury and no suspicion of this in the form of soft tissue abnormal fat pads (see Chapter 14) around the joint.

Treatment of pulled elbow is by attempting to relocate the radial head within the annular ligament. There is no consensus about the optimal means of achieving this. Most practitioners will immobilise the flexed elbow at approximately 90 degrees and will then supinate the forearm as they extend the elbow. Some pressure over the radial head during this procedure may facilitate successful relocation. A palpable and/or audible 'click' is felt as the radial head relocates. Alternate methods that are sometimes advocated include pronation rather than supination during relocation and flexion rather than extension as a means of relocation. In the absence of a conclusive evidence base for any one procedural method, it is recommended that the practitioner become familiar with the procedure adopted in their place of work and initially begin practice on this basis. Distraction therapy, perhaps enlisting the aid of colleagues, is invaluable during this procedure to gain the co-operation of the child. If the procedure can appear to have been a part of playful interaction with the child then this may also facilitate successful relocation.

If after two or three attempts the relocation is not successful then consideration should be given to consulting another practitioner to confirm or refute your diagnosis and to taking an x-ray of the joint to exclude other pathology. Successful relocation may be confirmed by the child using the affected limb normally. Children should be observed for a short period of time after relocation to ensure that this is the case. Post-relocation x-rays in a child that is using the limb normally again are not necessary and are unwarranted.

Parents or carers should be apprised of the probable cause of the injury if they were unaware of this at presentation. All parents or carers should be advised that a recurrence of the injury is likely if such circumstances are repeated. There is generally no need for review of the child and they may be discharged home with this advice.

Figure 12.7

The radial head retained in its normal anatomical position by the annular ligament.

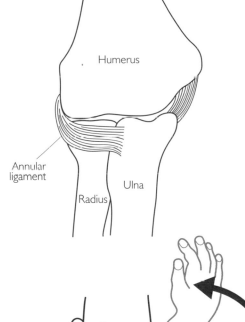

Figure 12.8

Flexion and supination of the forearm: one method advocated to facilitate relocation.

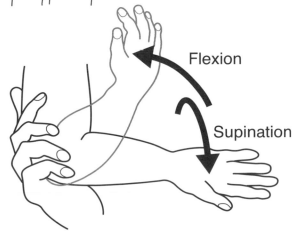

Paediatric minor emergencies

Fingertip injuries

Young children are more likely to sustain fingertip injuries than adults; they may suffer crush injuries in doors or when attempting to handle heavy objects in the home or at play. Children may sustain amputations of the tip, nail bed laceration or nail avulsion, sub-ungual haematomas or fractures of the terminal phalange. Treatment aims to preserve length in the digit, to preserve nail growth and function and avoid infection.

Assessment of the child with a fingertip injury will involve attempting to establish the mechanism of injury and providing adequate pain relief in order both to make the child comfortable and facilitate examination of the injury. Ideal analgesia for fingertip injuries is a digital block using local anaesthetic and this may be feasible in older children. In other children this obviously presents many challenges: the child may be frightened of needles and may not lie still or co-operate for the procedure. Under these circumstances, the practitioner will need to use persuasion in order to attempt to convince the child of the benefit of the procedure. The most important thing to remember is not to lie to, or mislead the child. Do not be tempted for instance to tell the child that the procedure will not hurt; you may gain their co-operation in this manner but subsequent to your lie being discovered (i.e. when the procedure does in fact cause pain) all future co-operation will be lost. If digital block cannot be achieved, consideration should be given to sedation of the child in order to repair the injury.

Amputation of the tip of the finger (i.e. beyond the distal interphalangeal joint) is assessed after analgesia and is managed by debriding the wound if necessary, cleaning the wound adequately and dressing it with a moist wound dressing. If the amputated portion of the finger has been retained then it should be wrapped in saline-soaked gauze, placed in a water-tight bag and then placed inside another container with ice and water within it. The feasibility of re-attaching the amputated portion should be assessed. Small amputations of the distal pulp will generally not be readily re-attached and the child, with good aftercare, will make a good cosmetic recovery without the need for this. More significant sized amputations should, if possible, be re-attached and this should be undertaken by specialist hand or plastic surgeons.

Where specialist services are not involved, arrangements should be made for the child to be reviewed in 48-72 hours anyway and parents/carers should be advised to provide the child with regular analgesia and to ensure that analgesia is given prior to the appointment for review. If the nail is involved in the injury then it should be sutured back in place if necessary. If there is any suspicion that the nail bed matrix has been involved in the injury then the nail should be removed, the matrix repaired, and the nail then re-inserted and sutured in place. Untreated nail bed lacerations can lead to deformed nail growth. Fractures of the proximal phalange with an overlying wound should be treated as an open fracture and will necessitate antibiotic therapy to avoid infection. Sub-ungual haematomas associated with other injuries of the digit may be trephined with the aid of the digital block. Isolated sub-ungual haematomas are more problematic. The benefit of a ring block in such circumstances is more questionable: inflicting two sub-cutaneous injections on a child to guard against the pain of a single procedure to drain the haematoma would not appear beneficial. Conversely trephining the nail without anaesthesia will not always be appropriate or feasible. Many children, and indeed some adults, will be fearful of the idea of having a hole made in the nail, and this will be compounded if, as in many departments and units, the hole is made by heating up a metal paper clip and applying it to the nail. If possible a trephining drill or even a hypodermic needle should be employed to do this. Trephining has the double benefit of achieving rapid pain relief and being associated with good cosmetic results for the child (Gamston 2006). Each injury, and each child, will have to be assessed differently to gauge their ability to co-operate with the procedure.

Figure 12.9

Management of sub-ungual haematoma where the nail bed and margin are intact

Management of sub-ungual haematoma where the nail bed and margin are intact (adapted from Gamston 2006)

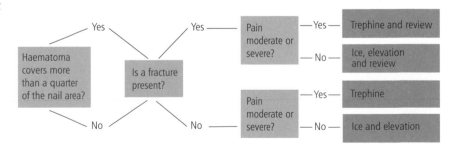

Paediatric minor emergencies

Animal bites

Children are more prone to animal bites than adults; they are more enquiring in nature and less aware of the potential dangers of approaching animals. They may not recognise the signs that warn adults that an animal is about to attack. Peak incidence of animal bites is in the 5–14 year age range (Stump 2006). Children will generally be bitten on hands or faces as they are stroking animals or putting their face close to the animal's face in play.

Animal bites vary in their nature depending on the animal that has inflicted them; most bites are inflicted by domestic dogs or cats. Cat bites, because of the animal's long incisor teeth, should be treated as penetrating injuries. Although the surface appearance of cat bites may be less remarkable than a dog bite, with perhaps only superficial puncture wounds from the incisors, the depth of penetration will generally be greater. Pain is caused by penetration to deep tissue and the potential for deep tissue to have been contaminated and to subsequently become infected is considerable. Antibiotic therapy is always warranted in the management of cat bites as they are associated with a high rate of infection particularly when they occur in the hand (Morgan 2005). Wounds should be cleansed or irrigated to as great an extent as possible given the nature of the wound.

Dog bites will tend to be more ragged in nature and are generally larger wounds. Large or powerful dogs may also inflict crush type injuries with the power of their bite. Under these circumstances, deeper structures may have been damaged. Neurovascular damage and damage to tendons should be excluded in such injuries. Crush injuries may also damage bone and an x-ray may be warranted to exclude this in severe injury. Bites of this nature will obviously need to be referred to specialist teams for management. Fresh bites (less than six hours old) that can be adequately debrided and cleansed, and where there are no risk factors for infection, may be closed on first presentation (Blackman 1998, Clinical Knowledge Summaries 2007a). Risk factors for infection include immunosuppression and diabetes. Bites to the hands and feet also carry a high risk of infection (Morgan & Palmer 2007). Antibiotic therapy is still widely advocated for dog bites though some minor or superficial bites may not warrant antibiotic treatment or may be treated by delayed prescription (Stump 2006). Where there are risks of infection subsequent to the child's medical history or the location of the injury then antibiotics should be prescribed. Bites that cannot be adequately debrided or cleansed, or where presentation is delayed, should be treated by delayed closure and will necessitate antibiotic therapy (Clinical Knowledge Summaries 2007a).

In all animal bites it should be ascertained that the child has followed the national immunisation schedule which will include prophylaxis against tetanus infection. If for any reason the child has not been immunised then a full course of tetanus vaccine should be commenced. An initial vaccination should be followed by two more at intervals of not less than four weeks. In children who have not been immunised, and are at high risk for tetanus infection because of the nature of the injury, then activated tetanus immunoglobulin should also be administered. Tetanus-prone wounds include (adapted from Salisbury & Begg 1996, Health Protection Agency 2003, Department of Health 2006):

- wounds needing surgical intervention where presentation is delayed for more than six hours
- wounds or burns with evidence of widespread devitalised tissue, or puncture wounds, especially those involving contact with soil, animal faeces, manure or compost
- wounds where there is an associated open fracture or foreign body
- wounds that are already clinically infected and/or patients who are systemically septic
- wounds in intravenous drug users.

Parents or carers and children should be made aware of the clinical signs and symptoms of infection developing in the wound and advised to re-attend under such circumstances.

Chapter 13
Injuries of the lower limb

Children may sustain injuries to the toes and foot from dropping heavy objects or by having the foot crushed between solid objects either at home or at play. Penetrating injury to the sole of the foot may occur when children inadvertently tread on sharp objects. Inversions of the ankle in young children generally result in different injuries than would occur in the adult with a similar mechanism. Certain fractures of the lower limb are peculiar to childhood and may be particularly difficult to identify on plain x-rays. Animal bites in the lower limb are assessed and treated in a similar manner to those in the upper limb (see pp. 106–107

Penetrating injury to the foot

Penetrating foot injuries

Children walking barefoot in the home or outdoors or even wearing footwear may inadvertently tread on sharp objects or fragments of broken material. A foreign body in the foot may need to be excluded in any young child that presents with sudden onset of limp or reluctance to weight bear on the affected limb. As the history is often difficult to elicit from the child themselves, or because the injury was unwitnessed or not remembered by parents or carers, the physical examination of the child may take on more importance when attempting to exclude this sort of injury. Common objects that may penetrate the sole of the foot and then fall out, or which may penetrate and be retained, are nails or small pieces of glass or metal.

In assessment of the child it will be necessary to formally examine the sole of the foot. Any obvious foreign bodies should be noted in terms of type and location and, if necessary, an attempt should be made to immobilise the foreign body with, for instance, a keyhole dressing. Do not attempt to remove anything but very superficial foreign bodies at this stage, and do not attempt removal without informing the child that you are going to do so. Again the consequences of such a manoeuvre may be to lose the future co-operation of the child. Neurovascular status in addition to motor function should be assessed distal to the injury to exclude damage to underlying blood vessels, nerves and tendons. In the presence of a penetrating foreign body it is advisable to provide the child with adequate pain relief prior to requesting an x-ray of the foot to exclude involvement of bone in the injury. Involvement of bone will make removal of the foreign body more difficult and will make antibiotic therapy in the management of the wound more imperative. Once such a child has returned from the x-ray department, consideration should be given to the means that will be employed to remove the foreign body. If the expertise is available then regional anaesthesia may be considered in a child who is otherwise co-operative. Otherwise systemic analgesia with sedation in the young or frightened child may also be considered. Some particularly anxious children with deep penetrating foreign bodies may need general anaesthesia to facilitate removal.

Where there is not an obvious foreign body, the child should be asked to identify where the foot is painful. Begin your surface examination of the foot away from this area in order to gain the co-operation of the child and in order that they begin to know what to expect from the examination. Gradually move towards the painful area, gently palpating the surface of the foot, attempting to identify any retained foreign bodies. If an adequate history is available concerning the nature of the foreign body then consideration should be given to asking for an x-ray of the foot in order to identify the size and location of a radio-opaque foreign body. Materials that are radio-opaque and may therefore be identified on a plain x-ray include metal, glass and ceramic compounds. Materials that are not radio-opaque, and in which there is therefore no indication for an x-ray include wood and plastic. If there is a palpable foreign body, whether it can be more specifically located by means of an x-ray or not, then in the older child the area may be anaesthetised by infiltration of the wound edges with local anaesthetic or by use of a regional block. In younger more anxious children this may again not be sufficient means to facilitate removal and consideration may have to be given to sedation or general anaesthesia.

Very small foreign bodies, radio-opaque or not, may not warrant formal exploration and removal. It may be more beneficial to leave the foreign body to gradually move closer to the surface of the foot during epithelialisation than to infiltrate the wound with sub-cutaneous injections, explore the wound and perhaps not be able to locate the foreign body due to its size. In such circumstances, the child, parents or carers will need reassurance about the prognosis for the child.

Superficial penetrating injuries involving only the epidermis do not warrant antibiotic treatment in their management. Deeper dermal injuries and particularly those that have also penetrated bone will necessitate antibiotic therapy. As in all such injuries, the tetanus status of the child should be verified and documented.

Inversion injury of the ankle

Inversion injury of the ankle in children can result in markedly different injuries from those seen in the adult. Children will invert their ankles for similar reasons to adults: whilst running or walking on uneven surfaces, at sport and at play. Assessment of the injured ankle will focus initially upon determining the exact mechanism of injury. Once it has been established that the injury has been caused by inversion of the ankle (it may be necessary to mimic inversion of the ankle to assist this process), enquiries should be made about the force involved: did the child jump and invert an ankle on landing, were they running when the ankle was inverted, or have they merely inverted the joint on walking? Some estimate of the force of inversion may give some insight into the level of injury to expect (though this should not mislead the practitioner into not assessing for injury outside of expected parameters). Was the child able to continue with the sport or activity that they were taking part in when the injury was sustained? Significant bony injury is unlikely if the child was able to continue what they were doing. Examination of the ankle joint should focus upon identifying where the injury is in terms of location and providing the child with adequate pain relief. Asking the child to identify the location of injury and pain will assist the examination as the practitioner may then work towards this point from other areas of the joint. Obvious areas of tenderness and swelling should be noted and neurovascular and motor function assessed distal to any injury.

The Ottawa ankle and foot rules (Stiell *et al.* 1993) have been devised as an assessment tool in ankle and foot injury to establish whether x-ray investigation is warranted or not. They are an accurate and effective means of identifying which patients should have such investigation. In children less than 12 years old they may be less reliable because of the potential for growth plate injury and avulsion fractures. They may however be used to provide some indication about the likelihood of bony injury and should be placed within the context of the physical findings on examination of the child.

The Ottawa ankle rules recommend requesting an ankle x-ray if there is pain in the malleolar zone plus:

- Bony tenderness at posterior edge or the tip of the lateral or medial malleoli (a 6cm length of the distal fibula or tibia) OR

- An inability to weight bear on presentation or at the time of the injury (defined as not being able to take more than four steps).

When inverting ankles, children, particularly young children, are less likely than adults to sustain a simple sprain of the lateral ligaments. They are as likely to sustain an epiphyseal (growth plate) injury of the distal fibula or an avulsion fracture of the base of the fifth metatarsal.

Epiphyseal injury to the distal fibula can be a missed initial diagnosis because of a lack of diagnostic findings on plain x-ray of the ankle. The injury, which is most commonly a Salter-Harris type I fracture, will need to be diagnosed on clinical findings: where there is a history of inversion injury in a young child, with maximal tenderness over growth plates, and a lack of positive x-ray findings then the child should be assumed to have sustained a Salter-Harris type I fracture and treated accordingly in plaster of Paris. The Salter-Harris classification of epiphyseal fractures and their management is discussed in more detail in Chapter 14 (see pp. 120–122.

Children's tendons are, relative to their bones, stronger than in the adult. Inversion of the ankle is therefore more likely to cause an avulsion fracture of the base of the fifth metatarsal, as the peroneus brevis tendon is stretched. Peroneus brevis has insertion points in the distal fibula and at the base of the fifth metatarsal of the foot laterally. Ottawa rules for decision making in radiography of the foot are as follows: request a foot x-ray if there is pain in the midfoot plus:

- bony tenderness over the navicular bone or base of the fifth metatarsal OR

- an inability to weight bear on presentation or at the time of the injury (defined as not being able to take more than four steps).

Figure 13.1 *right*

Normal apophysis: the line of the fragment of bone is perpendicular to the line of the metatarsal shaft.

Figure 13.2 *far right*

Avulsion fracture of base of the 5th metatarsal: the line of the fragment of bone is transverse to the line of the shaft of the metatarsal.

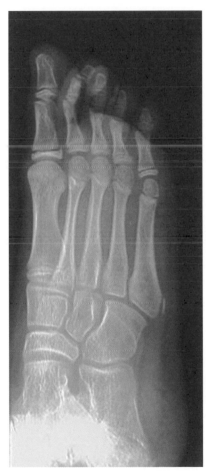

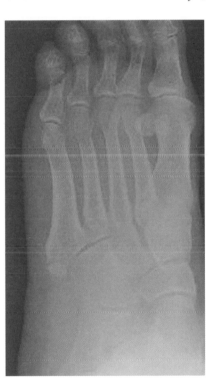

(Source: www.xray2000.co.uk used with permission.)

As in the ankle rules, the Ottawa foot rules should not be the definitive criteria on which the decision to order an x-ray investigation rests. Clinical findings should also be taken into account and the rules used with more caution than in adults. In interpreting the plain x-ray of the child's foot, where avulsion fracture of the base of the fifth metatarsal is suspected, the practitioner should be careful not to diagnose a normal paediatric apophysis as an avulsion fracture. Differentiation between the two is most readily achieved by remembering that in avulsion fractures the line of the fracture is usually transverse to the line of the metatarsal shaft and the edges of the avulsed fragment will have a ragged appearance. In a normal apophysis at the base of the fifth metatarsal the line of the apophyseal fragment will lie perpendicular to the line of the metatarsal shaft and the edges of the fragment will be smooth and well delineated.

Fractures of the base of the fifth metatarsal are generally managed either in a lower leg plaster of Paris cast or in a suitable lightweight splint should resources be available. One factor in considering which type of immobilisation to employ is that only children above the age of six or seven years will have the necessary co-ordination skills to be able to use crutches safely, though younger children may be able to use walking frames which offer greater stability. Although there is no consensus about the management of soft tissue injury or sprain of the ankle, recent literature reviews (Smith 2003, Pollard & Cronin 2005) found that compression therapy had been largely abandoned, that a period of initial rest and elevation and gradual return to normal activity was commonly advocated and ice therapy in addition to oral analgesia recommended to reduce swelling and pain from injury.

Crush injuries to the foot are not uncommon in children as a result of accidents in the home or at play. In some instances after severe crush injury and/or where there is an associated coagulopathy, children have developed a compartment syndrome of the foot requiring urgent surgical intervention (Bibbo et al. 2000). Where there is bony tenderness, deformity or an inability to weight bear a plain x-ray should be requested. Fractures of the toes tend to be managed conservatively except in the rare circumstances when they are compound. Salter-Harris type III, IV and V fractures should be referred for specialist care to avoid complications of post injury growth problems (Hatch & Hacking 2003).

Older children and adolescents, particularly athletes, may present with stress fractures of the lower limb. Half of all stress fractures in the lower limb are in the tibia and like all stress fractures are associated with sudden increased levels of activity, repetitive loading of the bone or inadequate footwear support during activity. Tibial stress fractures may require surgical fixation if they do not respond to initial conservative treatment (Sanderlin & Raspa 2003). In the foot stress fractures most commonly occur in the distal shaft of the second or third metatarsals and are managed conservatively. Children may give a history of gradual and worsening pain after activity as small microfractures gradually merge to form the stress fracture. X-ray appearances will be subtle and may show evidence of early regeneration and remodelling.

Severs disease describes heel pain in children caused by repetitive activity inflaming the apophysis of the calcaneum. Children, most commonly boys between the ages of 10 and 12 years of age, will complain of pain in the heel that is worse on activity (Cassas & Cassettari-Wayhs 2006). History taking and physical examination will help in the exclusion of calcaneal fractures or Achilles tendon injury. Treatment is conservative, involving analgesia, rest and a gradual return to activity (Noffsinger 2004).

The toddler's fracture

The toddler's fracture

First described in 1964 by Dunbar (Dunbar *et al.* 1964), the toddler's fracture is an oblique non-displaced fracture of the distal one-third of the tibia. Children will generally present with a limp or refusal to weight bear and the age group most often affected is, as the name suggests, toddlers from the age of approximately nine months to three years. A specific incident causing the injury may not be recollected by parents or carers because of its apparent insignificance at that time and because a child with a non-displaced fracture of the tibia may continue to weight bear upon it. Presentation may also therefore be delayed. These factors obviously raise the index of suspicion for non-accidental injury and historically the toddler's fracture was thought to be a consequence of child abuse. Work undertaken in the early 1990s (Mellick & Reesor 1990, Tenenbein *et al.* 1990) however

Paediatric minor emergencies

challenged this assertion, finding that most toddler's fractures were caused by the child trapping their foot and twisting as they fell, resulting in the oblique fracture characteristic of it. Many tibial fractures sustained as a result of abuse (the mechanism was thought to involve the abuser forcefully pulling and twisting the leg of the child) were found to be in the mid-tibia rather than the lower one-third and would obviously sometimes be accompanied by other signs of abuse.

In a plain x-ray of the tibia it may be very difficult to distinguish the fracture line in the toddler's fracture and some are missed. Like other paediatric fractures, such as the Torus fracture, which also have very subtle radiological findings, the diagnosis of toddler's fracture may of necessity be predominantly guided by clinical findings. The diagnosis should be considered in children in this age range presenting with a limp and who do not have a febrile illness.

Once pain relief has been established, the toddler's fracture, like other fractures of long bones, is treated by immobilisation in a plaster cast. Arrangements should be made for the child to be reviewed in an orthopaedic clinic.

Figure 13.3

The toddler's fracture: AP and lateral views show subtle undisplaced oblique fracture (arrowed) of the lower one-third of the tibia

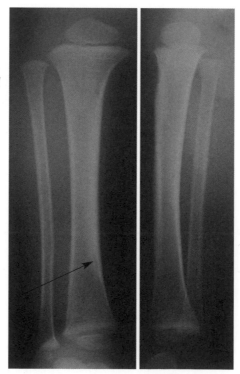

(Source: www.xray2000.co.uk used with permission.)

116

Chapter 14
X-ray requesting and interpretation

Children are more sensitive to the side effects of ionising radiation than adults. Requests for x-rays in the child, as in the adult, should be based on a sound clinical rationale derived from findings of the physical examination and history taking processes. They should not be a substitute for a careful physical examination in the child who is uncooperative or where the practitioner lacks the necessary skills in the examination of children. Neither should they be a substitute for assiduous history taking where, for instance, this may be problematic if the injury was not witnessed. All practitioners who request x-rays should have undertaken a radiation protection training lecture to make them aware of current legislation and professional guidelines relating to the requesting of x-rays. There is no requirement currently for practitioners to update radiation protection training, though it would seem good practice to formally update the training every two to three years and to take individual responsibility for remaining updated.

To reaffirm the importance of history taking and physical examination, it should be remembered that bone is formed by ossification of cartilage; cartilaginous bone, a feature of children's, particularly young children's, skeletal systems, may not be readily visualised on plain x-ray. Diagnosis therefore may have to be founded upon information gained during history taking and physical examination. This is also the case when dealing with suspected epiphyseal (growth plate) injuries where significant injury may have subtle appearance on plain x-ray.

In requesting a plain x-ray of the upper or lower limb in children, remember the importance of mechanism of injury in determining patterns of fractures and also how bony injury in children may differ to that in the adult despite a similar mechanism of injury (see Table 14.1 overleaf).

Paediatric minor emergencies

Table 14.1

Bony injuries in adults and children

Bony injuries in adults and children

Mechanism of injury	Likely injury in the adult	Likely injury in the child
Fall onto outstretched hand	Colles fracture Fracture of the radial head Scaphoid fracture Fractured neck of humerus	Torus fracture Supracondylar fracture Fractured clavicle
Axial loading injury (jump/fall from height)	Fractured calcaneum	Salter-Harris V injury
Inversion of the ankle	Sprain of the anterior talo-fibular ligament Fractured distal fibula	Avulsion fracture of the base of the fifth metatarsal Salter-Harris I injury to fibula

Knowledge of these factors will help to guide and focus the physical examination and should inform any requests for radiological investigation. In deciding upon the need for x-rays in the child the practitioner should be aware of the general indications for x-ray in both the adult and the child:

- bony tenderness
- swelling over bone
- loss of function
- deformity.

Any of these findings will necessitate x-ray investigation. In the child additional indications include:

- an incongruent or poor history concerning the mechanism of injury
- where non-accidental injury to other areas needs to be excluded.

The practitioner should note that they are required to distinguish bony tenderness from soft tissue tenderness. This may be difficult in the novice practitioner where, even with anatomical knowledge as background to practice, they may lack the confidence to make this distinction. In such circumstances advice should be sought from other, more experienced staff until this expertise and confidence is developed. The use of decision making tools in radiography, such as the Ottawa ankle and foot rules, is less reliable in children than adults because of the varying nature of injury. They may however be used as an assessment tool provided that physical examination and history taking findings are also used in the decision making process.

Radiographers are perfectly justified in asking practitioners to provide a rationale for their decision to request an x-ray and this may happen if they feel that requesters have not provided enough information on the request card, or appear not to have adhered to clinical guidelines for the requesting of x-rays such as the Ionising Radiation (Medical Exposure) Regulations (IRMER) 2000. Clinical findings and history taking should provide the information needed to answer such a challenge. Remember to always document the relevant clinical findings on the request card. It is also useful for the radiographer to have some idea of the injury suspected; this will enable them to position the patient optimally to identify injury and, if necessary, to take injury specific films that will more accurately inform your diagnosis. An example of this might be the patient who falls onto their outstretched hand and has tenderness in the distal radius. If the radiographer, from the information provided on the request card, knows that the practitioner is suspecting a fracture of the scaphoid then they can take certain x-rays that will enhance the view of the scaphoid bone.

When requesting x-rays in children always provide the child with an explanation of what they may expect when they get to the x-ray department, how long it will take to have their x-rays taken, and what will happen afterwards.

Interpretation of x-rays

Interpretation of x-rays

The practitioner attempting x-ray interpretation in children needs to employ the same systematic approach to interpretation that aids accurate diagnosis in adults. They also need to be aware of differences in the appearance of x-rays in children and the x-ray appearance of particular paediatric fractures. Knowledge of the aetiology and x-ray appearance of epiphyseal (growth plate) injuries will also enhance diagnosis of bony injury in children.

Paediatric minor emergencies

Systematic approach

Employing the same approach to interpretation of all x-rays will help to develop patterns of interpretation that take account of all relevant factors in this process; see Table 14.2.

Table 14.2

ABC of x-ray interpretation

ABC of x-ray interpretation

A **A**ttributability: Does the x-ray have the correct patient name and date on it? Is the x-ray of the correct (right or left) limb?

Adequacy: Is the film of a good enough quality to inform diagnosis? Is it too dark or too light? Have at least two views been taken?

Alignment: Have the correct views been taken?

B **B**ones: Is there any bony injury? Breaks in cortical lines? Deformity? Abnormal density?

C **C**artilage and soft tissue: Are joint spaces narrowed? Do joints have the correct anatomical alignment with each other? Are there any fat pads, bloody effusions or other swelling?

In addition to becoming familiar with this systematic approach to interpretation, practitioners should also be aware of relevant differences in paediatric x-rays. Epiphyseal growth plates, normal findings in the x-rays of children, may be mistaken for fractures if practitioners are unfamiliar with their appearance (see Figure 14.1).

Growth plate injuries

Growth plate injuries are obviously unique to children. Their appearance on x-ray depends upon the type of injury. Growth plate injuries have been classified into five types by Salter and Harris (1963), as shown in Figure 14.2 overleaf.

Figure 14.1

Growth plates at the base of the 5th metatarsal and the elbow. Unlike fracture fragments, the epiphyseal portion of the plate is regular and well defined. In the absence of injury they are in alignment with the metaphysis of the same bone. Avulsion fractures of the base of the 5th metatarsal tend to lie transverse to the shaft of the metatarsal; epiphyseal portions lie perpendicular to the shaft.

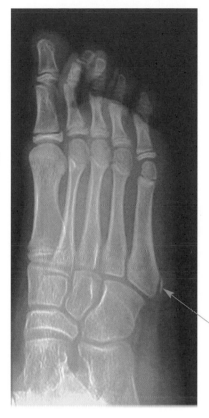

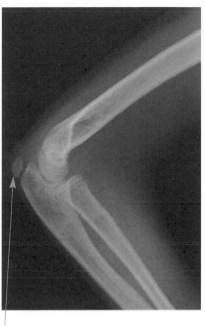

growth plates

(Source: www.xray2000.co.uk used with permission.)

Figure 14.2

Salter-Harris (1963) classification of growth plate injuries.

Salter-Harris (1963) classification of growth plate injuries

Type I: a fracture of the physis lying between the metaphysis and epiphysis. Usually caused by shearing forces the growth plate is not breached. Unless the epiphysis is displaced x-ray findings may be very subtle or not evident at all. Diagnosis therefore may be clinical: young children with tenderness over growth plates but negligible x-ray findings should be treated for a Salter-Harris I fracture.

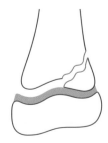

Type II: a fracture of the physis and metaphysis, the most common growth plate injury. Again the growth plate is not breached. X-ray findings are more evident than in the Salter-Harris I fracture. This sort of injury involving the metaphysis is more common in bones that have begun to ossify and the Salter-Harris II fracture is therefore seen predominantly in children of 10 years and above.

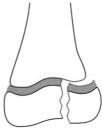

Type III: a fracture of the physis and epiphysis. The growth plate is breached and if the diagnosis is missed post-injury growth problems are therefore likely. X-ray findings are readily identifiable and all Salter-Harris III fractures should be referred to in-patient specialist teams for further assessment and management.

Type IV: a continuous fracture through the epiphysis, physis and metaphysis. The growth plate is breached and if the diagnosis is missed post-injury growth problems are therefore likely. X-ray findings are evident particularly if there has been displacement of the fracture fragments. Like Salter-Harris III fractures, these injuries should be referred to specialist teams.

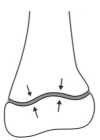

Type V: a crush injury of the physis. Associated with falls or jumps from height. X-ray findings may be minimal as growth plate narrowing may be the only sign. Comparison views of an unaffected limb, if available, may aid diagnosis. In symptomatic children, with a mechanism history making this injury likely, assume a Salter-Harris V fracture and refer to specialist teams.

In interpreting the x-ray of the child remember to always treat the patient and not the x-ray; the x-ray is nothing more than a diagnostic aid and the patient will give more information about diagnosis than an x-ray. Combine information you have gained from the history taking and the physical examination with that gained from x-ray investigation to form a clinical picture of the patient.

Remember that:

- You may not see all fractures on x-rays, which is why two views are taken. This is particularly true in some paediatric fractures such as supracondylar fractures and certain Salter-Harris growth plate injuries which may need to be diagnosed clinically.
- Children are more susceptible to the side effects of ionising radiation, therefore always be able to justify x-ray investigation.

Chapter 15
Burns and scalds

Each year approximately 50,000 children attend UK emergency departments with a burn or scald (Advanced Life Support Group 2005) and although this figure is in decline this still represents approximately 960 children a week needing emergency treatment. Children are more prone to burns and scalds because of limited risk awareness when very young, poorly supervised play and exposure to risks in the home, and because they may be the unwitting victims of others' behaviours, such as when they are trapped in house fires caused by cigarette smoking. As we have seen with other types of childhood injury, children may also be burnt or scalded maliciously when parents, carers or others intentionally burn or scald them.

Burns and scalds are classified according to their causative factor:

- thermal burns: caused by flames or hot liquids
- chemical burns: caused by potent acids or alkalis
- radiation burns: caused by ultraviolet radiation
- electrical burns: caused by high voltage electricity.

The management of all types of burns is founded on the same principles: support of the airway with cervical spine immobilisation where necessary, assistance with breathing and circulatory support. Obviously the need for such measures varies according to the type of the burn and its extent. The focus of this chapter will be upon differentiating between minor injury and more severe burns or scalds and the subsequent care of the child with a minor injury.

Paediatric minor emergencies

Thermal burns

Thermal burns are the type of burn most frequently seen in children. They may be caused by flames in house fires or more commonly by hot liquids such as cooking oils and water. In assessing the severity of the injury, an estimate needs to be made of the extent of the burn or scald in terms of the proportion of the body it has affected and an estimate of the depth to which the burn or scald has damaged the affected areas identified. Assessment of the body surface area (BSA) affected is most effectively and accurately undertaken by the use of body charts such as the Lund and Browder chart (Hettiaratchy & Papini 2004).

Figure 15.1

Lund and Browder chart. Equal value is given to the torso, abdomen, upper limb and feet whatever the age of the patient. Variations in the comparative size of the head, legs and thighs of children are shown in Table 15.1.

(Source: Lund, C.C. & Browder, N.C. (1944) 'Estimation of areas of burns' Fig. 1, p. 356, in *Surgery, Gynecology and Obstetrics*, 79, 352–358 (now the *Journal of the American College of Surgeons*).

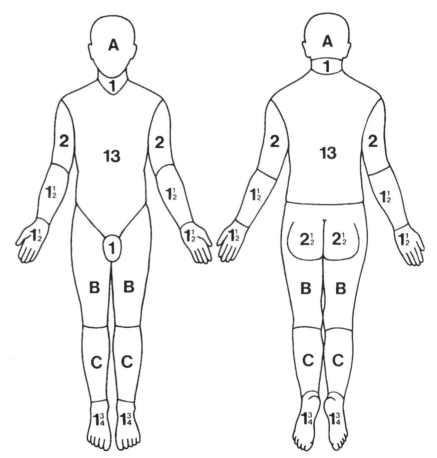

The Lund and Browder chart, unlike some of the body charts for estimation of BSA that preceded it (such as the Wallace's 'rule-of-nines' chart) takes into account the relatively different sizes both of children's body proportions from adults and children's differing proportions as they age from infants to young children to older children (Hettiaratchy & Papini 2004). In assessing the BSA in children it is therefore more accurate because it takes these important clinical variations into account. The body chart is easy to use and guidance is given about the relative importance of each area of the body. Obviously the age of the child needs to be known or estimated in order to use the chart most effectively. In the pre-hospital environment, or as a rapid estimation of BSA in the acute setting, an alternative way of estimating BSA affected is to equate a burnt or scalded area the size of the palm of the child to 1 % BSA (European Burns Association 2007). In emergency care settings where charts are available more accurate estimation should be made even if initial assessment is by this means.

Table 15.1

Percentages of BSA by age

Percentages of BSA by age

Area	Age 0	Age 1	Age 5	Age 10	Age 15	Adult
A: $^1/_2$ head	9.5	8.5	6.5	5.5	4.5	3.5
B: $^1/_2$ thigh	2.75	3.25	4	4.5	4.5	4.75
c: $^1/_2$ leg	2.5	2.5	2.75	3	3.25	3.5

The relevance of assessing the BSA is that it will assist in defining the volume of any fluid replacement required and will assist in differentiation of minor injury from more severe trauma. One of the criteria for the referral of a child to a specialist burn centre following injury is if the BSA is 10 % or greater (American Burn Association 1999). In defining BSA, however, some estimate of the depth of the burn also has to be made, as simple erythema should not be included in the estimation of BSA, either for the purpose of estimating fluid replacement requirements or as a criterion for referral to specialist services (European Burns Association 2007). Estimating the depth of a burn or scald is achieved by classifying the burnt or scalded areas as:

- **superficial**: involving only the epidermis with erythema and minimal blistering
- **superficial partial thickness**: involving upper part of the dermis, moderate blistering

- **deep partial thickness**: involving the whole dermis, widespread blistering and tissue loss
- **full thickness**: involving the deep fat layer also, extensive tissue loss and typical appearance of full thickness burns.

Of course many burns and scalds may be of mixed depth and the clinical assessment may be complicated by this. A child with 10% BSA affected after a cup of scalding tea has dropped on to them for instance may have areas of deep partial thickness loss where the liquid made initial contact but may also have areas of superficial loss where the liquid has splashed on to other areas of the body. Thus it is important when estimating BSA and depth to provide as accurate data as possible for other practitioners, as this will inform diagnosis of severity and subsequent treatment. The child who had scalding tea dropped on to them may therefore have a 6% area of deep partial thickness loss with a 4% area of superficial loss. On this basis the child would not be referred to a specialist centre, as the 4% superficial erythema would not be included in the estimate for referral purposes. In addition to the 10% total BSA criterion for the referral of a child to specialist care, any full thickness burn or scald should also prompt similar referral.

Another factor that is important in differentiating minor injury from more severe injury is the area of the body affected. Irrespective of the total BSA or depth of burn, burns and scalds to the following areas warrant referral for specialist treatment:

- eyes or ears
- scalds or burns to the airway, including smoke inhalation injury
- palms of hands or soles of feet
- genitals or perineum.

Scalds or burns that may affect the airway have the potential to cause more acute management problems in young children where the larynx is funnel shaped, becoming narrow distally, rather than having the cylindrical shape of older children and adults. In the narrow part of the larynx any swelling secondary to inhalation of hot gases, including smoke from house fires, will more readily occlude the airway than is the case in older children and adults. In all patients with a history of smoke inhalation or facial burns, signs of potential airway swelling should be looked for and if identified the child should be cared for by an anaesthetist or transferred to specialist facilities with anaesthetic support. Signs and symptoms of potential airway swelling include singing of facial hair such as the eyebrows and eyelashes, erythematous or blackened oral mucosa and tongue, erythematous or blackened external nasal structures, hoarseness, stridor, unexplained dyspnoea or tachypnoea, and low oximetry readings in the absence of other causes for this.

Chemical burns

Chemical burns

Chemical burns, caused by potent acids or alkalis, are more commonly seen in the adult population where they may be caused by accidents in the workplace. Principles of assessment and management however are the same whatever the age of the patient. In treating the patient with such an injury, it must first be established that the personal safety of the practitioner is not being jeopardised, either in the pre-hospital setting or in emergency departments, minor injury units or walk-in centres. If for instance the injury is the result of a chemical spillage, has the source been identified? Is the nature of the chemical apparent and has the leakage or spillage been stopped? If the patient has been exposed to large amounts of chemical, is it yet safe to treat the patient or do they need to undergo a decontamination process before this can be considered? If there is any doubt about the safety of caring for the patient (particularly for instance where patients may have been presented for emergency care without enlisting the aid of the pre-hospital emergency services) then advice should be sought from competent agencies who will be able to make the practitioner aware of precautions that may need to be taken. These agencies may include the fire service, toxicology services locally and the Health Protection Agency.

As in thermal burns an estimate needs to be made of the BSA affected and the depth and location of injury. Copious irrigation of affected parts of the body is the most important initial measure that can be taken. This may need to be prolonged, depending upon the nature of the chemical. The best solution to irrigate with is water and time should not be wasted attempting to locate buffer solutions for acids and alkalis which have no greater clinical efficacy than water.

Radiation burns

Radiation burns

The most common cause of such burns that the emergency practitioner is likely to encounter is burns caused by prolonged and/or unprotected exposure to the sun or ultraviolet radiation sources used in sunbeds. Other less common causes are iatrogenic radiation burns sustained when patients are undergoing treatment for malignant disease, accidental iatrogenic radiation burns when patients are given too large a dose of radiation or radiotherapy, and industrial accidents involving radioactive material such as that in Chernobyl, Russia in 1986.

Most parents and carers are aware of the risks associated with allowing children to be exposed for too long to the ultraviolet radiation of sunlight. These risks are short-term ones in which the child sustains a burn and longer-term ones where the child becomes more susceptible to dermatological malignancy such as malignant melanoma. A minority of parents or carers however seem less aware of simple precautions that need to be taken when children are exposed to sunlight or choose, for whatever reason, to ignore them. Occasionally therefore young children are still presented to GP surgeries, minor injury units, walk-in centres and emergency departments having sustained a sunburn. Sunburn will generally be of low significance in terms of its depth, with most being associated with superficial or superficial partial thickness loss. However the extent of the burn in terms of surface area affected, if parents or carers have allowed large parts of the child to be exposed to the sun, may render such a burn clinically significant, particularly in the infant and very young child. Clinical significance will be secondary to the amount of fluid lost from a burn covering such a large BSA and the associated pain (American Academy of Paediatrics 2007). This may also be exacerbated by associated illness such as diarrhoea and vomiting. In infants and very young children with a widespread burn, consideration should be given to the need for fluid replacement which may in exceptional circumstances warrant admission to an acute paediatric in-patient bed. More commonly mild fluid loss may be compensated by administration of supplements such as dioralyte and the encouragement of oral fluids.

Given the level of knowledge about the danger of exposing

young skin to the sun, and the simplicity and ready availability of measures to avoid over-exposure, allowing a child to become burnt in the sun may be deemed by some to constitute physical abuse of the child and the practitioner should offer parents and carers advice about avoiding a repetition of the injury. Parents and carers should also be made aware of where they may get further advice and support. It may be wise to check patient records to establish whether the child has ever sustained such an injury before and the case should be highlighted for the attention of the hospital or minor injury unit's child protection liaison services.

Electrical burns

Electrical burns

Electrical burns in children will predominantly be a consequence of accidents in the home and as such their prevention should be promoted by all practitioners. Younger children will be inquisitive about electrical apparatus within the home and this enquiring nature may take the form of putting fingers and hands into the workings of such apparatus or into plug sockets. In terms of prevention then unplugging apparatus that is not being used makes obvious sense and the use of socket guards will also mitigate against injury.

After an electrical burn the assessment of extent of injury is made difficult by the fact that much of the injury may be internal, where current has passed through body cavities, and is therefore not visible.

The relatively low alternating current within domestic circuitry in the UK means that many electrical burns are not fatal unless contact is prolonged. Higher rates of morbidity are associated with alternating current where tetany is stimulated and exposure is prolonged because of this, though this is more common at voltages in excess of 1000V (Benson 2006). Significant injury can however occur and the child should be inspected for obvious external injury. The length of time the child was exposed to the current should also be established if possible. If the child was thrown any distance by exposure to the current (though this is far more common in exposure to direct current) then other injuries such as fractures, lacerations and head injuries should be excluded'. The child's observations should be checked, in particular (Benson 2006):

- the pulse: electrical current passing through the thoracic cavity may precipitate arrhythmias
- urinalysis: electrical current damaging muscle may liberate myoglobin from muscle which causes a degree of renal damage and manifests as myoglobinuria – the urine takes on a pink to red colour depending upon the degree of damage.

Circumferential injuries

**Circumferen-
tial injuries**

In all burn injury the presence of a circumferential injury should be excluded. Circumferential injuries may again necessitate referral to a specialist burns centre. Circumferential injuries are, as the name implies, burns or scalds that affect the whole circumference of either a digit, a limb, or perhaps the abdomen or chest in larger injuries. As the burn or scald encompasses part of the body there is the potential for the area distal to this to become avascular or desensitised because of occlusion of blood vessels and nerves in the area affected by the burn or scald. This is particularly the case with deeper burns. Circumferential injuries can sometimes be caused by jewellery such as rings which when burnt cause circumferential injury because of their shape. In all injuries that are suspected of being circumferential neurovascular status distal to the injury should be assessed by palpation of pulses or estimation of capillary refill time and assessing sensation by touch.

Referral criteria

**Referral
criteria**

Criteria for referral to a burns unit may be used to distinguish minor burns and scalds from more severe injury and we have identified many of them during the course of this chapter and summarise them here (American Burn Association 1999):

- partial thickness burns > 10% BSA
- any full thickness burn
- burns to specific anatomical areas: soles of feet, palms of hands, genitalia, perineum, eye, ears and major joints
- inhalation injuries or suspected inhalation injuries

- chemical injuries where acids or alkalis are particularly potent, e.g. phenol burns
- electrical injuries associated with high voltage or clinical findings of myoglobinuria or cardiac arrhythmias
- circumferential injuries
- if the past medical history of the child contributes adversely to prognosis or there are multiple/significant traumatic injuries associated with exposure (e.g. from falls or being thrown across rooms)
- burned children in hospitals that do not have the facilities or resources to care for them or who will need specialist emotional care.

Using these guidelines it should be possible to ensure that children being cared for in emergency departments, minor injury units and walk-in centres are appropriately referred for specialist services. In the unlikely though not altogether excludable circumstance of a child presenting in a minor injury unit or walk-in centre with burn injury, requiring, or potentially requiring, anaesthetic care, the child may either to be transferred to the nearest emergency department. Alternatively, the anaesthetist may have to be transferred to where the child is, or, if such a service exists locally, the paediatric critical care retrieval services will need to attend the child and stabilise them prior to transfer. Guidelines and risk management strategies should be drawn up in advance of such eventualities rather than as a reaction to them. Using the sort of emergency care networks advocated by the Royal College of Paediatrics and Child Health (RCPCH 2002), a variety of these 'what if...' questions should be addressed in a prospective manner where minor injury and emergency department services co-exist. In all children with burns or scalds extensive enough to warrant referral for specialist care, the need for antibiotic administration to prevent opportunistic infection of the injury, and for anti-tetanus immunisation, should also be considered.

Using some of the recommendations made by the Royal College of Paediatrics and Child Health (RCPCH 2002), it is also possible to provide guidelines for the transfer of children from minor injury services to the emergency department or paediatric unit of a secondary care provider. Such children may not fit the criteria for referral for specialist care but would be more effectively and safely cared for where certain secondary care support services, such as paediatric services and facilities for observation of the child, are available. Such criteria will include:

- any full thickness burn or any burn < 10% BSA where fluid replacement is considered necessary
- any injury where the need for opiate and/or intravenous analgesia is ongoing
- any injury that is thought to have been inflicted non-accidentally
- any electrical injury.

The vast majority of burns and scalds in children will not require referral to a specialist centre and may be treated in the minor injury unit or emergency department.

Management of minor burns and scalds

Minor burns and scalds

During initial assessment the need for analgesia will also have been assessed. Using the British Association for Emergency Medicine (2004) guidelines (see p.29) such analgesia should be administered as soon as possible after presentation and its effectiveness monitored at regular intervals thereafter.

Non-pharmacological approaches to pain relief in burns include cooling the burn. Cooling a burn lessens pain and can decrease burn depth (McCormack et al. 2003). Cold water is an ideal way of cooling a burn and using tap water is an ideal means of doing this. Public education may mean that this measure has been undertaken already as a first aid measure by parents or carers. Where this has not happened, and presentation is within three hours of the injury, the child may still benefit from irrigation with cold tap water (McCormack et al. 2003). The irrigation should continue for 20–30 minutes. Ice and iced water should be avoided as water at less than 4 degrees celsius has been found to exacerbate injury as a result of promoting local vasoconstriction (McCormack et al. 2003). Children who have water-soaked dressings placed on the injury should have these changed regularly as the fluid within them warms up quickly.

Covering the surface of the skin affected may also reduce pain. Much of the pain from superficial burn injury is thought to derive from the convectional passage of air across the surface of the wound (Tsirigotou 1993). Placing an occlusive dressing over the injury will obviously overcome this problem and will provide some comfort to the child as they are no longer distressed by being able to see the injury. However some occlusive dressings are adherent and cause problems on removal and as they may need to be removed periodically for re-assessment or for inspection by other practitioners, this may cause distress to the child. Ideally clingfilm should be applied over the injury as it has the advantage of an occlusive dressing in inhibiting airflow across the area, but has relatively low adherent qualities, and enables re-assessment because of its transparency. The fact that the child can still visualise the injury themselves may be overcome by placing a non-transparent covering over the clingfilm which may be readily removed when necessary.

Other non-pharmacological approaches to pain relief in children with burns may include elevation of limbs where appropriate and use of distraction therapy which may be particularly important during treatment stages. These strategies are discussed in more detail in Chapter 5 (pp. 29–35).

After providing pain relief, attention will need to turn to the specific management of the injury. Depending upon the cause of the burn or scald, the wound may need to be cleansed prior to treatment. Cleansing should be undertaken by irrigating the wound with water (plain tap water is suitable for this purpose) and this may be achieved using a syringe and/or hypodermic needle depending on the nature of debris. If a hypodermic needle is used then the younger child may need reassurance (and a demonstration) concerning the way the needle is to be utilised. If debris cannot be removed using such methods, either because of anxiety on the part of the child or very adherent particles, then a decision needs to be made about the relative benefits of leaving minor debris in the wound and reviewing the wound at a later date, or sedating or anaesthetising the child to facilitate removal. The issue of whether or not blisters should be de-roofed, drained or left alone is contentious. Available evidence, of which there is little and which can be contradictory, does not justify the recommendation of any one method. In general the de-roofing or draining of blisters is discouraged on the basis that blister fluid promotes healing, and de-roofing or draining blisters is inherently painful (Cole 2003). Some authors advocate the draining of blisters where they overlie joints (Cole 2003) whilst others have noted an increased incidence of infection where blisters have been de-roofed or drained (Shaw 2006).

Injuries that constitute only superficial erythema do not need to be dressed but an occlusive cover of some sort may prevent irritation by clothing and the pain associated with air convection detailed earlier. Most superficial burn injuries in children will heal in three to six days. Superficial and deep partial thickness injuries should be dressed to assist in prevention of infection and to promote optimal wound healing environments. Much controversy also exists concerning appropriate wound care dressings in the management of minor burns. Best current evidence advocates the use of silicone coated nylon dressings in promoting effective wound healing and recommends against the use of silver sulfadiazine cream as it is associated with increased incidence of scar formation. Local wound guidelines should be followed but their rationale for use should be evidence based.

Table 15.2

A comparison of burns dressings
(Source: British Medical Journal 2007)

A comparison of burns dressings

Dressing product	Features	Brand names
Paraffin gauze	Simple and relatively inexpensive. Wound healing in approximately seven days. May dry out and become adherent.	Jelonet
Hydrocolloid dressings	Promote a moist environment for healing. Healing time about the same as for paraffin gauze.	Duoderm Granuflex
Clear film dressings	Allow visualisation of the injury. Wound healing in approximately 10 days. Increased incidence of scarring.	Opsite
Silicone coated nylon	Markedly less adherent than other types of dressings. Frequency of dressing change is reduced. Relatively expensive.	Mepitel
Silver impregnated cream	Used to avoid risk of infection. May be associated with prolonged healing times and increased pain.	Flamazine

The use of antibiotics in the management of minor burns is not warranted. Much recent literature finds little evidence of its effectiveness in preventing infection. Antibiotic administration should therefore be considered in established infection but otherwise should be avoided (Hudspith & Rayatt 2004, Clinical Knowledge Summaries 2007b).

Prior to discharge it should be decided whether or not the child needs to have their burn or scald reviewed and where this should happen. Children with superficial injuries do not need to be formally reviewed but parents and carers should be given appropriate aftercare advice along with the telephone number for NHS Direct/NHS 24 and the option to return to the department or unit if necessary. Children with more significant burn injuries will need to be reviewed in order to gauge wound healing progress and detect opportunistic infection. This may happen at the GP surgery or in the emergency department or minor injury unit where the child was first treated. This decision depends upon the size of injury, the resources for re-dressing the wound that the GP's surgery has, and practitioner and child preference; if a particularly good therapeutic rapport has been developed with the child this is as good a reason as any to bring the child back to the same department or unit, to see the same practitioner, when their first dressing is due for removal. Parents and carers should be advised to ensure that the child is given analgesia prior to a first dressing review.

Part III

Minor illness

Chapter 16
Assessment of illness in the child

Definition

Assessment and management of the child with a minor illness requires a different approach to that utilised in caring for the child with a minor injury. The assessment of minor illness and, crucially, its differentiation from more severe illness, is a more complex process that requires the practitioner to piece together relevant clues from history taking, to recognise how body systems may interact and cloud the clinical presentation of symptoms, and to be able to recognise and act upon signs and symptoms that indicate the child is suffering from more than a minor illness.

In the following chapters, minor illness in the child will be examined on a body systems basis: thus illness of the respiratory system will be dealt with in addition to ENT, abdominal, genito-urinary, musculo-skeletal and dermatological conditions. The assessment and management of children with minor illness pertinent to each system will be discussed. In each section 'red flag' signs and symptoms will be highlighted that should alert the practitioner to the presence or potential presence of severe illness. Additionally general parameters indicative of severe illness in the child will be dealt with in the section concerning recognition of the unwell child. In this way it is envisaged that the additional challenges associated with the assessment and management of illness rather than injury will be addressed by the practitioner in emergency care and the care of children in such environments be enhanced.

Assessment

The principles of clinical examination in the child have been outlined in Chapter 10 (pp. 69–79). The medical model of history taking may be applied as readily in the assessment of illness and injury though certain parts of the model may need to be expanded upon as follows.

PC: Presenting complaint

PC

What is the primary complaint of the patient? An ill child may have a multiplicity of complaints associated with one disease process and the child, or parents, will usually present these in order of importance to them. Thus a child with an exacerbation of asthma may have shortness of breath, an audible wheeze, an associated cough and fever, lethargy and malaise and it is worth considering what the principal complaint is, i.e. what has prompted the child or parents and carers to seek help at this time? Children with exacerbations of pre-existing illness may, along with their parents or carers, tolerate familiar symptoms well. Thus the child with asthma may not cause enough concern to prompt attendance for emergency care until a new or unusual symptom precipitates this. Parents may manage the child who is short of breath with a mild fever at home as this may be the usual course of exacerbation. If an audible wheeze is heard and this is not a usual feature of the child's illness then this may cause anxiety and prompt attendance. Information of this nature is potentially important in gauging the actual or potential severity of illness: parents and their children with pre-existing illness will have a familiarity with the usual pattern of disease not available to the practitioner. Notification of a new or unusual symptom or variance from usual patterns of disease should be considered with some gravity by the practitioner.

HPC: History of the presenting complaint

HPC

Minor injury is generally the result of a single and precipitate event. Presentation with illness may be the result of a period of ill-health with multiple complaints that has culminated in attendance for care. Many parents or carers may have attempted to care for their child themselves for a period of time. Attendance in secondary care may be subsequent to prior attendance in a primary care setting and vice versa. It is therefore important to ascertain how long the child has been unwell for and what changes in the clinical picture may have taken place. Repeat attendance, whatever the setting, should be considered with caution; many parents may have recognised deterioration in the child and where the repeat attendance is in a different setting and previous documentation is not available extra caution should be taken. If the child has received treatment from another provider and has now presented again in a different setting then they may have a partially treated illness that may not have the classic clinical signs and symptoms associated with it. Recent or recurrent treatment with antibiotics should for instance prompt referral of the infant who has suffered a febrile convulsion as partially treated meningococcal disease may not present with the classical signs and symptoms of this disease (Prodigy 2006a).

PMH: Past medical history, SH: social history, DH: drug history

PMH, SH and DH

Although these historical and sociological factors are important to define when assessing the child with a minor injury, it is more likely that they will be directly relevant to presentation in illness. An obvious example of this is the child with an exacerbation of a pre-existing illness. Additionally however it may be that the presentation may be the result of disease being transmitted within a family or other social group such as a school. Where relevant therefore, information about peers, siblings and other family members should be sought. Certain illnesses such as asthma may also have a familial or hereditary pre-disposition. If a child is taking medication for a pre-existing illness or for any other reason then to what extent may this have precipitated the presentation for care? For example, the child taking immunosuppressive medication will be more prone to minor illness secondary to opportunistic infections. The child taking antibiotics for another illness may develop gastro-intestinal symptoms such as diarrhoea which again prompts attendance for care.

Paediatric minor emergencies

OE: on examination

OE

Examination of the child with a minor injury, once history taking has excluded associated injuries, will focus very much upon the area injured. Illness may be more multi-faceted than this, either because of idiosyncrasy in the presentation of illness in childhood or because illness in one body system may cause signs and symptoms in a different system. Thus up to 25% of children with abdominal pain may be suffering from upper respiratory infection, sinusitis or otitis media (Erkan *et al.* 2004). The child with meningococcal disease may present with lesions principally of the dermatological system, e.g. a petechial rash.

In circumstances such as these it is therefore important not to focus only on the presenting complaint or the body system affected. It may be necessary to enquire about signs and symptoms in other body systems and to undertake a physical examination of these systems.

IMP: impression

IMP

Provisional diagnosis or the impression gained from history taking and physical examination can involve many statements about what may be wrong with the child. Diagnosis may lack the certainty associated with many minor injuries and may be a statement of probable or possible diagnoses. More importantly the impression will have identified or excluded the presence of severe illness and in this respect, by excluding such illness, the impression may be a statement of what is not wrong with the child.

Plan

Plan

Investigations in uncomplicated minor injury are limited: x-rays may or may not be requested, urinalysis may reveal complications of traumatic injury to the abdomen. As minor illness gives rise to a more complex array of presentations, and there is the need to exclude more severe illness, investigations in such circumstances include the appropriate use of blood sampling and analysis, urinalysis, x-rays and other forms of radiological intervention, audiometric and ophthalmological tests and tests of respiratory function such as peak expiratory flow estimations.

Investigations planned should have a rationale based on information gleaned from the history taking and physical examination. They should be justifiable in these terms and should not take the place of an adequate clinical examination. The results of investigations may narrow down the differential diagnoses to a point where a likely diagnosis is reached or they refute them altogether, making a re-assessment of the child obligatory.

Diagnostic decision making

**Diagnostic
decision
making**

Evans (2005) discussed clinical decision making and categorised four strategies for this:

- pattern recognition
- decision analysis theory
- hypothetico-deductive reasoning
- intuition.

In pattern recognition, patients are categorised according to how similar their presentation is to those seen previously and this approach may be most effectively applied to less complex presentations. Decision analysis theory involves estimates of probability of illness based upon clinical reasoning and judgements concerning the likelihood of different disease processes. Hypothetico-deductive reasoning involves the construction of a hypothesis based upon information gained during history taking and physical examination. Subsequent investigation may confirm or refute the presumptive diagnosis. Intuition, states Evans (2005), has been mostly associated with nursing and an inability to quantify its rationale has often led to it lacking credibility amongst other professions. Paraphrased as 'gut feeling', some writers speculate that this is a legitimate strategy based upon the clinical experience of the practitioner (Harbison 2001). Evans (2005) highlights the fact that in practice the four strategies may be intermingled or used selectively based upon their appropriateness to the presentation and the experience of the practitioner. Decision analysis theory for instance may not always be most effectively applied in emergency care settings where speed of decision making may be of the essence, provided that the practitioner has the skills and experience to utilise the more appropriate methods available.

An additional resource in reaching diagnosis in minor illness may be the passage of time. Just as in the child with a minor head injury, a period of observation may reinforce the decision to discharge the child, having allowed an opportunity to receive analgesia and interact with parents, carers or siblings, so the child with a fever or a mild exacerbation of asthma may benefit from a period of observation, or re-assessment after a fixed period of time, in order to gauge the benefits of interventions made. Strategies such as these, when used appropriately, will also have the benefit of alleviating parental anxiety and allow the practitioner a period of time to reflect upon care and if necessary reconsider certain aspects of the case episode.

Chapter 17
Recognition of the unwell child

Initial assessment of the child should include a rapid exclusion of red flag signs and symptoms indicative of severe illness. Whilst this process may not result in definitive diagnosis it will, effectively applied, exclude life-threatening illness in the child.

The 3-minute toolkit

The 3-minute toolkit

Consultant in Paediatric Emergency Medicine Ffion Davies edited a joint Department of Health and Royal College of Paediatric and Child Health DVD entitled *Spotting the Sick Child* (Davies 2004). In this visual presentation, aimed at the timely identification of the child with life-threatening illness, a checklist called the 3-minute toolkit is presented to assist in the systematic assessment of children. After history taking and visual assessment of the child the checklist follows this order:

A: assessment of the airway

B: assessment of breathing

C: assessment of circulation

D: assessment of disability or level of consciousness

ENT: assessment of the ears and throat

T: take the temperature.

Using this toolkit, which with experience may take no longer than three minutes to complete, will assist in the identification of the child who has more than a minor illness.

Assessment of the airway and breathing will involve looking at the child and gauging respiratory rate and effort. Increased respiratory effort associated with dyspnoea in children is evidenced by flaring of the nostrils, the use of accessory muscles in the thorax to assist breathing and intercostal and costal muscle recession secondary to marked respiratory effort. Looking at the child will also elicit information about airway and respiratory status by observation of skin colour and the exclusion or identification of symptoms associated with airway obstruction such as drooling.

Listening to the child will also yield information about airway and breathing: noisy breathing, an audible wheeze or stridor are all symptomatic of respiratory distress. An expiratory grunt is a red flag marker also. In an attempt to increase airway pressure during severe respiratory distress, infants may partially close the glottis during expiration. This produces a characteristic expiratory grunt. If the child is talking to the practitioner or parents, are they able to talk in complete sentences? An inability to complete sentences between breaths is another marker of severe respiratory distress. Formal auscultation of the chest and the identification or exclusion of red flag signs (such as a silent chest) also forms a part of this assessment. Additional estimates of respiratory function should include pulse oximetry readings. The Manchester Triage Group define low oxygen saturation as being < 95% in air and very low saturation as being < 90% in air or < 95% on oxygen therapy (Manchester Triage Group 2005).

Assessment of circulation may be achieved by again initially looking at the child: does the child's skin colour indicate effective perfusion or is it pale or dusky? Make an estimate of the capillary refill time by pressing on a nail bed for five seconds and then releasing it. The nail bed should re-perfuse within two seconds (Manchester Triage Group 2005). Where peripheries are cool then this assessment may need to be undertaken more centrally, for instance over the sternum. Palpate a major pulse in the child and exclude tachycardia or bradycardia which in the child may be a pre-morbid sign.

Assessment of disability or level of consciousness may be quickly achieved by the use of the AVPU classification (Advanced Life Support Group 2005):

A: **A**lert

V: responds to **V**oice

P: responds to **P**ain

U: **U**nresponsive.

Recognition of the unwell child

This classification is used in initial assessment as an alternative to the Glasgow Coma Score (GCS) as this is more time consuming and is sometimes difficult for practitioners to apply in the pre-verbal child. If the child is anything but alert then this should prompt further assessment of the child to elicit a cause for this deficit.

A rapid examination of the ears and in particular the throat will assist in the exclusion of severe illness that has the potential to cause, for instance, respiratory problems. This includes tonsillitis and other throat infections in addition to the presence of a foreign body in the airway. It should be noted that any child with red flag symptoms of stridor or drooling should not undergo a formal examination of the throat as this may precipitate complete airway obstruction secondary to agitation and inflammation. Where stridor or drooling is secondary to foreign body obstruction, examination of the throat may force the foreign body further into the airway and again may cause complete occlusion. Any child displaying such symptoms should be kept as calm as is possible, be provided with supplemental high-flow oxygen in as non-threatening a manner as is possible and immediate advice should be sought from colleagues in ENT and anaesthetic medicine. Examination of the ears may identify the inflammatory changes associated with infection of the middle ear such as those seen in otitis media.

Checking the temperature of the child is most readily achieved with a tympanic thermometer. High fever, and fever which persists despite the administration of an anti-pyretic such as paracetamol, may be indicative of more severe illness. In undifferentiated fever the National Institute for Health and Clinical Excellence advocate a 'traffic light' approach to assessment of the child (NICE 2007a). See Table 17.1 (overleaf).

The NICE guidelines advocate the referral of a child with any red light signs and symptoms to a paediatric specialist. Where there are amber signs and symptoms, parents/carers should be given an option to return, the child should be formally reviewed, or advice should be sought from a paediatric specialist. Those with green light signs and symptoms may be safely managed at home.

Note that the absence of a high fever does not preclude serious illness, as there is little evidence that serious illness in the child is always associated with a high fever and the severity of illness should not be gauged by temperature readings alone (National

Paediatric minor emergencies

Table 17.1

Traffic light assessment
(Source: National Institute
for Health and Clinical
Excellence 2007a, used
with permission)

Institute for Health and Clinical Excellence 2007b). A hot rather than warm child is defined by the Manchester Triage Group (2005, p. 16) as a child with a temperature greater than 38.5° C.

Traffic light assessment

	GREEN – LOW RISK	AMBER – INTERMEDIATE	RED – HIGH RISK
COLOUR	• Normal colour of skin, lips and tongue	• Pallor reported by parent/carer	• Pale/mottled/ashen/blue
ACTIVITY	• Responds normally to social cues • Content/smiles • Stays awake or awakens quickly • Strong normal cry/ not crying	• Not responding normally to social cues • Wakes only with prolonged stimulation • Decreased activity • No smile	• No response to social cues • Appears ill to a healthcare professional • Unable to rouse or if roused does not stay awake • Weak, high-pitched or continuous cry
RESPIRATION		• Nasal flaring • Tachypnoea: – RR > 50 breaths/minute age 6–12 months – RR > 40 breaths/minute age > 12 months • Oxygen saturation ≤ 95% in air • Crackles	• Grunting • Tachypnoea: – RR > 60 breaths/minute • Moderate or severe chest indrawing
HYDRATION	• Normal skin and eyes • Moist mucous membranes	• Dry mucous membrane • Poor feeding in infants • CRT ≥ 3 seconds • Reduced urine output	• Reduced skin turgor
OTHER	• None of the amber or red symptoms or signs	• Fever for ≥ 5 days • Swelling of a limb or joint • Non-weight bearing/ not using an extremity • A new lump > 2 cm	• Age 0–3 months, temperature ≥ 38°C • Age 3–6 months, temperature ≥ 39°C • Non-blanching rash • Bulging fontanelle • Neck stiffness • Status epilepticus • Focal neurological signs • Focal seizures • Bile-stained vomiting

Note: CRT: Capillary refill time, NWB: Non-weight bearing

Recognition of the unwell child

Note that blood pressure estimation does not form a part of the assessment; recording this may cause additional distress in the child. Children maintain normal pressure in severe illness more readily than adults (Advanced Life Support Group 2005) and normal blood pressure readings cannot be safely relied upon as an indicator of well-being. Decreasing blood pressure is often a pre-terminal sign in children (Advanced Life Support Group 2005). It should be measured if other findings indicate the child is profoundly unwell.

In undertaking initial assessment of the child, knowledge of normal physiological parameters is needed in order that abnormal findings are readily identified. See Table 17.2.

Table 17.2

Normal physiological parameters

Normal physiological parameters

Age	Respiratory rate	Heart rate	Systolic BP	Temperature	Oxygen saturation	Capillary refill time
Neonate	60	160	70	> 37.5° C = Warm	< 95 % in air = low	Normal = < 2 seconds
< 1 year	35–45	110–160	75			
					< 90 % in air	
1–5 years	25–35	95–140	80–90			
					< 95 % on O$_2$ =	
5–12 years	20–25	80–120	90–110	> 38.5° C = Hot	very low	
> 12 years	adult	adult	100–120			

Note: *Normal systolic blood pressure may be estimated by the formula 80 + (age in years × 2)*
(adapted from Davies 2004, Advanced Life Support Group 2005, Manchester Triage Group 2005.)

Chapter 18
Febrile convulsion

Between 2% and 4% of children will suffer a febrile convulsion with the peak of incidence being at around the age of 18 months (Armon *et al.* 2001, Waruiru & Appleton 2004). Febrile convulsions are rare after the age of five or six years as thermoregulatory mechanisms mature. Febrile convulsions are a common cause of childhood attendance for emergency care accounting for up to 5% of all paediatric presentations (Armon *et al.* 2001). The processes governing how a febrile convulsion occurs are unclear but there is an underlying pathology that has caused feverish illness in the child. These illnesses in decreasing order of incidence are (Armon *et al.* 2003):

- viral illnesses
- otitis media
- tonsillitis
- urinary tract infection
- gastroenteritis
- lower respiratory tract infection
- meningitis
- following a childhood immunisation.

Most febrile convulsions will be limited to a period of three to six minutes though in more complex presentations this may persist for up to 30 minutes (Prodigy 2006a). An obvious priority in the management of febrile convulsion is to eliminate bacterial meningitis as a cause for fever and illness. Although Armon *et al.* (2003) found meningitis to be one of the least likely causes of febrile convulsion and others have found the risk of bacterial meningitis to be between 0.6% and 7% after febrile seizure

(Offringa & Moyer 2001, Baumer *et al.* 2004) best practice urges caution in the interpretation of such data (Prodigy 2006a) as it did not include children managed outside of secondary care environments. In Armon's 2003 work (Armon *et al.* 2003) a Delphi study of 30 senior clinicians resulted in the recommendation that:

> A child who presents with seizure and fever and has any of the following on history or examination should be treated as having meningitis until proven otherwise: drowsy preseizure, neck stiffness, petechial rash, bulging fontanelle, a Glasgow Coma Scale of < 15 (more than one hour post seizure)

Practitioners' priorities for care are to secure the airway of the child if they are still convulsing and to give respiratory support where necessary. Subsequent history taking and examination should focus upon attempting to establish the underlying reason for fever and convulsion. Assessment of the respiratory system, the ear, nose and throat, and the abdomen will assist in this endeavour. Visual examination of the skin to exclude purpural rash, and dipstick urinalysis may further clarify underlying diagnosis. History taking should focus upon signs and symptoms in the child prior to convulsion in order to inform diagnosis.

As the majority of children with a febrile convulsion have a minor illness of childhood such as viral illness or otitis media it is recommended that most children who suffer such a seizure should be discharged home (Prodigy 2006a). Only when meningitis has been excluded as a cause of fever should this outcome be considered. In addition to the criteria mentioned above, the following should also prompt referral to specialist services rather than discharge home:

Referral criteria

- Any infant less than 18 months old should be referred, as there is some evidence that meningitis may present atypically in this age group (Armon *et al.* 2003).

- If the child has received recent antibiotic therapy then there is again some evidence suggesting that such children may have meningism masked. It is recommended that such children are admitted for observation (Armon *et al.* 2003).

- If the convulsion was sustained for an unusually long period or if the fitting is recurrent or if the child remains drowsy then referral is advised.

- If parents or carers are too anxious to adequately care for the child at home referral is advised.

Parents of children who have suffered febrile convulsions are often particularly anxious and may even believe that their child is about to die during the seizure (Parmar *et al.* 2001). Many make no intervention before calling an ambulance to take the child to hospital and there is widespread anxiety about the child having long-term complications such as epilepsy (Parmar *et al.* 2001). Parents taking children home should have written advice emphasising the need to administer regular anti-pyretic medication, to ensure the child is drinking enough whilst feverish, and to keep the child in a cool environment without overdressing them. The use of fans, cold bathing and sponging has no evidence base and may distress the child (Prodigy 2006a). Parental anxiety should be addressed by:

Parental anxiety

- reassurance and advice concerning the importance of rolling the child into the recovery position during a convulsion to protect the airway
- advising parents to stay with the child until the fit has stopped and then to call NHS Direct or their General Practitioner
- advising parents to call an ambulance if the seizure is prolonged and this is defined as being more than 10 minutes (Prodigy 2006a)
- reassuring them that there is an association between febrile convulsion and the development of epilepsy in only 1 % of those children who have more than one fit (Prodigy 2006a)
- reassuring them that there is only a one in three chance of the child having another febrile convulsion (Prodigy 2006a)
- reassuring them that anti-convulsant medication to prevent further seizures is not warranted
- reassuring them that childhood immunisations are not contraindicated subsequent to a febrile convulsion.

Chapter 19
ENT and respiratory illness

Children, and in particular very young children, have immature immune systems that pre-dispose them to infection in general and this includes illnesses of the ear, nose and throat and respiratory systems. More specifically children have a eustachian tube lying at a less acute angle to the auditory canal than the adult. This facilitates infective transmission between the middle ear and the upper respiratory tract.

The tapering trachea of the infant and young child, narrowing toward the larynx, differs from that of the adult where the trachea is of a uniform lumen. This gradual narrowing pre-disposes to:

● partial or full occlusion of the airway during inflammatory disease – the gradually narrowing lumen of the trachea means that the airway of the child becomes exponentially narrower during inflammation at a much faster rate than in the adult

● impaction of foreign bodies – the narrow part of the trachea at the larynx serves as a point of impaction for appropriate sized foreign bodies that children will sometimes ingest. In any child who presents with sudden onset of stridor, drooling and dyspnoea, foreign body ingestion should be suspected.

In addition second-hand tobacco smoke, still unfortunately a feature of many children's lives, can aggravate sinusitis and rhinitis, increase the incidence of sore throat amongst children, may trigger or exacerbate asthma and increases the incidence of otitis media. In fact children who live in a house with a smoker of 20 cigarettes a day are twice as likely to be hospitalised for respiratory illness than their peers who live in tobacco smoke-free households (American Academy of Otolaryngology 2007). Recent legislation prohibiting tobacco smoking in public places in England has gone some way to protecting vulnerable people, including children, from the effects of secondhand smoke. However if it becomes apparent during consultation that a child is living in a household with a smoker then it is incumbent upon the practitioner, as an advocate for the child, to highlight the risks associated with this to parents and carers and to:

- encourage smokers to stop smoking and provide them with information about resources they may require to achieve this
- where it is not possible to encourage smokers to quit then encourage them to smoke outside of the house
- encourage smokers not to smoke in cars with child occupants.

Sore throat

Sore throat

The vast majority of sore throats occur in association with an upper respiratory tract infection and are viral in origin. Pharyngitis and laryngitis are terms used to describe sore throat where symptoms are predominantly in the oropharynx (pharyngitis) or where patients complain of symptoms at a lower point, sometimes in association with hoarseness (laryngitis). Additionally tonsillitis may be evidenced by swelling and the presence of exudate (Prodigy 2006b).

Children may present with soreness, dysphagia, fever, headache, malaise and hoarseness if there is laryngeal involvement but be aware also that up to almost one-quarter of children with upper respiratory illness will complain of abdominal pain as a feature of the presentation (Erkan *et al.* 2004). In acute sore throat tonsillar exudate may be found on examination and palpation of tonsillar, sub-mandibular and anterior cervical lymph nodes may also elicit tenderness.

During the consultation ask the child or parents/carers about any self-help strategies that may have been used and about the child's medical history. Enquire about associated symptoms such as stridor, drooling, grunting and shortness of breath that may be indicative of severe illness. Adoption of Fowler's position by the child is a red flag marker of respiratory distress also; patients adopt this position (sometimes called the tripod position) by sitting upright with the torso held slightly forward in an attempt to maximise respiratory potential when acutely short of breath.

ENT and respiratory illness

Make an assessment of respiratory status using the measures outlined in Chapter 17 on the recognition of the unwell child such as respiratory rate and effort and pulse oximetry readings. It is always worth checking that the child has kept to recommended immunisation schedules as this is helpful in the exclusion of certain illnesses that can cause respiratory and ENT problems such as diphtheria and pertussis. Careful questioning and observation of the child can therefore exclude certain illnesses prior to examination.

Anaphylaxis (see also Chapter 21, pp. 193–196) may also present with respiratory symptoms and the laryngeal oedema associated with it may present as sore throat. Children with anaphylaxis may have a history of this disorder if this is not the first presentation. Patients will display other associated symptoms in anaphylaxis that will assist in excluding or identifying this life-threatening condition:

- swollen lips and/or tongue
- signs of hypovolaemia secondary to distributive shock: tachycardia, tachypnoea, hypotension, delayed capillary refill time, diaphoresis, angio-oedema causing swelling of dependent parts, collapse
- urticarial rash
- rhinitis, conjunctivitis, wheeze
- nausea, vomiting and abdominal pain
- a sense of impending doom.

Other causes of sore throat that may need to be excluded include sexually transmitted disease secondary to sexual abuse of the child. If consultation prompts concerns about the potential for symptoms to be secondary to abuse (see Chapter 6) then this cause of sore throat should be considered and child protection guidelines implemented. Where the child or parents complain of recurrent infections of the upper respiratory tract or elsewhere, especially when other causes for recurrence cannot be identified (e.g. secondhand smoke) then it may be worth considering the exclusion of neutropenia as a cause for this. Parents and children may be reassured in the knowledge that in the majority of instances recurrent fever in children resolves without serious consequence (Sadovsky 2003).

Paediatric minor emergencies

In examining the throat of a child, do so gently with a tongue depressor. Routine swabbing of throats is not necessary (Prodigy 2006b) and is likely to cause unnecessary distress in the child. Note the presence of any enlargement of the tonsils or exudate on them, note any reddening and inflammation of the oropharynx and any deviation of the uvula away from the midline which is associated with peritonsillar abscess (quinsy) formation.

Figure 19.1

Normal midline uvula. Note the presence of any deviation of the uvula. Here it is seen in its normal position in the midline of the throat.

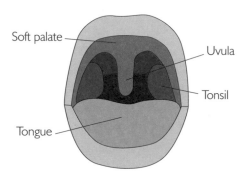

Streptococcal throat infection

As much as one-quarter of sore throats may be attributable to streptococcal infection (Prodigy 2006b). This may subsequently cause the development of peritonsillar abscess, pneumonia or meningitis. Such infection is accompanied by scarlatine (vivid red) coloured rash in skin folds and a white or strawberry coloured tongue. History taking may yield information about the sudden onset of the illness.

Figure 19.2

'Strep throat': note the inflammation of the oropharynx and the white appearance of the tongue

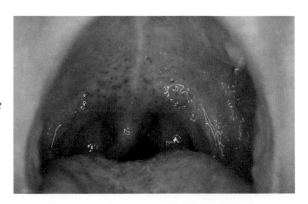

Source: http://www.childhoodhealth.com/health-information/diseases-and-symptoms/sore-throat/#comment-2883 Used with permission.

ENT and respiratory illness

Management of sore throat is founded upon the fact that resolution without treatment occurs in 40% of patients within three days and 85% within one week and this is true even if the sore throat was attributable to streptococcal infection (Prodigy 2006b). Reassurance and advice about provision of anti-pyretics are the only form of treatment that most children and their parents or carers will need. Red flag signs and symptoms of respiratory distress should be highlighted to parents or carers and they should be advised to return if any of these become evident. A contact telephone number should be provided and it may be beneficial to also provide the telephone number for NHS Direct or NHS 24 in Scotland for telephone support and advice.

Antibiotics are not routinely indicated for sore throat and their prescription should be limited to patients who fulfil the following criteria (NICE 2001):

- patients who are systemically unwell
- patients with unilateral peritonsillitis
- patients with a history of rheumatic fever
- patients at increased risk of infection such as those with diabetes mellitus or neutropoenia.

Red flag signs and symptoms in sore throat

- Stridor, drooling
- Dyspnoea and tachypnoea
- Adoption of Fowler's position
- Low oximetry readings
- Any symptoms associated with anaphylaxis
- Any suspicion of sexual abuse
- Any suspicion of peritonsillar abscess: uvula deviation, dysphagia, high fever, unilateral pain.

Croup

Croup

Croup is a viral illness that most often affects children between three months and six years of age in autumn and winter months (Beattie *et al.* 1999, Knutson & Aring 2004). It is characterised by inspiratory stridor, hoarseness of the voice and a barking 'seal like' cough. Symptoms tend to be worse at night and most patients will present at this time. The stridor and pronounced cough are often distressing to the child and parents and a calm approach to consultation whilst providing information about likely prognosis will help to alleviate anxiety and avoid exacerbation of symptoms. History taking may yield information about there having been upper respiratory symptoms of a common cold for a few days and a low grade fever (Beattie *et al.* 1999). A respiratory assessment should take place in a similar manner to that for the child with a sore throat but remember not to examine the throat of a child who has stridor or drooling. Important differential diagnoses that need to be excluded include bacterial tracheitis, epiglottitis, anaphylaxis and a foreign body in the throat. As in sore throat, the exclusion of these may be achieved by careful and focused history taking prior to any examination of the child, as follows (adapted from Beattie *et al.* 1999):

- Does the child have a history of allergy or anaphylaxis and are there any other signs or symptoms of these?

- Is there any chance of foreign body ingestion? Was the child alone for a period of time? Have symptoms come on very suddenly with no history of common cold symptoms as seen in croup?

- Is the child's immunisation schedule up to date? – Immunisation against Haemophilus influenza B (HIB) and diphtheria, tetanus and pertussis (DTP) means that epiglottitis and diphtheria are extremely unlikely diagnoses.

- Is there a high fever (i.e. > 38.5° C) and does the child appear systemically unwell? High fever and systemic illness are associated with epiglottitis and bacterial tracheitis.

Additionally the presence of the barking cough is of great diagnostic value as this is not a feature of either epiglottitis or bacterial tracheitis. Auscultation of the chest should reveal the inspiratory stridor associated with croup.

As most children with croup may be managed safely at home, whilst a minority with severe symptoms will need hospital admission, attempts have been made to develop scoring systems to help clinicians gauge the severity of illness and most appropriate management. A commonly utilised tool is the modified Westley croup scoring system (Westley *et al.* 1978, Patientplus 2004). See Table 19.1.

Table 19.1

Westley croup scoring system.

(Source: Westley *et al.* 1978)

Westley croup scoring system

SIGN OR SYMPTOM	SEVERITY	SCORE
Stridor	None	0
	At rest on auscultation	1
	At rest without auscultation	2
Intercostal / costal muscle recession	None	0
	Mild	1
	Moderate	2
	Severe	3
Air entry	Normal	0
	Decreased	1
	Severely decreased	2
Cyanosis	None	0
	With agitation	4
	At rest	5
Level of consciousness	Normal	0
	Altered	5

< 4	Mild croup
4–6	Moderate croup
6–17	Severe croup

There is no consensus about the management of croup. Corticosteroid administration is widely advocated for moderate and severe croup and should be considered for those with mild symptoms also (Victoria Department of Human Services 2007). The corticosteroid advocated for its efficacy in the management of croup is dexamethasone and this should be given in a dose of 0.15mg–0.60mg/kg body weight (Patientplus 2004, Victoria

Paediatric minor emergencies

Department of Human Services 2007). Children with mild croup, who are otherwise well, whose parents are happy to care for the child at home and are aware of circumstances that should prompt them to return for emergency care, may be discharged home (Fitzgerald & Kilham 2003). Parents and carers should be advised that a worsening of symptoms such as stridor or cyanosis at rest, increasing dyspnoea and decreased level of consciousness should prompt re-attendance. The development of symptoms such as drooling, high fever or systemic illness will also necessitate urgent re-attendance.

Whilst there is much anecdotal evidence for the benefit of humidified and/or warmed air therapy in children with croup there is no evidence base for this. Research that has been undertaken in this area has found no quantifiable benefit for this treatment (Fitzgerald & Kilham 2003) and other authors highlight the potential for scald injury inherent in attempting to implement the treatment (Beattie *et al.* 1999).

In addition to corticosteroids, children with moderate or severe croup need supplemental oxygen to maintain acceptable oximetry readings. Children with severe symptoms will benefit from nebulised adrenaline and either oral corticosteroid therapy in the form of dexamethasone or a nebulised corticosteroid such as budesonide if they are vomiting (Victoria Department of Human Services 2007). A low threshold should be maintained for the involvement of anaesthetic services in the management of children with severe symptoms.

Table 19.2

Features of croup, bacterial tracheitis and epiglottitis

Features of croup, bacterial tracheitis and epiglottitis

(adapted from Beattie et al. 1999, Fitzgerald & Kilham 2003, Patientplus 2004)

	Temperature	Oximetry	Barking cough	Onset	Position	Systemic illness
Croup	Low grade fever	>95% air	Present	Gradual	Variable	Unlikely
Bacterial tracheitis	High	Low	Absent	Gradual	Fowler's	Likely
Epiglottitis	High	Low	Absent	Sudden	Fowler's	Possible

Red flag signs and symptoms in croup

- Sudden onset of symptoms
- Adoption of Fowler's position
- Low oximetry readings
- Any symptoms associated with anaphylaxis
- High fever
- Child is systemically unwell.

Otitis media

Otitis media

Otitis media is an infection of the middle ear. It is associated with upper respiratory tract infections and such respiratory tract infections may precede or follow an episode of otitis media. Children are particularly prone to the passage of infection between the respiratory tract and middle ear because the eustachian tube of a child lies at a less acute angle to the auditory canal than in the adult. This makes the passage of infective organisms between the two structures more likely. Apart from a respiratory tract infection, otitis media may also be caused, or pre-disposed to, by the use of a dummy and secondhand smoke (Prodigy 2006c).

Figure 19.3

The outer, middle and inner ear

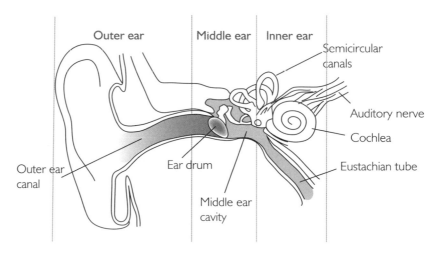

Children with otitis media will present with a painful ear, a low grade fever and some hearing loss. In more severe episodes of illness they may also suffer vertigo and vomiting secondary to involvement of the vestibular apparatus in disease. As visualisation with an otoscope is likely to be painful, this aspect of examination should be delayed as long as possible in order to maintain the trust and co-operation of the child and minimise distress. It will also be beneficial to administer analgesia where this has not been done by parents or carers or where this has been ineffective.

Examination of the auditory canal will reveal a red, bulging tympanic membrane and there may be an associated purulent discharge. In severe otitis media the membrane may be perforated, resulting in deafness. This perforation resolves spontaneously over a period of weeks.

Management of otitis media is founded upon the provision of effective analgesia whilst the condition resolves. Although mastoiditis may be a consequence of otitis media, the routine prescription of antibiotics to treat it is not warranted as this has no effect on the subsequent development of mastoiditis (Prodigy 2006c). Indications for the use of antibiotics in otitis media are (Prodigy 2006c):

● if the child is less than two years of age

● if symptoms are bilateral

● if fever is high i.e. $> 38.5°$ C.

Where antibiotics are indicated then the child should be prescribed amoxicillin or erythromycin for seven days. Consideration may be given to delayed prescription; a prescription may be issued but parents and carers advised not to request dispensation of the drugs for three days when symptoms may have resolved spontaneously negating the need for antibiotics. This is one method by which the appropriate use of antibiotics may be reinforced, though delayed prescription will need to be discussed with, and understood by, parents and carers of the child.

Four out of five children will however enjoy a spontaneous recovery from the illness in approximately 72 hours (Prodigy 2006c). Parents and carers should be advised to provide the child with regular analgesia. Avoidance of air travel and swimming, both of which may exacerbate symptoms, is also advocated.

Red flag signs and symptoms in otitis media

- Any suspicion of mastoiditis: severe vertigo, vomiting, high fever
- Systemic ill health may indicate mastoid disease.

Asthma

Asthma

Asthma, which often first presents in childhood, ranges in severity from a minor illness to a severe illness with life-threatening features. It is estimated that one in eight children in the UK suffer with asthma (Cambridge Consultants 2007). Every two weeks one child dies as a result of asthma in the UK and many of these deaths are avoidable given prompt recognition and appropriate treatment (Asthma UK 2004).

Asthma may be triggered by factors such as cold, exercise, specific allergens, viral infections, animals, air pollutants, pollen, and certain medicines. Smoking either directly or as a result of exposure to secondhand smoke is responsible for initiating and exacerbating asthma (American Academy of Otolaryngology 2007, Asthma UK 2007).

Presentation of asthma reflects the extent to which it varies in its severity. Children may present with mild features such as a slightly raised respiratory rate, an expiratory wheeze audible only on auscultation and a slight tachycardia or with more severe features such as severe dyspnoea and tachypnoea, an audible wheeze, a marked tachycardia and use of accessory muscles to assist in breathing. Initial assessment of severity should be made by reference to oximetry readings, heart rate, respiratory rate, identification of the use of accessory muscles to assist breathing and where appropriate in children peak expiratory flow recordings (British Thoracic Society 2005):

- PEFR > 75% predicted value: mild asthma
- PEFR 33%–75% predicted value: moderate–severe asthma (severe < 50% predicted)
- PEFR < 33% predicted value: severe life-threatening asthma

Paediatric minor emergencies

Table 19.3

Peak expiratory flow recordings: predictive values

Peak expiratory flow recordings: predictive values

Height of child	Predictive PEFR value
3 feet 8 inches	160
4 feet 4 inches	267
5 feet	373
5 feet 6 inches	454

Source: Leiner *et al.* 1963

The diagnostic and predictive value of these recordings is obviously dependent upon the child's ability to use a peak flow recording machine effectively. Technique may be poor or the child may be too young to provide a PEFR. Other markers of asthma severity, which should be taken into account in all presentations, become more crucial in the assessment process. The British Thoracic Society's (2005) asthma guidelines indicate that for asthma in children to be considered moderate, rather than severe or life-threatening, pulse oximetry readings should be 92% or more. In two- to five-year-olds heart rate should be less than 130 and less than 120 in children of five years and above for asthma to be considered moderate rather than severe. See Table 19.4.

Table 19.4

Features of acute asthma in children

Features of acute asthma in children

Severity	SpO$_2$	Heart rate	Respiratory rate	PEFR
Moderate	≥ 92%	< 130 2–5 yrs < 120 5 yrs and older	< 50 2–5 yrs < 30 5 yrs and older	≥ 50%
Severe	< 92%	> 130 2–5 yrs > 120 5 yrs and older	> 50 2–5 yrs > 30 5 yrs and older	< 50%
Life-threatening	< 92%	> 130 2–5 yrs > 120 5 yrs and older	> 50 2–5 yrs > 30 5 yrs and older	< 33%

Notes:

Severe asthma in the child may also involve the child being too breathless to talk or eat and the use of accessory muscles to assist breathing. The child may also begin to become exhausted and this is evidenced by poor respiratory effort.

Life-threatening asthma may feature cyanosis, agitation, altered levels of consciousness secondary to hypoxia, poor respiratory effort and reduced respiratory rate secondary to exhaustion and a silent chest on auscultation.

(Source: British Thoracic Society 2005, reprinted with permission.)

If the presentation is not severe, focused history taking, asking pertinent questions of the child and/or their parents/carers, can yield much information about the presentation before the potentially more distressing physical examination. The practitioner should attempt to elicit information concerning any previous episodes of asthma and in particularly their severity. Is there for instance a history of admission to intensive care facilities for intermittent positive pressure ventilation (IPPV)? If so then this should raise concern that the child may become profoundly unwell even if apparently only moderately unwell on initial presentation. If the child is able to provide the history themselves, are they able to talk in complete sentences? An inability to do so is a marker of severe or life-threatening asthma (British Thoracic Society 2005). Does the patient smoke or are they exposed to secondhand smoke in the home? Secondhand smoke can trigger or exacerbate asthma (American Academy of Otolaryngology 2007, Asthma UK 2007). If the child is re-attending for care subsequent to recent treatment and discharge, then safe governance dictates that the child is reviewed by a senior clinician. Re-attendance with partially treated asthma may indicate more severe disease than is immediately apparent.

Physical examination in the child with asthma will include the observational skills already discussed such as the identification of accessory muscle use to assist breathing. Auscultation of the chest should identify an expiratory wheeze. The presence of an inspiratory wheeze should prompt a re-evaluation of the patient and consideration of differential diagnoses. Crackles heard on auscultation, when accompanied by a fever in the child, indicate an infective exacerbation of the illness. A silent chest, indicative of minimal movement of air in the inspiratory or expiratory phase of respiration, is an ominous sign and is associated with exhaustion in the child.

A moderate exacerbation of asthma should be treated with 2–10 puffs of a β_2 agonist such as salbutamol and in children this should be delivered with a spacer device where available. The child should then be re-assessed after 15 minutes. If the response to intervention has been good and the child's condition is improving then they should be given 20 mg of oral prednisolone and on discharge advised to take the β_2 agonist four-hourly on a PRN basis and consideration should be given to providing a 20 mg dose of prednisolone for three days (British Thoracic Society 2005). Inhaler technique should be checked and poor technique rectified where necessary and the parents should be advised to make an appointment for primary care review of their child within one week (British Thoracic society 2005). Parents/carers, and children where appropriate, should be additionally advised to re-attend for urgent care if the condition is deteriorating rather than improving after discharge. Contact telephone numbers should be provided and also that of NHS Direct in England and Wales or NHS 24 in Scotland.

Any child displaying symptoms of more severe asthma should receive a nebulised β_2 agonist, an appropriate dose of soluble prednisolone, this being 20 mg in two- to five-year-olds and 30 mg–40 mg in children older than five years (British Thoracic Society 2005) and arrangements made for referral to paediatric specialist services. Where available, anaesthetic services should also be considered. If in a primary care setting then an emergency (999 or 112) ambulance should be requested. The practitioner should stay with the child until the ambulance arrives and in addition to providing a verbal account of the consultation to the pre-hospital staff, should also provide documentation concerning the episode for receiving staff in secondary care (British Thoracic Society 2005).

Anxiety and fear will compound symptoms in asthma. It will be beneficial where possible to spend time explaining to the child and parents their likely trajectory through the emergency care setting, i.e. who they will meet on referral and approximately how long processes will take. Children develop unrealistic ideas about what will happen to them in healthcare settings (Bentley 2004). It will also be of benefit to explain to the child the nature of likely investigations on referral. Thus telling the child that they may undergo further assessment and investigation, and being honest about the nature of these, may have the benefit of enhancing co-operation and compliance when the child is referred.

Red flag signs and symptoms in asthma

- Use of accessory muscles to assist breathing, nasal flaring and an expiratory grunt
- Audible wheeze
- Tachypnoea, tachycardia, SpO_2 < 92%, PEFR < 50% of predicted
- Adoption of Fowler's position, inability to talk in sentences
- Slow respiratory rate, bradycardia, exhaustion.
- Silent chest.

Bronchiolitis

Bronchiolitis

Bronchiolitis describes an acute infection of the lower respiratory system that predominantly affects infants and small children in the 2–24 month age group (Louden 2007). Like some other childhood illnesses such as croup, its incidence peaks in autumn and winter. It is associated with viral infection caused in 75% to 85% of cases by the respiratory syncytial virus (RSV) (Scottish Intercollegiate Guidelines Network 2006, Louden 2007). As the disease is most prevalent in such a young age group, presenting symptoms may be vague and non-specific and include problems with breathing, nasal secretions and discharge, irritability, poor feeding and cough. Although it has been estimated that bronchiolitis may affect up to one-third of all infants during the first year of life and re-infection is common, it is, in most instances, a self-limiting illness, with morbidity and mortality being related to age (mortality may be as high as 2% in the very young aged less than six months) and the existence of other health problems that contribute to mortality such as those associated with prematurity. In such infants bronchiolitis may present as apnoea (Scottish Intercollegiate Guidelines Network 2006, Louden 2007).

The infant presenting with such symptoms will, on examination, have an associated fever. It is unusual however for this to be a high fever and the absence of fever does not exclude the diagnosis of bronchiolitis. Pulse oximetry values may be decreased and any infant with a saturation ≤ 92% needs admission to hospital. Chest auscultation will also reveal inspiratory crackles and/or an expiratory wheeze (Scottish Intercollegiate Guidelines Network 2006).

The diagnosis of bronchiolitis is a clinical one and is based upon the following criteria, some of which have been discussed already (adapted from Fitzgerald & Kilham 2004, Paediatric Society of New Zealand 2005, Scottish Intercollegiate Guidelines Network 2006):

- **Age** – The disease is most prevalent in the 2–24 month age group.
- **Fever** – High fever is rare and should prompt re-assessment. The absence of fever does not exclude bronchiolitis.
- **Rhinorrhoea** – A nasal discharge is common in the illness.
- **Cough** – This is generally of a dry and wheezy nature.
- **Tachypnoea and recession** – Tachypnoea is an important marker of lower respiratory illness in infants. Subcostal/intercostal recession may be seen in bronchiolitis.
- **Poor feeding** – This is not specific to this illness but feeding may need to be supported in acute bronchiolitis.
- **Wheeze** – This is a common feature of bronchiolitis.
- **Seasonal variation** – The illness is most prevalent between November and March.
- **Secondhand smoke** – There is a quantified association between exposure to secondhand smoke and the development of RSV infection.

Most infants and young children with bronchiolitis may be safely managed at home and parents/carers should be advised that symptoms will persist for up to two weeks. Where secondhand smoke exposure is a feature of presentation then parents/carers should be advised of the association between exposure and the development of illness and encouraged not to further expose their children to smoke.

Some infants and children are admitted to hospital for support with feeding and fluid balance, suctioning of nasal secretions and respiratory support in the form of supplemental oxygen. The use of antibiotics, steroids, inhaled bronchodilators or nebulised epinephrine is not advocated in bronchiolitis (Scottish Intercollegiate Guidelines Network 2006). Where any red flag signs or symptoms are identified, where there are other factors present that affect morbidity and mortality (e.g. prematurity, other existing illness, exposure to secondhand smoke) or where diagnosis is uncertain then referral should be made to specialist paediatric services in secondary care.

Red flag signs and symptoms in bronchiolitis

- Oximetry values ≤ 92% on air, cyanosis
- Poor feeding – < 50% usual fluid intake in last 24 hours
- Apnoea, chest wall recession, nasal flaring, grunting
- Respiratory rate > 70/minute
- Lethargy.

Things that shouldn't be there:
Foreign bodies in the ear, nose and throat

Foreign bodies

Young children are inquisitive and have a tendency to insert foreign bodies into their own auditory canals, nasal passages and throats, in addition to occasionally inserting these objects into similar places in peers or siblings. These foreign bodies (FBs) include such items as toys, toy parts, crayons, coins, beads, and almost anything else narrow enough to fit the appropriate lumen. Children between the ages of six months and four years account for much of this activity though it is not unheard of in older children (Conners 2006).

Children may present for care having been witnessed ingesting a foreign body or placing it into the ear or nose. Others may only present with the later consequences of foreign body ingestion with the event having been unwitnessed. Most children who ingest FBs will have no serious consequence to this and the item will pass harmlessly through the GI tract. Exceptions to this are sharp objects such as glass, objects that become lodged in the GI tract, or objects that are toxic, or potentially toxic in nature such as batteries.

History taking should therefore focus upon exactly what may have been ingested and how long ago this occurred. The funnel shaped trachea of the infant and young child, tapering toward the larynx, pre-disposes to impaction of an FB in this age group. A child who is drooling, with stridor and dyspnoea should be transferred to an area where resuscitation facilities are available and anaesthetic and ENT services summoned urgently. Such children should be managed with their parents or carers in attendance in order to reduce distress and anxiety which may exacerbate respiratory symptoms. If an FB cannot be directly visualised then under no circumstances should attempts be made to blindly remove the item. This may have the consequence of impacting the item further into the tapering larynx and convert a partially occluded airway to one that is fully occluded.

Lateral and AP chest x-ray investigation is recommended where there is a history of FB ingestion (Munter 2005, Conners 2006, Sersar *et al.* 2006). In late presentation this may help to identify or exclude the development of pneumonia secondary to aspiration of a foreign body. Radio-translucent items that become lodged in the oesophagus will be highlighted on plain x-ray, though a request for a soft tissue x-ray of the neck may be of more value where the location of the FB is thought to be in the upper airway or GI tract (Munter 2005). Where items are lodged in the upper GI tract, or have been aspirated into the airway, or need to be removed because of their toxicity, then children will need to be referred for endoscopic or bronchoscopic removal of the FB.

Figure 19.4

A coin in the oesophagus of a child. AP and lateral plain x-rays of the chest should be requested.

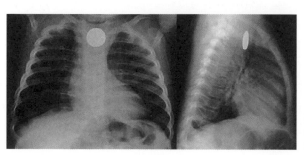

(Source: www.xray2000.co.uk used with permission.)

ENT and respiratory illness

Children who insert foreign bodies into the ear or nose, like those that insert items into their mouths, may present straight after the event as it was witnessed, or may present later as a result of complications of FB insertion. The removal of foreign bodies from the ear and nose may be distressing for the child. In emergency care settings the removal of foreign bodies in the nose has been carried out with greater success than those in the ear, without the need for referral to ENT services (Mackle & Conlon 2005). Where distress makes co-operation unlikely then it is advisable to refer the child to specialist ENT services for removal rather than persist in attempting to remove the item which may lead to trauma to the tympanic or nasal membranes and make removal, under anything other than general anaesthesia impossible (Uslu Coskun *et al.* 2006). Where the co-operation of the child can be gained and the FB visualised then an attempt to remove the item with forceps or a magnet may be made. This should be done with the co-operation and assistance of the parents or carers.

Other techniques that have been advocated to remove foreign bodies from the ears or noses of children include suction at 100–140 mm/hg, though this can be distressing to the child, the use of positive pressure such as the parent or carer blowing into the child's mouth in order to raise intra-nasal pressure and dislodge an FB, and the use of irrigation techniques to retrieve FBs where it can be established that the tympanic membrane is intact and that the foreign body is not constituted of material, such as vegetable matter, that will expand when wet (Davies & Benger 2000). In all such instances the sedation of the child may need to be considered to facilitate whichever technique is deemed most appropriate (Davies & Benger 2000). It is also recommended that once a foreign body has been removed, the ear or nose should be visualised again to ensure there are not multiple FBs present and the contralateral nostril or ear should also be examined to exclude bilateral foreign bodies (Davies & Benger 2000).

Children with foreign bodies in the ear or nose may only present some time after insertion of the item when there is a purulent discharge from the ear or nose or a problem with the child's hearing has been identified (Munter 2005, Uslu Coskun *et al.* 2006). In children with unilateral nasal discharge, or recurrent infection of the nose or ear, FB presence as a focus for infection should be excluded.

Chapter 20
Abdominal and genito-urinary illness

Up to 25% of children presenting with abdominal pain have otitis media, sinusitis or an upper respiratory tract infection (Erkan *et al.* 2004). Additionally, much non-abdominal pathology presents with abdominal pain: pneumonia, pharyngitis, sickle cell anaemia and diabetic keto-acidosis may all have abdominal pain as a feature of presentation (Leung & Sigalet 2003). Half of all patients with abdominal pain are incorrectly diagnosed on initial presentation (University of Leeds 2007). Added to this uncertainty in diagnosis is the contention by some authors that abdominal pain in children may be functional in nature, i.e. it has a non-organic cause (Huang *et al.* 2000) and the knowledge that abdominal pain in the child may be a marker of sexual abuse (Kellogg 2005).

History taking should include an attempt to elicit how long symptoms have been present and whether they are becoming more severe. Any associated signs and symptoms should also be noted and may include diarrhoea, vomiting, constipation, fever, dysuria, polyuria or oliguria. Past medical history should be examined for relevance to the current episode and, as many causes of abdominal pain in the child may be secondary to communicable disease, for instance gastroenteritis, it is important to take a social history and check immunisation schedules.

Physical examination of the child should occur in the sequence 'look, listen, feel'; attempting to palpate the abdomen of a child early on in the consultation may cause distress, anxiety and pain which subsequently makes the child less co-operative for the remaining part of the consultation. Leaving the potentially distressing part of the examination until last may avoid this happening.

Looking at the child's abdomen may yield important information about the nature and severity of illness: an abdomen that is held rigid and where diaphragmatic movement is limited because of pain is likely to be indicative of peritonitis. Costal recession in the abdominal border with the thorax, in conjunction with tachypnoea, indicates a seriously ill child. A distended abdomen may indicate obstruction in the bowel of the child. Practitioners should also note any bruising or lacerations to the abdomen that may indicate that symptoms are a result of traumatic injury.

Given that abdominal symptoms may be a result of respiratory pathology, any auscultation of the abdomen should be combined with examination of the chest. In listening to the abdomen, the presence of bowel sounds needs to be identified along with their nature – for instance, are they markedly increased or decreased? Do the findings from auscultation confirm or refute any initial diagnostic thinking made during history taking and visual assessment? Do they fit the pattern of what has so far been established?

In palpating the abdomen, palpate all four quadrants (see Figure 20.1), starting furthest away from where the child reports pain in order to maximise co-operation. Any guarding of the abdomen or rebound tenderness after palpation is indicative of peritonitis.

Figure 20.1

The four quadrants of the abdomen and underlying structures.

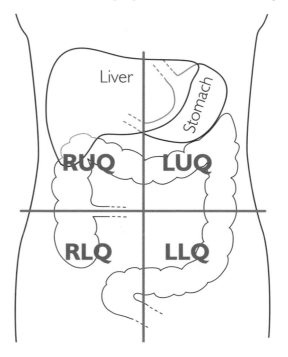

Notes:

RUQ: Right upper quadrant   **LUQ**: Left upper quadrant

RLQ: Right lower quadrant   **LLQ**: Left lower quadrant

Abdominal and genito-urinary illness

In attempting to reach a decision about diagnosis in the child with abdominal pain the practitioner may want to consider the value of investigations in aiding this process. Investigations should be appropriate and justifiable. They should be a logical consequence of the history taking and examination process rather than a prelude to this. Abdominal distension for instance, a red flag finding and unusual in the child, should prompt a request for an abdominal x-ray in an attempt to confirm diagnosis with the identification of fluid levels in the bowel. In the child this may be associated with volvulus formation or intussusception, both of which may lead to partial or complete bowel obstruction. Where such findings are evident then the child should be referred to in-patient specialist teams. More common investigations in the child with abdominal pain may include urinalysis where urinary tract infection is suspected or a pregnancy test where this is suspected in the post-pubescent female.

In addition to certain investigations a period of observation may be helpful in decision making. A child presenting with non-specific abdominal pain for instance may undergo a period of observation after red flag signs and symptoms have been excluded and analgesia has been provided. This period of time will allow for reflection upon care by the practitioner and may reassure parents and carers particularly if it is a prelude to discharge. A child who deteriorates during such a period of observation should be referred to in-patient specialist teams.

Red flag signs and symptoms need to be excluded during decision making and it may be that the exclusion of serious illness is the end point of the consultation with no specific diagnosis, or several probable or possible diagnoses, being made.

Red flag signs and symptoms in abdominal pain

- Guarding or splinting of the abdomen, rebound tenderness
- Malaena or fresh blood per rectum which may indicate gastro-intestinal bleeding or intussusception
- Bile stained or faecal vomiting which is indicative of bowel obstruction
- Projectile vomiting which may be indicative of pyloric obstruction in the infant

● Any indication of respiratory distress or signs and symptoms of severe illness.

Appendicitis

Appendicitis

Appendicitis is the most common surgical cause of abdominal pain in children (Leung & Sigalet 2003). Children may initially present with diffuse abdominal pain and it is often difficult to identify a specific cause for it due to its widespread nature. As the disease progresses, pain does generally become specific to the right lower quadrant. Possibly because of the delays in diagnosis that presentation in children make more likely, a perforated appendix is more common in children (Craig 2006). The child may be nauseated or vomiting. Vomiting follows the onset of abdominal pain; if vomiting precedes abdominal pain then intestinal obstruction should be considered as a diagnosis (Craig 2006). A loss of appetite is noted in many children and some also have associated diarrhoea or constipation. The inflamed appendix will cause rebound tenderness on examination of the abdomen and this will be associated with pain on percussion of the abdominal wall. Remember to provide the child with analgesia prior to examination.

Children with suspected appendicitis should be cannulated and blood samples taken for a full blood count and urea/electrolytes. A white cell count of greater than 12,000 is an additional diagnostic aid (Tzanakis *et al.* 2005). Children should also receive intravenous fluid therapy and if there are signs of local peritonitis such as rebound tenderness and guarding then intravenous antibiotics should also be administered. A referral should be made to in-patient surgical teams.

Differential diagnosis in children includes gastroenteritis, respiratory tract infection or mesenteric adenitis. A substantial proportion of children with appendicitis are misdiagnosed with these conditions (Craig 2006).

Authors in Greece (Tzanakis *et al.* 2005) have developed a scoring system to assist diagnosis in acute appendicitis. Four criteria were used to assist the diagnosis and each given a numerical value:

● Ultrasound evidence of acute appendicitis: 6 points

- Rebound tenderness: 3 points
- Pain in the right lower quadrant: 4 points
- White cell count > 12,000: 2 points

The authors used a score of eight or more as being indicative of acute appendicitis and found a high degree of specificity associated with this. This may seem reasonably unremarkable when the score includes the fairly unequivocal finding of inflammation of the appendix on ultrasound. With ultrasound not always immediately available to the practitioner, the criteria of rebound tenderness, pain in the right lower quadrant and raised WCC, in combination with findings from the history and physical examination, should be useful in guiding the diagnosis of appendicitis. In the absence of diagnostic ultrasound facilities, or where the child is clinically too unwell for discharge, a referral should be made to in-patient surgical specialist teams with a presumptive diagnosis of appendicitis.

Gastroenteritis

Gastro-enteritis

Although accidental injury is the leading cause of death amongst children in the 'developed' world, between 2000 and 2003 diarrhoea accounted for 18% of the 10.6 million annual deaths of children under the age of five years throughout the world (Bryce *et al.* and the World Health Organisation 2005). This means that almost 2 million children died each year during this period as a consequence of diarrhoea, the predominant symptom in gastroenteritis. Apart from being a testament to the efficacy of treatment in gastroenteritis in children, this data also reminds us that gastroenteritis still has the potential to cause morbidity and mortality in children where access to healthcare is limited and other factors contributing to morbidity are also evident.

Gastroenteritis is characterised by diarrhoea of rapid onset associated with nausea, vomiting, abdominal cramps and pain, bloating, flatulence, fever and a loss of appetite. Four out of five cases in children are viral in origin, though other causes may include Escherichia coli (E. coli). Campylobacter and salmonella infection is more common in adults (Prodigy 2006d). Most cases are self-limiting and treatment is focused upon the alleviation of symptoms.

History taking and physical examination should identify factors that may be pertinent in the aetiology of the illness in addition to excluding some of the more serious consequences of it:

- Is there marked weight loss and/or is the child systemically unwell and visibly dehydrated?
- Does the child suffer from immunosuppression?
- Is there any blood or mucus in the stool?
- Do any of the child's family, their pets, or their peers in nursery or school have diarrhoea also?
- Is there a history of ingestion of high risk foods, foreign travel, or recent treatment with medication?

Blood or mucus in the stool may be indicative of the severity of the illness but may also evidence inflammatory bowel disease as a cause of symptoms. Intussusception, most common in infants less than one year of age, may also feature blood in the stool, classically described as 'currant jelly stool' – this mix of blood and mucus is evident in 50% of children with intussusception (King 2006).

High risk foods include shellfish, cooked eggs and products made with eggs (e.g. mayonnaise), certain dairy products such as cream, cooked meat and poultry and cooked meat products such as sandwich fillings (Christchurch Community Council 1998).

Assessment of whether the child is dehydrated or not, and the severity of any dehydration, involves reference to clinical features associated with this; see Table 20.1.

Table 20.1

Dehydration in children: clinical features

Dehydration in children: clinical features

	< 5% dehydration	5%–10% dehydration	> 10% dehydration
Mouth	Moist	Dry	Very dry
Extremities	Warm, good refill	Delayed refill	Mottled, poor refill
Tears	Normal	Normal to absent	Absent
Eyes	Normal	Sunken	Sunken, very dry
Level of consciousness	Well, alert	Restless, irritable	Lethargic, floppy
Skin pinch	Goes back quickly	Goes back slowly	Marked delay
Heart rate	Normal	Moderate tachycardia	Marked tachycardia
Urine output	Slight reduction	Moderate reduction	Marked reduction

(adapted from World Health Organisation 1993, Farthing *et al.* 1996, Cincinnati Children's Hospital 2002)

Abdominal and genito-urinary illness

All children who have greater than 5% clinical dehydration and/or risk factors that will exacerbate disease severity, such as diabetes mellitus or immunosuppression, should be referred to in-patient paediatric specialists for further care. Consideration should be given to instituting rehydration therapy by intravenous fluids depending upon the severity of dehydration. Children with less than 5% dehydration and who do not have any risk factors to exacerbate illness may be managed at home. Principles of management include (Prodigy 2006d):

- Promotion of normal feeding including breast feeding as there is no evidence that fasting has any influence on disease progress or outcome (if children have associated vomiting small frequent feeds may be better tolerated).

- In infants and small children oral rehydration therapy may be warranted and should take the form of 30–50 ml of the therapy (e.g. Dioralyte) per kg body weight over 3–4 hours. If the child is breastfeeding this should be alternated with the therapy.

- The promotion of effective handwashing technique for the whole family is important to prevent further spread. The child should not attend nursery or school until there have been 48 hours free from diarrhoea.

- Anti-motility drugs are not indicated in children and antibiotics should only be prescribed for high risk patients or those whose stool has been cultured. Routine culture of stools is not necessary but is justified in children with a fever or where there is blood or mucus in the stool.

Parents and carers should be advised to re-attend if the child's condition is deteriorating or if they develop any new symptoms such as blood or mucus in the stool. They should be provided with contact numbers and the telephone number of NHS Direct in England and Wales or NHS 24 in Scotland.

Red flag signs and symptoms in the child with diarrhoea

- Clinical features suggesting >5% dehydration (see Table 20.1)
- Blood or mucus in the stool

- A concurrent history of disease such as diabetes mellitus or immunosuppression.

Urinary tract infection

Urinary tract infection

The majority of urinary tract infections (UTI) occur as a result of Escherichia coli infection and in children UTI is most common amongst the very young who are still in nappies. Younger infants will generally present with a low grade fever (though this may be absent or high as well) and will be miserable. Parents may give a history of vomiting and a loss of appetite in the child with infants taking fewer milk feeds (National Institute for Health and Clinical Excellence 2007d). Older children will complain of abdominal pain associated with frequency of micturition and dysuria.

One of the principal differential diagnoses to consider is pyelonephritis and this is characterised by:

- high fever
- flank pain/loin pain
- nausea/vomiting
- pain below the lower ribs on the affected side.

If a diagnosis of pyelonephritis is being considered then the child should be provided with analgesia and referred to in-patient specialist teams for intravenous antibiotic therapy.

UTI in the child may be a marker of sexual abuse (Klevan & DeJong 1990). Identification of recurrent infection during history taking or in medical records should prompt consideration of this as a factor in the illness. Other markers of abuse (see Chapter 6) should be identified or excluded and if necessary a referral to child protection services, following local guidelines and policies, should be made.

Urine should be collected and analysed; urine collection pads may be used in very young infants where a sample is otherwise difficult to obtain. Suspicion of infection in a child less than three months of age should mandate referral to specialist paediatric services for management. This is because younger infants with UTI may develop systemic sepsis which has an associated high morbidity rate (Prodigy 2006e).

Abdominal and genito-urinary illness

Based upon the National Institute for Health and Clinical Excellence guidelines for the management of urinary tract infection in children, those aged between three months and three years who have specific urinary symptoms should begin antibiotic treatment and also have urine collected for culture and microscopy (National Institute for Health and Clinical Excellence 2007d).

Children over three years of age should have their urine analysed using a dipstick and then cared for using the guidelines shown in Table 20.2.

Table 20.2

UTI treatment guidelines

UTI treatment guidelines

Leucocyte and nitrite positive urine	*Begin antibiotic treatment. Culture urine if there is risk of serious illness or previous UTI.*
Leucocyte negative, nitrite positive urine	*If fresh sample was analysed begin antibiotic treatment. Culture urine.*
Leucocyte positive, nitrite negative urine	*Culture urine. Withhold antibiotic in absence of clinical evidence of UTI. Treat based on culture result.*
Leucocyte and nitrite negative urine	*Do not culture urine. Do not give antibiotic treatment for UTI. Reassess for other causes of illness.*

Source: National Institute for Health and Clinical Excellence 2007d

Treatment with trimethoprim or cefalexin is generally advocated. A three-day course of treatment should be prescribed for infants and children over the age of three months and arrangements made for the child to be seen again within a week (Prodigy 2006e, National Institute for Health and Clinical Excellence 2007d). Routine follow up in terms of imaging studies such as ultrasound is not advocated unless the infant is less than six months old or where presentation is atypical or recurrent in nature.

Paediatric minor emergencies

Red flag signs and symptoms in UTI

- High fever
- Nausea or vomiting
- Associated signs and symptoms of abuse
- Child is under three months old
- Signs of systemic illness
- Flank pain/loin pain
- Recurrent illness.

Constipation

Constipation

Poor dietary fibre intake and a sedentary lifestyle pre-dispose to constipation. The increasing prevalence of both of these factors in the paediatric population (British Nutrition Foundation 2004, Oon 2005) may therefore be expected to lead to an increasing incidence of constipation amongst children. Other factors that may pre-dispose to constipation in children include diseases such as autism, attention deficit hyperactivity disorder, dehydration and cystic fibrosis (University of Michigan Health System 2003). Certain medication may also cause constipation (Talley *et al.* 2003):

- anti-epileptics such as carbamazepine
- calcium and iron supplements
- aluminium based antacids
- anti-spasmodics
- opioids such as codeine.

Enquiries about medical and drug history may reveal a potential cause for the condition and provide an opportunity to avoid recurrence.

In addition children may develop what is termed 'functional faecal retention' (Rasquin-Weber *et al.* 1999) where because of a fear of the consequences of defecation children attempt to avoid or delay defecation and become constipated.

Children may present with faecal incontinence/soiling, abdominal pain and pain on defecation. Examination may reveal a palpable mass in the left lower quadrant. Per rectum examination is not warranted in uncomplicated constipation. It may be warranted as part of a diagnosis of underlying disease process that is a contributory factor in constipation (see above) but these circumstances are rare.

Mild, isolated episodes of constipation amongst children should initially be dealt with by advice concerning diet, fluid intake and exercise (Prodigy 2006f). Oral laxatives may be considered in more acute or recurrent presentation. Lactulose is licensed for use in all age groups and is recommended for use in infants and younger children where the administration of bulk-forming laxatives may be problematic (Prodigy 2006f). Bulk-forming and stimulant laxatives (Senna) are recommended in older children (Prodigy 2006f) and some are only licensed for use in this age group. Practitioners should check that medication is appropriate for the age of the child being treated and where necessary the advice of a pharmacist should be sought.

Longstanding, recurrent or severe constipation, which in the absence of an underlying cause may have a degree of functionality associated with it, may need more intensive intervention; dietary advice and laxatives may be supplemented by psycho-social interventions such as discussion with the parents and carers and encouraging the child to use the toilet regularly. Enemas and suppositories are not recommended in children (Prodigy 2006f). Such children should obviously be reviewed on a regular basis. Indications for the referral of a child for specialist care from a gastro-enterologist include (Australian Prescriber 2002):

- where other treatment has failed
- where constipation is prolonged for more than six months
- where frequent soiling is a problem and the condition is causing distress and embarrassment to the child and interrupting schooling and social circumstances
- where there are significant feeding problems.

Red flag signs and symptoms in constipation

- Any suspicion of underlying causative factors such as dehydration

- Any suspicion of intestinal obstruction as a cause of constipation (guarding, abdominal distension, rebound tenderness, associated vomiting).

Testicular torsion

Testicular torsion

Testicular torsion is a urological emergency. It is most often seen in young males, with peaks of incidence being at the ages of 14 years and in boys less than one year of age (Rupp & Zwanger 2006). As the affected testicle rotates upon the spermatic cord, this causes a strangulation of blood vessels, leading to ischaemia of the testicle (see Figure 20.2). In patients who undergo surgery to correct torsion within six hours of the onset of pain, there is a success rate of 100% in terms of the restoration of testicular function. This decreases markedly to only 20% if delayed until 12 hours after pain onset, and if there is a delay of more than 24 hours the testicle is not salvageable (Rupp & Zwanger 2006). Implications for practice are that a high degree of suspicion for testicular torsion should exist in any acute scrotal presentation and that diagnosis needs to be made in a timely fashion to maximise the opportunity to retain a functioning testicle.

Figure 20.2

Testicular torsion: rotation of the testicle on the spermatic cord causing venous obstruction, pain, swelling, ischaemia and ultimately death of the testicle.

Patients will present with a sudden onset of severe, unilateral testicular pain. This may be associated with scrotal swelling, nausea and vomiting, fever and polyuria (Galejs & Kass 1999, Rupp & Zwangler 2006). In 50% of cases a history of previous short, self-resolving, episodes of similar pain may be given and these are attributable to episodes of torsion that are self-resolving (Rupp & Zwangler 2006). Where the onset of pain is more gradual, and in particular where there is an associated fever, a diagnosis of epididymitis rather than torsion should be considered.

History taking may also reveal certain pre-disposing factors for torsion which include (Rupp & Zwangler 2006):

- sexual arousal or activity
- congenital abnormality or undescended testicle
- trauma or exercise.

Practitioners should be aware that an adolescent male with a disorder of the scrotum may seek to avoid embarrassment by trivialising symptoms or not disclosing the true source of pain. They may for instance claim to have pain in the lower abdomen rather than the scrotum. Patients should be approached in a sensitive manner and information should be sought from other sources, such as parents or carers, where possible. The need for privacy should be accommodated and wherever possible the adolescent patient cared for by a male practitioner.

On examination the affected side of the scrotum may be swollen and erythematous, the affected testicle may be lying horizontally, or may have an abnormally high position. In epididymitis pain is relieved when elevating the affected testicle; this is known as the Prehn sign. No improvement in pain as a result of elevating the testicle may therefore aid in the diagnosis of torsion (Galejs & Kass 1999). Urinalysis should be undertaken; abnormal findings from urinalysis are not commonly associated with torsion and may represent a different pathology.

In managing the patient, a high priority needs to be given to the alleviation of pain. Guidelines for the relief of severe pain should be followed. The patient should also be provided with information about the prognosis in testicular torsion and should be given some idea of the circumstances that will surround their admission to hospital. Pain relief in this anxiety-provoking disorder will be enhanced by the provision of information that addresses anxiety. Subsequent to clinical examination, any patient with a history of a short duration of pain and no abnormal findings on urinalysis should be assumed to have torsion until proven otherwise (Galejs & Kass 1999). The patient should be referred urgently to urological specialists for operative reduction of the torsion as soon as is possible.

The abdominal x-ray

Abdominal x-ray

A plain x-ray of the abdomen may be requested as a part of the assessment of abdominal pain in the child if there is the need to identify or exclude an acute abdomen where this cannot be achieved by history taking and physical examination alone. Causes of an acute abdomen in the child may be intussusception, volvulus formation or a perforated appendix.

As has been noted, an abdominal x-ray in suspected intussusception has up to a 20% false negative rate and adds little value to the assessment and management of the child (Broomfield & Maconochie 2002), hence the threshold for requests should be high and only made where clinical examination does not establish diagnosis.

Figure 20.3 *right*
The abdomen in volvulus: note the air accumulation associated with an obstructed bowel which will clinically cause abdominal distension.

Figure 20.4 *far right*
The crescent sign: note the air accumulation in the shape of a crescent associated with an obstructed bowel secondary to intussusception.

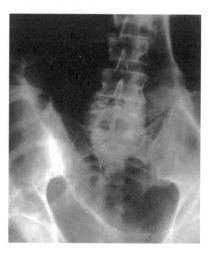 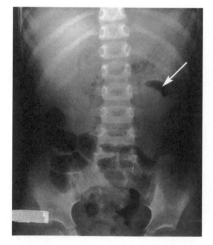

(source: www.xray2000.co.uk, used with permission.)

Chapter 21
Dermatological minor illness

The ability to recognise, identify and describe dermatological lesions is more than an academic exercise. Certain types of lesion are associated with certain disorders and their identification will enhance diagnostic skills. See Table 21.1. In addition to this, certain disorders have characteristics in terms of the distribution of lesions. Herpes zoster (shingles) for instance is almost always unilateral and has a dermatomal distribution following the pathway of one of the cranial nerves. Ascending lymphangitis, or the 'tracking' of infective processes that follow lymphatic vessels is associated with worsening cellulitis.

Table 21.1

Typology of dermatological lesions

Typology of dermatological lesions

Bullae	Bullae are fluid-filled lesions greater than 1cm in diameter
Vesicle	A fluid filled lesion less than 1cm in diameter
Pustule	A raised lesion, well defined margins, commonly infected
Nodule	A raised solid lesion greater than 1cm in diameter
Maculae	A flat rash on the skin
Petechiae	Small lesions produced by bleeding into the epidermis
Purpura	Larger lesions produced by bleeding into the epidermis
Wheal	An area of oedema in the epidermis
Burrow	A tunnel in the epidermis associated with infestation
Plaque	A raised segmented lesion

Other lesions may be indicative of underlying illness rather than being a primary dermatological illness. Thus a purpural, non-blanching rash in a child may be indicative of meningococcal septicaemia.

Dermatological illness, unlike some other minor illnesses, may be visible to both the child and to other people. Older children, particularly where disease is recurrent or chronic, may encounter psycho-social problems in addition to the physical manifestations of the disease. Where possible these factors should be addressed; there are web-based support groups that offer advice and expertise on dealing with psycho-social aspects of diseases such as psoriasis and eczema: the Psoriasis Association at http://www.psoriasis-association.org.uk/index.html or Talk Eczema at http://www.talkeczema.com/

Impetigo

Impetigo

This is a staphylococcal or streptococcal infection of the epidermis that may present as a primary disease or may opportunistically infect other skin lesions such as eczema. It is typically found on the face or trunk, and history taking may reveal that the child has been in contact with other children with impetigo at school or nursery.

Figure 21.1

The characteristic 'honey-coloured' encrustation of impetigo. The disease is more common in children and is most often found on the face and trunk.

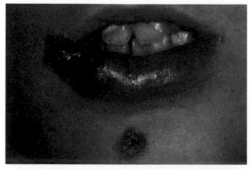

Treatment is with topical fusidic acid or oral flucloxacillin, though resistance is more likely to develop in association with topical preparations (Prodigy 2006g). The crusting lesions of impetigo are highly contagious and parents should be advised to keep the child away from school until two days after antibiotic treatment has finished. Members of the family should also be advised to wash hands after any dealings with the child and should use separate items for washing such as flannels and towels. Rare complications of impetigo infection include staphylococcal scalded skin syndrome (Painter *et al.* 2007) and cellulitis, though both are rare in incidence.

Herpes simplex

Herpes simplex

Caused by the herpes simplex virus, this lesion, commonly known as 'cold sores', is most often seen on the face around the lips and mouth. A causal infection in early childhood may facilitate the development of dormant lesions which may be re-activated by certain triggers such as stress, sunlight, menstruation, respiratory infection or physical trauma (Prodigy 2006h).

Figure 21.2

The herpes simplex virus. Most often seen as vesicular or pustular lesions in the proximity of the lips. These sort of lesions are likely to recur in a similar place with certain trigger factors causing re-activation of dormant lesions formed originally after early childhood infection.

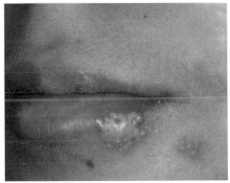

(Source: http://www.pediatrics.wisc.edu/education/)

As the virus is transmitted in saliva, it is important to avoid kissing during the most contagious period of one to four days after the appearance of the lesions. It is particularly important to avoid contact with pregnant women and infants where the development of neonatal herpes may lead to central nervous system damage, mental retardation or death. Any immunosuppressed people should also be treated with similar caution as contagion may lead to chronic and persistent lesions that may become life-threatening.

If taken within 48 hours of the appearance of the lesions then acyclovir may be effective in treating the infection, though practitioners need to be aware that it is contra-indicated in pregnancy. The goal of treatment otherwise is to provide effective analgesia to the patient and minimise opportunities for transmission of the virus to others. Although the period of maximal contagiousness is only between one and four days, patients may remain contagious for up to one week and symptoms of disease such as pain may persist for several weeks.

Children, parents and carers should be advised that the infection will probably recur at the same site in the future and they may be able to identify certain trigger factors that precipitate this, making timely intervention possible.

Scabies

Scabies

Scabies is a process of infestation with a parasite called Sarcoptes scabiei, otherwise known as the scabies mite. Infestation generally happens where people are living in cramped conditions, in poverty and where there is a degree of malnutrition. As with other dermatological conditions, immunosuppressed people are more prone to disease and may develop a more severe form of scabies, called crusted scabies, involving infestation with far more mites than is generally the case. This sort of crusted infestation, though rare in children, has been reported in children on long-term cortisone therapy for other dermatological disorders (Dragos *et al.* 2004)

Children will present with lesions that generally first appear in the web spaces of fingers and in the flexor folds of the wrist. They may also appear on elbows, armpits, the groin and genitalia. Where children have infestation that may have been transmitted through sexual contact, such as mites in the groin and genitalia, then sexual abuse of the child should be considered as a cause for this and if necessary other sexually transmitted infections excluded.

The burrows of the mite appear like grey linear markings in the epidermis and extreme pruritus, which is especially worse at night (when the mite is more active), is often also reported. It is not uncommon for itching to result in surface lesions that become opportunistically infected by bacteria. This sometimes leads to the development of cellulitis or more rarely staphylococcal scalded skin syndrome and if present should be treated with flucloxacillin. Scabies itself is treated with topical cream (permethrin) and Malathion solution and patients should be warned that itching may last up to three weeks after treatment (Prodigy 2006i). As it is likely that close family members will be infested as well, they should also be treated at the same time. The scabies mite cannot survive for more than 48–72 hours away from its human host and therefore any items that cannot be washed should be isolated and not used for a few days. All items of bedding and clothing should be washed in hot water (> 50°C)

Figure 21.3

Sarcoptes Scabiei: the scabies mite.

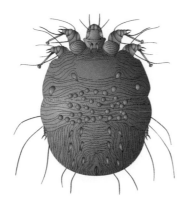

About the size of a pinhead, mites can burrow into the skin in less than three minutes. Females produce two or three eggs a day which hatch after 48 hours and burrow to the surface of the skin.

(Source: Janice Money, used with permission.)

Allergy and anaphylaxis

Allergy and anaphalaxis

Although not primarily a dermatological complaint allergic responses to certain antigens may manifest as skin rashes. Additional symptoms such as a respiratory wheeze are associated with more severe allergic reaction. Common allergens include:

- pollen and grass
- animal fur
- bee and wasp stings
- certain foods – eggs, nuts, shellfish, milk, wheat
- household chemicals such as detergents
- medication such as antibiotics.

History taking may pinpoint a cause for the onset of symptoms but in many cases specific allergens are never identified. Children with mild allergic type symptoms such as urticarial rash and rhinitis should be treated with oral chlorphenamine. See Table 21.2 (overleaf).

Paediatric minor emergencies

Table 21.2

Oral chlorphenamine dosages in mild allergy

Oral chlorphenamine dosages in mild allergy

Age	Dose of chlorphenamine
1 month–2 years	1 mg: then 1 mg BD
2–6 years	1 mg: then 1 mg up to 4 hourly with a maximum daily dose of 6 mg
6–12 years	2 mg: then 2 mg up to 4 hourly with a maximum daily dose of 12 mg
12–18 years	4 mg: then 4 mg up to 4 hourly with a maximum daily dose of 24 mg

(Source: British National Formulary for Children 2006)

It should be noted that because of its sedatory effects chlorphenamine syrup is not licensed for use in children less than one year of age and tablets are not licensed for use in children less than six years of age. Additionally chlorphenamine injection is not licensed for use in neonates (British National Formulary for Children 2006).

Where symptoms of more severe allergy are present, or where anaphylaxis is evident, then children should receive adrenaline as a first line treatment and this may be augmented with chlorphenamine by sub-cutaneous, intra-muscular or intravenous injection in the dosages shown in Table 21.3.

Table 21.3

Oral chlorphenamine dosages in severe allergy or anaphylaxis

Chlorphenamine dosages in severe allergy or anaphylaxis

Age	Dose of chlorphenamine
1 month–1 year	250 mcg/kg to a maximum of 2.5 mg repeated up to four times a day if required
1–6 years	2.5 mg–5 mg repeated up to four times a day if required
6–12 years	5 mg–10 mg repeated up to four times a day if required
12–18 years	10 mg–20 mg repeated up to four times a day to a maximum daily dose of 40 mg

(Source: British National Formulary for Children 2006)

Dermatalogical minor illness

It should be noted that in anaphylaxis the preferred route for administration of chlorphenamine is intravenous, as the speed of onset in sub-cutaneous or intra-muscular injection is no faster than oral administration (British National Formulary for Children 2006). It should also be noted that first line treatment in anaphylaxis is intramuscular adrenaline (McLean-Tooke *et al.* 2003, Bryant 2007) and that chlorphenamine may be given as an adjunct to, rather than a replacement for this. The dosage of adrenaline for injection in children in anaphylaxis is calculated at 0.01mg/kg (McLean-Tooke *et al.* 2003) but has been approximated for ease and speed of use as shown in Table 21.4.

Table 21.4

Adrenaline dosage in anaphylaxis

Adrenaline dosage in anaphylaxis

Age	Dose of IM adrenaline 1:1000
Children > 12 years	0.5ml
Children 6-12 years	0.3ml
Children < 6 years	0.15ml

Repeat after 5 minutes if necessary

(Source: Resuscitation Council 2008, used with permission.)

As management varies and prognosis differs, it is important to be able to distinguish what is a moderate or severe allergic response from an anaphylactic episode. McLean-Tooke *et al.* (2003) define anaphylaxis as existing when respiratory distress and/or hypotension are present. Other authors note that skin wheals or hives, oedema of the face, lips and eyes, along with abdominal pain and vomiting may all be present in a severe allergic rather than anaphylactic type reaction (Anaphylaxis Australia 2003, Bryant 2007).

In managing the care of children with anaphylaxis, the prevention of recurrence and its prompt recognition and treatment if it does recur are crucial parts of care. Children who have suffered an episode of anaphylaxis should be referred for allergen testing in an attempt to identify causative factors if this has not become evident during the acute episode. They should also be prescribed an epi-pen containing a suitable dose of adrenaline in case of recurrence. The child, their parents and carers, siblings, peers and teachers will all need to be made aware of how to use this device and under what circumstances it needs to be employed.

In addition children should be advised to

- read food/drug and packaging labels where these were a factor in presentation or where the allergen is not known

- ask what is in food that has been made by someone else and be vigilant when eating out

- be alert to their symptoms and educate those around them about signs, symptoms and treatment

- wear an alert bracelet

- be careful kissing others and avoid getting drunk and letting their guard down.

(Anaphylaxis.org.uk 2006):

Table 21.5

Features of allergy and anaphylaxis

Features of allergy and anaphylaxis

Allergy	Anaphylaxis
Gradual onset	Sudden onset
Rhinitis	Rhinitis
Conjunctivitis	Conjunctivitis
Orbital oedema	Orbital oedema
Facial oedema	Facial oedema
Oedema of lips	Oedema of lips
Abdominal pain and vomiting	Abdominal pain and vomiting
Pruritic skin hives and wheals	Pruritic skin hives and wheals
	Respiratory distress/noisy breathing
	Hypotension/collapse/floppy child
	Laryngeal oedema, hoarse voice
	Swelling of the tongue
	Palpitations
	Sense of impending doom

(adapted from Anaphylaxis Australia 2003, McLean-Tooke *et al.* 2003, Anaphylaxis.org.uk 2006)

Meningococcal rash

**Meningo-
coccal rash**

Not primarily a dermatological illness, recognition of the petechial or purpural rash associated with meningococcal septicaemia is however crucial in the early identification and prompt treatment of this illness that still accounts for significant morbidity and mortality in children. Whilst mortality from meningococcal disease in the United Kingdom, at 12 per annum, is significantly lower than the global average of 31 deaths a year (World Health Organisation 2004), morbidity from the disease, which includes hearing loss, speech defects, loss of limbs and mental retardation might be significantly reduced from its prevalence in approximately 15% of survivors (World Health Organisation 2004) by prompt recognition and treatment.

Whilst a non-blanching purpural rash aids diagnosis of meningococcal disease, practitioners should be aware that up to 50% of patients with disease do not have a skin rash (Granier *et al.* 1998). Where the rash does occur, it may often first appear as petechial lesions over pressure points on the skin such as waistbands, belts, collars and socks before becoming more generalised and purpural in nature (Meningitis Research Foundation 2006). Apart from the identification of the skin rash, recommendations for the early recognition and treatment of meningococcal disease also include (Granier *et al.* 1998, Meningitis Research Foundation 2006):

- When a haemorrhagic rash is present, do not be deterred from diagnosing meningococcal disease and starting antibiotic treatment if the child is otherwise well or if the rash is scanty or has an unusual distribution.

- An unwillingness to interact or make eye contact, altered mental state, and pallor with a high temperature have been noted as early precursors of the disease.

- Actively listening to parents and carers and their knowledge of normal patterns of behaviour and interaction for their child is important in identifying early symptoms of disease.

- Cool extremities and a delayed capillary refill are early markers of compensated shock. Hypotension is a pre-terminal sign in children and an apparently normal blood pressure should not be relied upon as a marker of wellness.

Paediatric minor emergencies

If there is any doubt about the diagnosis of meningitis then the child should be treated as if they had the disease, given antibiotic medication, and referred to in-patient specialist services for further assessment and management. Recommended antibiotic therapy is intravenous cefotaxime at 50 mg/kg or intravenous ceftriaxone at 80 mg/kg. If there is a history of anaphylactic type reaction to cephalosporins such as cefotaxime then chloramphenicol may be used (British National Formulary 2007). In pre-hospital or community settings it is recommended that children be given benzylpenicillin either intravenously or intramuscularly where such access cannot be established. See Table 21.6.

Table 21.6

Benzylpenicillin dosages in meningitis

Benzylpenicillin dosages in meningitis

Child 10 years or older	1200 mg benzylpenicillin
Child 1–9 years	600 mg benzylpenicillin
Infant < 1 year	300 mg benzylpenicillin

(Source: Meningitis Research Foundation 2006)

Penicillin allergy should not mean that therapy is withheld. Only where there is a history of severe allergy or anaphylactic type reactions to penicillin, should either cefotaxime or chloramphenicol be used as an alternative (Meningitis Research Foundation 2006, British National Formulary 2007).

Red flag signs and symptoms in skin disease

- Any suspicion of meningococcal disease – non-blanching petechial or purpural rash
- Ascending lymphangitis
- Any suspicion of severe allergy or anaphylaxis
- Immunosuppressed child
- Non-resolving illness, fever or skin sloughing that may be associated with staphylococcal scalded skin syndrome.

Chapter 22
Musculo-skeletal illness in children

Musculo-skeletal illness is not uncommon in children, with almost one child in every five reporting limb pain at some point in their childhood (Malleson & Beauchamp 2001, Junnila & Cartwright 2006). Much of this pain is attributed to 'growing pains' or manifestations of viral illness (Junnila & Cartwright 2006) but certain musculo-skeletal illnesses of childhood need to be promptly identified and appropriately managed.

In attempting to exclude limb- or life-threatening diagnoses, the practitioner should consider whether the presentation may be attributable to trauma, infection or malignancy. Effective history taking and physical examination will be of value in the identification or exclusion of these factors. Infective processes will be evident in the child with fever and localised pain and erythema. Diffuse pain that extends beyond joint lines and is worse at night may be suggestive of malignant processes such as osteoma, sarcoma or leukaemia.

The limping child

The limping child

The assessment of the limping child is complicated by the fact that the cause of the limp may range from a severe illness such as osteomyelitis to something as minor as a superficial foreign body in the plantar aspect of the foot. Identification of the cause of the presentation with limp will be enhanced by thorough history taking and an effective physical examination.

History taking should include pertinent factors such as:

- Enquiring about how long the child has been limping for: sudden onset of limp is more likely to be associated with a traumatic event.

- Whether symptoms are improving or becoming worse: a worsening of symptoms, particularly if this has also involved multiple previous presentations for care, should act as a red flag for practitioners and the exclusion of severe pathology becomes a priority.

- Whether pain and other symptoms show any temporal variation: pain that is worse in the morning is classically associated with arthritic disease, whereas pain that is worse at night is associated with malignancy.

- Whether there are any other associated symptoms: fever and malaise are indicative of infective processes.

- Has the child been recently unwell? Recent viral illness may have pre-disposed to the development of septic arthritis or to transient synovitis (irritable hip).

- Is there a family history of relevant illness? Certain musculo-skeletal illnesses have a familial association.

Remember during physical examination that hip pain may be referred to the knee, and any child complaining of knee pain should have hip pathology excluded from the diagnosis. Simple observation forms the basis of initial examination; observation of the child walking will yield information about gait. Children with hip pathology will tend to spend as little time in the stance phase of walking (i.e. with their foot on the ground) as possible and will increase the time spent in the swing part of walking (i.e. with the foot off the ground) (Leet & Skaggs 2000).

In an examination of the lower limb, areas of erythema and local warmth should be noted and may be indicative of inflammation or infection. Where these areas involve a joint, of the ankle, knee or hip for instance, consideration should be given to a diagnosis of an infective or juvenile arthritis or synovitis of the joint.

If the child's condition permits it, put affected joints actively and passively through their full range of motion (remember the need to consider analgesia prior to the examination of any patient). Is there any limitation of movement in the hip, knee or ankle? In the absence of positive findings from such an examination, a spinal pathology should be considered as a cause for limp. Does the child have back pain and is it aggravated by flexion or extension of the spine? Assessment of the plantar reflexes in the lower limb should be undertaken also.

In addition to such activity, the age of the child will give some indication of what may or may not be wrong. Certain pathologies causing limp are very much related in their onset to the age of the child. See Table 22.1.

Table 22.1

Causes of acute limp by age of onset

Causes of acute limp by age of onset

	1–5 years	5–10 years	10–15 years
Trauma	■	■	■
Transient synovitis	■	■	
Osteomyelitis or septic arthritis	■	■	■
Developmental hip dysplasia	■		
Juvenile rheumatoid arthritis	■		
Legg-Calve-Perthes disease		■	
Slipped femoral epiphysis			■
Chondromalacia			■
Malignancy			■

Adapted or Reprinted with permission from 'Evaluation of the Acutely Limping Child', February 15 2000, American Family Physician. Copyright © 2000 American Academy of Family Physicians. All Rights Reserved.

Investigations should be governed by the differential diagnoses being considered. A plain x-ray may be useful in identifying:

- Traumatic injury: the toddler's fracture of the tibia for instance often presents as a limp and history taking may not reveal the episode that caused the injury. In children unable to verbalise, AP films of the entire lower limb have revealed fractures in 20% of such cases presenting as limp (Leet & Skaggs 2000). This investigation should be a last resort where history taking and examination have failed to identify another cause for the presentation.
- Bone fragmentation and joint space widening: may be evident on plain x-rays of the hip and may identify Legg-Calve Perthe's disease, septic processes or a slipped femoral epiphysis (see Figures 22.1 and 22.2 overleaf). Slipped femoral epiphysis is

more common amongst obese or rapidly growing children and is 2.5 times more common in boys than girls (Marano *et al.* 2006). Legg-Calve-Perthe's disease (LCPD) is seen most commonly in children between 3 and 12 years of age and involves necrosis of the femoral epiphysis for which there is not an identified cause (Nochimson 2006). Muscle wasting secondary to lack of use may be evident in LCPD and one in five children have disease affecting both hips.

Figure 22.1

Slipped femoral epiphysis.

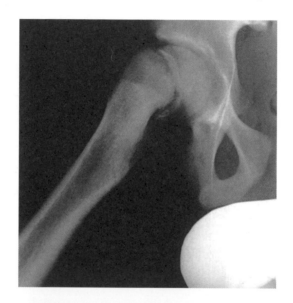

Figure 22.2

Legg-Calve-Perthes disease: note the degeneration of the femoral head.

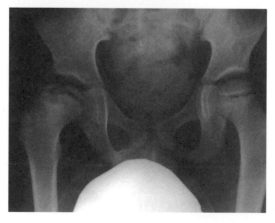

(Source: www.xray2000.co.uk used with permission.)

In the absence of any abnormal findings and where the child is not systemically unwell, a diagnosis of transient synovitis (otherwise known as irritable hip syndrome) may be considered and this is the most common atraumatic cause of hip pain in young children – adolescents are rarely affected (Judd & Wright 2005). Transient synovitis usually develops after a viral infection or minor trauma, though its exact cause is not known. As the condition is self-limiting, treatment is conservative. Where infective processes or malignancy are suspected, or cannot be excluded by the examination, then children should be referred for in-patient specialist orthopaedic opinion. Suspicion of slipped femoral epiphysis or Legg-Calve-Perthe's disease should also prompt referral.

Anterior knee pain in children

Anterior knee pain

Osgood-Schlatters disease is seen in adolescents between 11 and 18 years and is more common in boys than girls. Children will generally report that they have had low level pain on activity for a number of months but that some minor traumatic event has exacerbated this, prompting presentation for care (Chang 2007). The condition is associated with periods of rapid growth in adolescence. An avulsion fracture of the tibial tuberosity is thought to occur secondary to contraction of the patellar tendon during activity. There may be swelling and tenderness over the tibial tuberosity where the tendon inserts. A quarter of children have bilateral symptoms (Chang 2007). Treatment is conservative and involves rest and gradual re-mobilisation and an attempt to avoid the activities that caused pain initially.

Osteochondritis dissecans involves a part of the epiphysis fragmenting due to repetitive trauma and may therefore also be associated with overuse injury. The fragmented part of bone forms a loose body in the joint. Although it may occur in any weight bearing joint it is seen most commonly in the knee joints of adolescents and young adults where the femoral condyles are usually involved (Bui-Mansfield 2005). A plain x-ray of the joint may be useful in identifying loose bodies, though these are more likely to be identified by ultrasound. Treatment is generally conservative and patients should be advised to try and avoid exacerbatory patterns of activity.

Chondromalacia of the knee or **patello-femoral syndrome** is an overuse syndrome seen most commonly in very active children (Moses 2007). Malalignment of the patella during activity causes increasing pain during exercise. Pain from chondromalacia may be referred to the hip. Treatment for this condition is generally conservative and children should be provided with knee strengthening exercise advice and/or access to physiotherapy.

Figure 22.3 *right*

Malignant sarcoma of the tibia.

Figure 22.4 *far right*

Osgood-Schlatters disease – note the appearance of the tibial condyle.

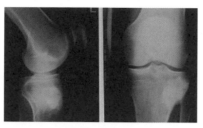

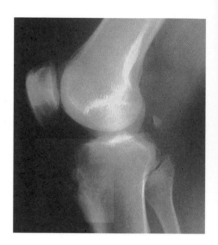

(Source: www.xray2000.co.uk used with permission.)

Costochondritis

Costo-chondritis

Costochondritis is an inflammation of the costal cartilage at its attachment to the sternum. There is no acknowledged cause for this disorder though it may occur after trauma to the chest, after a viral infection, and has sometimes been associated with disease such as fibromyalgia and inflammatory bowel disease (Flowers & Wippermann 2005, Shiel 2006).

Onset of pain and soreness at the sternal margins unilaterally or bilaterally is generally sudden and when the adolescent or young adult is examined (the mean age for presentation is 14 years) there will be specific tenderness over the affected area. This pain is exacerbated by movement, coughing, sneezing and deep inspiration.

Although some authors use the terms costochondritis and Tietze's syndrome interchangeably (Pillinger 2005) others stress that in Tietze's syndrome a slightly older age group is affected and that the syndrome is characterised by swelling of the costosternal margins, whereas this is not the case in costochondritis (Flowers & Wippermann 2005, Shiel 2006).

Presenting symptoms of chest pain that is worse on inspiration and that may follow a history of trauma will prompt the practitioner to exclude other causes for the presentation such as pneumothorax, pulmonary embolism (particularly in the presence of other risk factors), fractures of the ribs or soft tissue chest wall injury or where appropriate a cardiac origin for pain. History taking, observation of the patient and physical examination including auscultation and percussion of the chest will clarify diagnosis.

The management of costochondritis and Tietze's syndrome is similar and involves rest, the administration of analgesia in the form of non-steroidal anti-inflammatory drugs (unless contraindicated) and a gradual return to normal activity. The disease is self-limiting within two to three weeks. Children and their parents and carers may need a great deal of reassurance concerning the prognosis for the condition. Where appropriate the patient should be advised to stop smoking as this will exacerbate symptoms.

Henoch-Schonlein Purpura

Henoch-Schonlein Purpura

Primarily a vascular disorder with musculoskeletal symptoms, Henoch-Schonlein Purpura (HSP) can affect any age group, though 75% of cases occur in children less than 10 years old and it is the most common vasculitic disorder of childhood (Tizard 1999). Although the disease is idiopathic in nature, there is an association with recent viral respiratory tract infection, drug and food allergy and insect bites (Dyne & KesslerDeVore 2006, Bossart 2007). Children presenting with HSP generally complain of:

- Joint pain: particularly involving the knees and ankles (Bossart 2007). Joint symptoms occur in the majority of children and may precede the rash of HSP in some (Kraft *et al.* 1998).

- Rash: this is most evident on the buttocks and the extensor surfaces of the legs and is purpuric in nature (Robinson *et al.* 2005). The rash is also more evident around pressure points such as the waistline, and becomes non-blanching. It is therefore necessary to distinguish HSP from the rash of meningococcal septicaemia (Kraft *et al.* 1998). Parents and carers will need a degree of reassurance where the disease can be isolated as HSP, though where there is any doubt the child should be treated for meningococcal disease.

- Abdominal pain: bleeding into the gut is also a feature of HSP and children may complain of abdominal pain and have malaena stools and haematemesis (Robinson *et al*. 2005, Bossart 2007). In severe cases children may suffer intussusception and associated symptoms of intestinal obstruction (Kraft *et al*. 1998). Bleeding into the scrotum also occurs in some boys and symptoms may mimic testicular torsion (Bossart 2007).

Involvement of the kidneys, evidenced by haematuria and proteinuria is the most pertinent indicator of morbidity in this otherwise self-limiting illness. Children who develop renal problems will need specialist referral and all children with HSP should be screened periodically after discharge for the development of such problems (Kraft *et al*. 1998, Tizard 1999).

Although a small proportion of children develop chronic HSP and some have associated chronic renal problems, the child and their parents or carers may be reassured that most children who suffer HSP have a single episode which resolves in a few weeks with no ongoing problems (Bossart 2007).

Plain x-rays of joints

Plain x-rays of joints may be particularly valuable in establishing diagnosis in musculo-skeletal illness. An x-ray investigation should not however be a substitute for a thorough clinical examination of the child and, in view of the increased sensitivity to the side effects of ionising radiation in childhood, practitioners should have sound clinical justification for requests.

Figure 22.6 *right*

Plain x-ray of the hip in Legg-Calve-Perthe's disease – bony degeneration at the head of the femur.

Figure 22.7 *far right*

Plain x-ray of the hip showing displacement of the epiphysis in slipped femoral epiphysis.

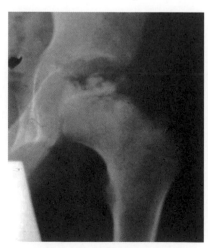

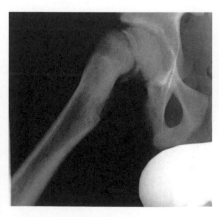

(Source: www.xray2000.co.uk used with permission.)

Red flag signs and symptoms in musculo-skeletal disease

- Night pain
- Unexplained weight loss
- Repeated attendance and/or worsening of symptoms
- Associated systemic ill health and/or fever
- Severe pain.

Chapter 23
Ophthalmic illness

The most common ophthalmic presentations to emergency care involve foreign bodies in the eye or conjunctivitis and children are prone to both of these minor ophthalmic complaints. Before examination of any child with an eye complaint, visual acuity should be estimated using a Snellen's chart.

Foreign bodies in the eye

Foreign bodies in the eye

Children with a corneal foreign body will present with a mildly painful or irritated red eye. Visual acuity assessment should be normal though the child may complain of blurring of vision. History taking may reveal a specific, witnessed episode where a foreign body has entered the eye. Conversely history may not elicit such information, and careful questioning about recent activities should rule out the possibility of a penetrating injury to the eye.

Figure 23.1

Foreign body on the surface of the cornea. In children these should be removed gently with a cotton bud

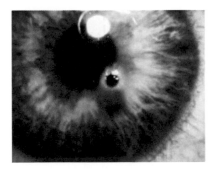

(Source: www.tedmontgomery.com/the_eye, used with permission.)

A great deal of persuasion and negotiation may be needed to gain the co-operation of the child in the assessment of the eye, and this is particularly the case in younger children. The eye should be anaesthetised with a topical preparation and stained with fluorescein. Any foreign body in the eye will then be highlighted green and should be removed gently with a cotton bud. The assistance of parents or carers during this process will be invaluable. Ensure there is not a corneal abrasion associated with the foreign body.

Where there is foreign body sensation but fluorescein staining does not reveal it, then the presence of a corneal abrasion or a sub-tarsal foreign body should be excluded. In order to identify a sub-tarsal foreign body the eyelid will need to be everted. This is best achieved by standing behind the child and asking them to look down. The eyelid should be folded back gently and everted over the shaft of a cotton bud. Remember to revert the lid afterwards!

Where there is the possibility of multiple foreign bodies, for instance when the child has sand blown into their eyes, then sub-tarsal irrigation to facilitate removal of foreign bodies should be undertaken routinely.

A corneal abrasion may mimic the symptoms of a foreign body on the surface of the cornea and will also be highlighted with fluorescein staining. It may have been caused by a foreign body scratching the surface before dislodging. Abrasions may otherwise be caused when the fingernail of a sibling has accidentally scratched the surface or when the child's eye is scratched by thorns and other plant material.

Large corneal abrasions and/or those that present infected may need to be referred for specialist ophthalmic care and at the least their advice about management should be sought. Smaller non-infected abrasions may be treated with chloramphenicol or fusidic acid and arrangements should be made for the child to be reviewed in order to identify any deterioration in condition such as an opportunistic infection.

Usual ophthalmic anaesthetic preparations include Benoxinate and Tetracaine. Allergies should be enquired about before administration. Both of these preparations cease to be effective after 20–25 minutes (Oxford Eye Hospital 2004) and there is therefore no need to pad the eye if treatment has extended beyond this time period.

Conjunctivitis

Conjunctivitis

Conjunctivitis may be infective or allergic in nature. Infective conjunctivitis is further sub-divided into being viral or bacterial in origin.

Allergic conjunctivitis

In addition to a red eye, children with allergic conjunctivitis will also complain of the eye itching. Unlike infective conjunctivitis, discharge from the eye is minimal. Children with allergic conjunctivitis may also have a history of asthma, eczema or hayfever (Prodigy 2006j).

Figure 23.2

Allergic conjunctivitis: note the raised nodules present in allergic conjunctivitis that are not seen in infective conjunctivitis.

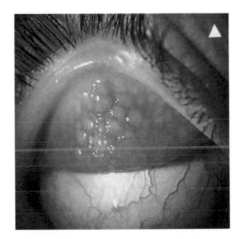

(Reprinted from *Practical Opthalmology*, Anthony Pane & Peter Simcock, 2005, used with permission.)

In the assessment of allergic conjunctivitis, its association with a severe allergic or anaphylactic response to an allergen should be excluded. Treatment involves administration of anti-histamine ophthalmic drops.

Infective conjunctivitis: viral and bacterial

Children with viral conjunctivitis may give a history of having had a viral type illness of the respiratory or ENT system prior to the development of symptoms in the eye. Symptoms will also tend to be bilateral in nature, whereas in bacterial conjunctivitis symptoms generally start in one eye and may spread to the other (where symptoms are unilateral exclude an FB as a focus of the infection). Although there is a discharge associated with both forms of infective conjunctivitis they may be distinguished by the fact that the discharge is clear and watery in viral conjunctivitis but purulent and sticky in the bacterial form. See Table 23.1.

Table 23.1

Characteristics of viral and bacterial conjunctivitis

Characteristics of viral and bacterial conjunctivitis

Characteristic	Viral conjunctivitis	Bacterial conjunctivitis
Discharge	Clear	Purulent and sticky
Onset	Bilateral	Unilateral
Duration	7 days	7–14 days

The potential for corneal penetration and development of pneumonia or meningitis makes the referral of neonates with viral or bacterial conjunctivitis mandatory (Prodigy 2006j). Viral conjunctivitis is otherwise a self-limiting condition that parents and children should be advised will settle in approximately seven days. Analgesia should be recommended for the mild pain associated with the condition and, as both forms of infective conjunctivitis are highly contagious, advice about not sharing hygiene items such as towels with the child should also be given.

After checking for allergy, bacterial conjunctivitis is commonly treated with chloramphenicol or fusidic acid. Recent recommendations however advocate the consideration of delayed prescription when managing bacterial conjunctivitis (Prodigy 2006j). In delayed prescription, patients will be given a prescription for chloramphenicol or fusidic acid but advised only to have the drug dispensed if the condition does not settle spontaneously within a week. Others have found that both bacterial and viral conjunctivitis are self-limiting illnesses that resolve in two to seven days and that antibiotics need not be prescribed in either instance (Sheikh & Hurwitz 2001).

Red flag signs and symptoms in ophthalmic illness

- Any eye infection in a neonate or infant
- Signs of anaphylaxis associated with allergic conjunctivitis
- Any suspicion of penetrating injury
- Reduced visual acuity or loss of vision.

Figure 23.3

The clear, watery discharge associated with viral conjunctivitis.

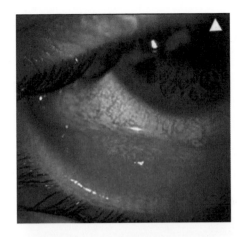

Figure 23.4

Purulent, sticky discharge associated with bacterial conjunctivitis.

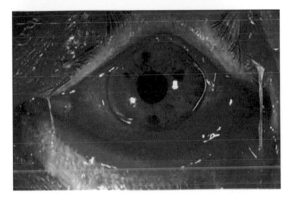

(Reprinted from *Practical Opthalmology*, Anthony Pane & Peter Simcock, 2005, used with permission.)

References

Advanced Life Support Group (2005). *Advanced Paediatric Life Support*. 4th edn. London: BMJ Books.

American Academy of Otolaryngology (2007). *Children and secondhand smoke* [online, accessed 13 February 2007] available from: http://www.entnet.org/healthinfo/tobacco/secondhand_smoke.cfm

American Academy of Paediatrics (2007). *Protecting your child from the sun* [online, accessed 4 May 2007] available from: http://www.aap.org/family/protectsun.htm

American Burn Association (1999) *ABA referral criteria* [online, accessed 24 March 2007] available from: http://www.shrinershq.org/files/hospitals/Cincinnati/pdf/ABA_Referral_Criteria.pdf

Anaphylaxis Australia (2003). *What is anaphylaxis?* [online, accessed 17 March 2007] available from: http://www.allergyfacts.org.au/whatis.html

Anaphylaxis.org.uk (2006). *Anaphylaxis* [online, accessed 16 March 2007] available from: http://www.anaphylaxis.org.uk/

Armon, K., Stephenson, T., Gabriel, V., MacFaul, R., Eccleston, P., Werneke, U. & Smith, S. (2001). 'Audit: Determining the common medical presenting problems to an accident and emergency department' in *Archives of Diseases in Childhood*, 84, 390–392.

Armon, K., Stephenson, T., MacFaul, R., Hemingway, P., Werneke, U. & Smith, S. (2003). 'An evidence and consensus based guideline for the management of a child after a seizure' in *Emergency Medical Journal*, 20, 13–20.

Asthma UK (2004). *Where do we stand?: asthma in the U.K. today* [online, accessed 22 February 2007] available from: http://www.asthma.org.uk/health_professionals/ordering_materials/where_do_we.html

Asthma UK (2007). *Smoking* [online, accessed 23 February 2007] available from: http://www.asthma.org.uk/all-about-asthma/asthma-triggers-az/smoking.html

Auburn, T. & Bethel, J. (2007). 'Hand injuries in children: A reflective case study' in *Emergency Nurse* 14 (9), 30–32.

Australian Prescriber (2002). 'Managing constipation in children' in *Australian Prescriber* 25 (4), 87–90.

Baldry, A. & Winkel, F. (2003). 'Direct and vicarious victimization at school and at home as risk factors for suicidal cognition among Italian adolescents' in *Journal of Adolescence*, 26, 703–716.

Barkin, S., Smith, K. & DuRant, R. (2002). 'Social skills and attitudes associated with substance use behaviors among young adolescents' in *Journal of Adolescent Health*, 30, 448–454.

Barnes, K. (2003). *Paediatrics: A Clinical Guide for Nurse Practitioners*. London: Butterworth-Heinemann.

Barton, E., Colwell, C., Wolfe, T., Fosnocht, D., Gravitz, C., Bryan, T., Dunn, W., Benson, J. & Bailey, J. (2005). 'Efficacy of intranasal naloxone as a needleless alternative for treatment of opioid overdose in the prehospital setting' in *Journal of Emergency Medicine*, 29 (3), 265–271.

Basile, K., Black, M., Simon, T., Arias, I., Brener, N. & Saltzman, L. (2006) 'The association between self-reported lifetime history of forced sexual intercourse and recent health-risk behaviors: Findings from the 2003 National Youth Risk Behavior Survey' in *Journal of Adolescent Health*, 39, 752e1-752e7

Baumer, J.H. and Paediatric Accident and Emergency Research Group (2004). 'Evidence based guideline for post-seizure management in children presenting acutely to secondary care' in *Archives of Disease in Childhood* 89 (3), 278–280.

BBC (2002). *Binge drinking causes rapid damage* [online, accessed 4 April 2007] available from: http://news.bbc.co.uk/1/hi/health/1930417.stm

BBC (2006). *UK youths 'among worst in Europe'* [online, accessed 8 April 2007] available from: http://news.bbc.co.uk/1/hi/uk/6108302.stm

Beattie, J., Gibson, N., Paton, J. & McDevitt, A. (1999). *Emergency Management of Croup* [online, accessed 19 January 2007] available from: http://www.gla.ac.uk/departments/yorkhill/pdf/croup.pdf

Begg, J. (2005). *Accident and Emergency X-Rays Made Easy*. Edinburgh: Churchill Livingstone.

Bell, T. & Millward, J. (1999). 'Women's experiences of obtaining emergency contraception: a phenomenological study' in *Journal of Clinical Nursing*, 8, 601–609.

Benson, B. (2006). *Burns, electrical* [online, accessed 4 November 2007] available from: http://www.emedicine.com/ped/topic2734.htm

Bentley, J. (2004). 'Distress in children attending A&E' in *Emergency Nurse*, 12 (4), 20–26.

Bethel, J. (2006). 'Emergency practice' (letter to the editor) in *Paediatric Nursing*, 18 (10), 8.

Bibbo, C., Lin, S. & Cunningham, F. (2000). 'Acute traumatic compartment syndrome of the foot in children' in *Pediatric Emergency Care*, 16 (4), 244–248.

Blackman, J. (1998). 'Man's best friend?' in *Journal of the American Board of Family Practitioners* 11 (2), 167–169.

Blenner, J. (1991). *Culturally sensitive care* [online, accessed 22 March 2007] available from: http://www.cno.org/docs/prac/41040_CulturallySens.pdf

Bossart, P. (2007). *Henoch-Schonlein purpura* [online, accessed 18 March 2007] available from: http://www.emedicine.com/emerg/topic845.htm

Brick, J. (2005). *Alcohol overdose* [online,accessed 4 April 2007] available from: http://alcoholstudies.rutgers.edu/onlinefacts/od.html

Brilliant, L. (2007). *Fractures, Clavicle* [online, accessed 5 April 2007] available from: http://www.emedicine.com/emerg/topic190.htm

Brindis, C., Llewellyn, L., Marie, K., Blum, M., Biggs, A. & Maternowska, C. (2003). 'Meeting the reproductive health care needs of adolescents: California's family planning access, care, and treatment program' in *Journal of Adolescent Health*, 32S, 79–90.

British Association for Emergency Medicine (2004). *Guideline for the management of pain in children* [online, accessed 4 March 2007] available from:

References

http://www.emergencymed.org.uk/BAEM/CEC/assets/cec_pain_in_children.pdf

British Medical Association (2004). *Doctors' responsibilities in child protection cases*. [online, accessed 2 March 2007] available from: http://www.bma.org.uk/ap.nsf/Content/childprotection

British Medical Journal (2007). *What treatments work for minor burns and scalds?* [online, accessed 3 November 2007] available from: http://besttreatments.bmj.com/btuk/conditions/1000404670.html

British National Formulary (2007). *Meningitis: initial 'blind' therapy* [online, accessed 5 November 2007] available from: http://www.bnf.org/bnf/bnf/54/102038.htm

British National Formulary for Children (2006). *Chlorphenamine maleate* [online, accessed 16 March 2007] available from: http://bnfc.org/bnfc/bnfc/current/3036.htm?q = %22chlorphenamine%22#_hit

British Nutrition Foundation (2004). *Dietary fibre* [online, accessed 14 March 2007] available from: http://www.nutrition.org.uk/upload/Fibre-PDF.pdf

British Thoracic Society (2005). *Asthma guidelines* [online, accessed 26 February 2007] available from: http://www.brit-thoracic.org.uk/iqs/sid.051859406781453942034/49/Guidelinessince%201997_asthma_html

Broomfield, D. & Maconochie, I. (2002). *Role of plain abdominal radiograph in the diagnosis of intussusception* [online, accessed 21 March 2007) available from: http://www.bestbets.org/cgi-bin/bets.pl?record = 00388

Bryant, H. (2007). 'Anaphylaxis: recognition, treatment and education' in *Emergency Nurse*, 15 (2), 24–28

Bryce, J., Boschi-Pinto, C., Shibuya, K., Black, R. & the WHO Child Health Epidemiology Reference Group (2005). 'WHO estimates of the causes of death in children' in *The Lancet* **365** (9465), 1147–1152.

Bui-Mansfield, L. (2005). *Osteochondritis dissecans* [online, accessed 17 March 2007] available from: http://www.emedicine.com/radio/topic495.htm

Bywaters, P. & Rolfe ,A. (2005). *Look Beyond the Scars: Understanding Self-injury and Self-harm*. London: NCH.

Cambridge Consultants (2007). *Taking the tears out of asthma* [online, accessed 22 February 2007] available from: http://www.cambridgeconsultants.com/news_pr96.shtml

Cannell, F. (1990). 'Concepts of parenthood, the Warnock Report, the Gillick Debate and Modern Myths' in *American Ethnologist*, **17** (4), 667–687. Reprinted in Fallon, D. (2003) op. cit.

Cassas, K. & Cassettari-Wayhs, A. (2006). 'Childhood and adolescent sports related overuse injuries' in *American Family Physician*, **73** (6), 1014–1022.

Cerel, J. & Roberts, T. (2005). 'Suicidal behavior in the family and adolescent risk behavior' in *Journal of Adolescent Health*, 36, 352e8–352e14.

Chang, K. (2007). *Osgood-Schlatter disease* [online, accessed 20 October 2007] available from: http://www.emedecine.com/EMERG/topic347.htm

Child Development Institute (2006). *Normal stages of human development (Birth to 5 years)* [online, accessed 24 March 2007] available from: http://www.childdevelopmentinfo.com/development/normaldevelopment.shtml

Christchurch Community Council (1998). *Serving safe food* [online, accessed 5 March 2007] available from: http://www.ccc.govt.nz/Health/serving.asp

Cincinnati Children's Hospital Medical Center (2002). *Evidence based clinical practice guideline for children with acute gastroenteritis (AGE)* [online, accessed 18 January 2007] available from: www.cincinnatichildrens.org

Clinical Knowledge Summaries (2007a). *Bites – Human and Animal* [online, accessed 7 November 2007] available from: http://www.cks.library.nhs.uk/bites_human_and_animal/about_this_topic

Clinical Knowledge Summaries (2007b). *Burns and Scalds, minor* [online, accessed 9 November 2007] available from: http://cks.library.nhs.uk/clinical_summary/burns_and_scalds_minor.pdf

Cole, E. (2003). 'Wound management in the A&E department' in *Nursing Standard*, **17** (46), 45–55.

Conners, G. (2006). *Paediatrics, foreign body ingestion* [online, accessed 19 March 2007] available from: http://www.emedicine.com/emerg/topic379.htm

Craig, S. (2006). *Appendicitis, Acute* [online, accessed 8 March 2007] available from: http://www.emedicine.com/emerg/topic41.htm

Crawford, T., Geraghty, W., Street, K. & Simonoff, E. (2003). 'Staff knowledge and attitudes towards deliberate self-harm in adolescents' in *Journal of Adolescence*, **26**, 619–629.

Davies, F. (2003). *Minor trauma in children*. London: Arnold.

Davies, F (2004). *Spotting the sick child*. DVD. London: Department of Health.

Davies, P. & Benger, J. (2000). 'Foreign bodies in the nose and ear: a review of techniques for removal in the emergency department' in *Emergency Medical Journal*, **17**, 91–94.

Department for Constitutional Affairs (2006). *The UK Statute Law database: The Family Law Reform Act* [online, accessed 24 March 2007] available from: http://www.statutelaw.gov.uk/LegResults.aspx?LegType = All + Primary&Page Number = 57&NavFrom = 2&activeTextDocId = 1277000

Department for Education and Skills (2005). *Teenage Pregnancy* [online, accessed 12 April 2007] available from: http://findoutmore.dfes.gov.uk/2005/08/teenage_pregnan.html

Department of Health (1989). *The Children Act*. London: HMSO.

Department of Health (1990). *Access to health records act* [online, accessed 2 March 2007] available from: http://www.opsi.gov.uk/acts/acts1990/Ukpga_19900023_en_1.htm

Department of Health (2001). *Reforming Emergency Care*. London: HMSO.

Department of Health (2003). *The Victoria Climbie Inquiry* [online, accessed 24 March 2007] available from: http://www.victoria-climbie-inquiry.org.uk/finreport/finreport.htm

Department of Health (2006a). *Direction of travel for urgent care: a discussion document* [online, accessed 24 March 2007] available from: http://www.dh.gov.uk/prod_consum_dh/groups/dh_digitalassets/@dh/@en/documents/digitalasset/dh_4139429.pdf

Department of Health (2006b). *Immunisation against infectious disease – 'the*

green book' [online, accessed 24 March 2007] available from:
http://www.dh.gov.uk/en/Policyandguidance/Healthandsocialcaretopics/Greenbook/Greenbookgeneralinformation/DH_4097254

Donovan, J. (2004). 'Adolescent alcohol initiation: A review of psychosocial risk factors' in *Journal of Adolescent Health*, 35, 529e7–529e18.

Dragos, V., Kecelj, N. & Zgavec, B. (2004). 'Crusted scabies in an 8-year old child' in *Acta Dermatoven APA*, 13 (2), 66–70.

Dube, S., Miller, J., Brown, D., Giles, W., Felitti, V., Dong, M. & Anda, R. (2006). 'Adverse childhood experiences and the association with ever using alcohol and initiating alcohol use during adolescence' in *Journal of Adolescent Health*, 38, 444e1–444e10.

Dunbar, J., Owen, H. & Nogrady, M. (1964).'Obscure tibial fracture of infants: the toddler's fracture' in *Journal of the Canadian Association of Radiologists* 15, 136–144.

Dyne, P. & KesslerDeVore, H. (2006). *Paediatrics, Henoch-Schonlein purpura* [online, accessed 18 March 2007] available from:
http://www.emedicine.com/emerg/topic767.htm

Erkan, T., Çam, H., Özkan, H., Kiray, E., Erginoz, E., Kutlu, T., Tastan, Y. & Çullu, F. (2004). 'Clinical spectrum of acute abdominal pain in Turkish pediatric patients: A prospective study' in *Pediatrics International*, 46, 325–329.

European Burns Association (2007). *European Practice Guidelines for Burn Care* [online, accessed 2 November 2007] available from:
http://www.euroburn.org/download.php

Evans, C. (2005). 'Clinical decision making theories: Patient assessment in A&E' in *Emergency Nurse*, 13 (5), 16–19.

Faculty of Family Planning and Reproductive Health Care (2004). 'Contraceptive choices for young people' in *Journal of Family Planning and Reproductive Health Care*, 30 (4), 237–251.

Fallon, D. (2003). 'Adolescent access to emergency contraception in A and E departments: reviewing the literature from a feminist perspective' in *Journal of Clinical Nursing*, 12, 4–11.

Farthing, M., Feldman, R., Finch, R., Fox, R., Leen, C., Mandal, B., Moss, P., Nathwani, D., Nye, F., Percival, A., Read, R., Ritchie, L., Todd, W., & Wood, M. (1996). 'The management of infective gastroenteritis in adults. A consensus statement by an expert panel convened by the British Society for the Study of Infection' in *Journal of Infection* 33 (3), 143–152.

Fitzgerald, D. & Kilham, H. (2003). *Croup: assessment and evidence based management.* [online, accessed 22 February 2007] available from:
http://www.mja.com.au/public/issues/179_07_061003/fit10207_fm.html

Fitzgerald, D. & Kilham, H. (2004). 'Bronchiolitis: assessment and evidence based management' in *Medical Journal of Australia*, 180 (8), 399–404.

Flowers, L. & Wippermann, B. (2005). *Costochondritis* [online, accessed 21 January 2007] available from: http://www.emedicine.com/emerg/topic116.htm

Galejs, L. & Kass, E. (1999). *Diagnosis and treatment of the acute scrotum* [online, accessed 14 March 2007] available from:
http://www.aafp.org/afp/990215ap/817.html

Gamston, J. (2006). 'Subungual haematomas' in *Emergency Nurse*, 14 (7), 26–34.

Garber, J., Little, S., Hilsman, R. & Weaver, K. (1998). 'Family predictors of suicidal symptoms in young adolescents' in *Journal of Adolescence* 21, 445–457.

Garnefski, N. & Arends, E. (1998). 'Sexual abuse and adolescent maladjustment: differences between male and female victims' in *Journal of Adolescence*, 21, 99–107.

Garnefski, N. & DeWilde, E. (1998). 'Addiction-risk behaviours and suicide attempts in adolescents' in *Journal of Adolescence*, 21, 135–142.

Granier, S., Owen, P., Pill, R. & Jacobson, L. (1998). *Recognising meningococcal disease in primary care: qualitative study of how general practitioners process clinical and contextual information* [online, accessed 20 January 2007] available from: http://www.bmj.com/cgi/content/abstract/316/7127/276

Greene, K., Krcmar, M., Walters, L., Rubin, D. & Hale, J. (2000). 'Targeting adolescent risk-taking behaviors: the contributions of egocentrism and sensation-seeking' in *Journal of Adolescence*, 23, 439–461.

Gruber, E., Thau, H., Hill, D., Fisher, D. & Grube, J. (2005). 'Alcohol, tobacco and illicit substances in music videos: A content analysis of prevalence and genre' in *Journal of Adolescent Health*, 37, 81–83.

Guly, H. (1996). *History Taking, Examination and Record Keeping in Emergency Medicine*. Oxford: Oxford University Press.

Harbison, J. (2001). 'Clinical decision making in nursing: theoretical perspectives and their relevance to practice' in *Journal of Advanced Nursing*, 35 (1), 126–133.

Hartley, V. (2002). 'Paracetamol overdose' in *Emergency Nurse*, 10 (5), 17–24.

Hatch, R. & Hacking, S. (2003). 'Evaluation and management of toe fractures' in *American Family Physician*, 68 (12), 2413–2418.

Healthcare Commission (2007). *Improving services for children in hospital* [online, accessed 24 March 2007] available from: http://www.healthcarecommission.org.uk/_db/_documents/children_improving_services_Tagged.pdf

Health Protection Agency (2003). 'Cluster of cases of tetanus in injecting drug users in England' in *Communicable Disease Report Weekly*, 13, 47–48.

Helman, C. (2007). *Culture, Health and Illness*. 5th edn. London: Hodder-Arnold.

Hettiaratchy, S. & Papini, R. (2004) Initial management of a major burn: II – assessment and resuscitation. in *British Medical Journal*, 329, 101-103

Hockenberry, M. (2004). *Wong's Clinical Manual of Paediatric Nursing*. 6th edn. Missouri USA: Mosby.

Home Office (1998). *Data Protection Act* [online, accessed 2 March 2007] available from: http://www.opsi.gov.uk/ACTS/acts1998/19980029.htm

Huang, R., Palmer, L. & Forbes, D. (2000). 'Prevalence and pattern of childhood abdominal pain in an Australian general practice' in *Journal of Paediatrics and Child Health*, 36, 349–353.

Hudspith, J. & Rayatt, S. (2004). 'First aid and treatment of minor burns' in *British Medical Journal*, 328, 1487–1489.

Joughin, V. (2003). 'Working together for child protection in A&E' in *Emergency Nurse*, 11 (7), 30–37.

Judd, J. & Wright, L. (2005). *Irritable hip: Family information leaflet* [online, accessed 18 March 2007] available from: http://www.suht.nhs.uk/SCH/media/pdf/9/0/IRRITHIP2_1.pdf

Junnila, J. & Cartwright, V. (2006). *Chronic musculoskeletal pain in children* [online, accessed 16 March 2007] available from: http://www.aafp.org/afp/20060701/115.html

Karbakhsh, M. & Zandi, N. (2007). 'Acute opiate overdose in Tehran: the forgotten role of opium' in *Addictive Behaviours,* 32 (9), 1835–1842.

Kellogg, N. (2005). *The evaluation of sexual abuse in children* [online, accessed 1 March 2007] available from: http://pediatrics.aappublications.org/cgi/reprint/116/2/506

Key, J., Washington, C. & Hulsey, T. (2002). 'Reduced emergency department utilization associated with school-based clinic enrollment' in *Journal of Adolescent Health*, 30, 273–278.

King, L. (2006). *Pediatrics, intussusception* [online, accessed 6 March 2007] available from: http://www.emedicine.com/emerg/topic385.htm

Klevan, J.L. and de Jong, A.R. (1990). 'Urinary tract symptoms and urinary tract infection following sexual abuse' in *American Journal of Diseases in Children* 144 (2), 242–244.

Kliewer, W. & Murrelle, L. (2007). 'Risk and protective factors for adolescent substance use: Findings from a study in selected Central American countries' in *Journal of Adolescent Health*, 40 (5), 448–455.

Knutson, D. & Aring, A. (2004). *Viral croup* [online, accessed 19 January 2007] available from: http://www.aafp.org/afp/20040201/535.html

Kokkevi, A., Gabhainn, S., Spyropoulou, M. & the World Health Organisation Risk Behaviour Focus Group of the Health Behaviour in School-aged Children study (2006). 'Early initiation of cannabis use: A cross-national European perspective' in *Journal of Adolescent Health*, 39, 712–719.

Kraft, D., McKee, D. & Scott, C. (1998). *Henoch-Schonlein purpura: a review* [online, accessed 18 March 2007] available from: http://www.aafp.org/afp/980800ap/kraft.html

Labbe, J. (2003). *Determining whether a skin injury could be physical abuse* [online, accessed 16 February 2007] available from: http://www.contemporarypediatrics.com/contpeds/article/articleDetail.jsp?id = 111810

Leet, A. & Skaggs, D. (2000). 'Evaluation of the acutely limping child' in *American Family Physician*, 61 (4), 1011–1026.

Leiner, G., Abramowitz, S., Small, M., Stenby, V. & Lewis, W. (1963). 'Expiratory peak flow rate' in *American Review of Respiratory Disease*, 88, 644, tables reproduced in *Healthcare South* (2001) *Predicted average peak expiratory flow* [online, accessed 26 February 2007] available from: http://www.healthcare-south.com/pages/asthmaaverpeak.htm

Leung, A. & Sigalet, D. (2003). 'Acute abdominal pain in children' in *American Family Physician,* 67 (11), 2321–2326.

Louden, M. (2007). *Pediatrics: Bronchiolitis* [online, accessed 3 November 2007] available from: http://www.emedicine.com/EMERG/topic365.htm

Lund, C.C. & Browder, N.C. (1944) 'Estimation of areas of burns' in *Surgery, Gynecology and Obstetrics*, **79**, 352–358.

Mackle, T. & Conlon, B. (2005). 'Foreign bodies of the nose and ears in children. Should these be managed in the accident and emergency setting?' in *International Journal of Pediatric Otorhinolaryngology*, **70**, 425–428.

Malleson, P. & Beauchamp, R. (2001). *Rheumatology 16: diagnosing musculo-skeletal pain in children* [online, accessed 16 March 2007] available from: http://www.cmaj.ca/cgi/content/full/165/2/183

Manchester Triage Group (2005) *Emergency Triage*. 2nd edn. London: Blackwell Publishing & BMJ Books.

Marano, H., Lin, D. & Schwartz, E. (2006). *Slipped capital femoral epiphysis* [online, accessed 17 March 2007] available from: http://www.emedicine.com/sports/topic122.htm

Marcell, A., Klein, J., Fischer, I., Allan, M. & Kokotailo, P. (2002). 'Male adolescent use of health care services: where are the boys?' in *Journal of Adolescent Health*, **30**, 35–43.

Margo, J., Dixon, M., Pearce, N. & Reed, H. (2006). *Freedom's Orphans: Raising Youth in a Changing World*. London: Institute for Public Policy Research.

Maurice, S., O'Donnell, J. & Beattie, T. (2002). 'Emergency analgesia in the paediatric population. Part 1 current practice and perspectives' in *Emergency Medical Journal*, **19** (1), 4–9.

McCormack, R., La Hei, E. & Martin, H. (2003). 'First-aid management of minor burns in children: a prospective study of children presenting to the Children's Hospital at Westmead, Sydney' in *The Medical Journal of Australia*, **178** (1), 31–33.

McElhatton, P. (1990). 'Paracetamol poisoning in pregnancy: an analysis of the outcomes of cases referred to the teratology information service of the national poisons information service' in *Human and Experimental Toxicology*, **9**, 147–153.

McGee, R. & Williams, S. (2000). 'Does low self-esteem predict health compromising behaviours among adolescents?' in *Journal of Adolescence*, **23**, 569–582.

McLean-Tooke, A., Bethune, C., Fay, A. & Spickett, G. (2003). *Adrenaline in the treatment of anaphylaxis: what is the evidence?* [online, accessed 16 March 2007] available from: http://www.bmj.com/cgi/content/full/327/7427/1332

McNairn, J., Cavanaugh, R. & Rosenbaum, P. (2004). 'Lack of a confidant: an important marker for getting depressed or upset easily and having thoughts of self harm in adolescents' in *Journal of Adolescent Health*, **34** (2), 138–139.

Mellick, L. & Reesor, K. (1990). 'Spiral tibial fractures of children: A commonly accidental spiral long bone fracture' in *American Journal of Emergency Medicine*, **8**, 234–237.

Meningitis Research Foundation (2006). *Early management of meningococcal disease in children* [online, accessed 20 January 2007] available from: http://www.meningitis.org/health-professionals

Mental Health Foundation (2006). *Truth Hurts: Report of the National Inquiry into Self-harm among Young People.* London: The Mental Health Foundation.

Merkel, S., Voepel-Lewis, T., Shayevitz, J. & Malviyas, R. (1997). 'The FLACC: A behavioural scale for scoring postoperative pain in young children' in *Paediatric Nursing,* 23 (3), 293–297.

Morgan, M. (2005). 'Hospital management of animal and human bites' in *Journal of Hospital Infection,* 61 (1), 1–10.

Morgan, P. & Palmer, J. (2007). 'Dog bites' in *British Medical Journal* 334 (7590), 413–417.

Moses, S. (2007). *Patellofemoral syndrome* [online, accessed 17 March 2007] available from: http://www.fpnotebook.com/ORT257.htm

Munter, D. (2005). *Foreign bodies, trachea* [online, accessed 19 March 2007] available from: http://www.emedicine.com/EMERG/topic751.htm

National Institute for Health and Clinical Excellence (2001). *Referral advice* [online, accessed 21 February 2007] available from: http://www.nice.org.uk/page.aspx?o = ReferralAdvice

National Institute for Health and Clinical Excellence (2003). *Head injury: triage, assessment, investigation and early management of head injury in infants, children and adults* [online, accessed 3 March 2007] available from: http://www.nice.org.uk/guidance/CG4/guidance/pdf/English

National Institute for Health and Clinical Excellence (2007a). *Feverish Illness in Children: Assessment and Initial Management in Children Younger than 5 years.* London: National Institute for Health and Clinical Excellence.

National Institute for Health and Clinical Excellence (2007b). *Feverish illness: assessment and initial management in children younger than five years of age: 1st draft* [online, accessed 21 February 2007] available from: http://www.nice.org.uk/page.aspx?o – 388165

National Institute for Health and Clinical Excellence (2007c). *Head injury: Triage, assessment, investigation and early management of head injury in infants, children and adults* [online, accessed 21 October 2007] available from: http://guidance.nice.org.uk/CG56/guidance/pdf/English

National Institute for Health and Clinical Excellence (2007d). *Urinary tract infection in children: Diagnosis, treatment and long-term management* [online, accessed 3 November 2007] available from: http://www.nice.org.uk/guidance/index.jsp?action = byID&o = 11819

National Society for the Prevention of Cruelty to Children (2006). *What is child abuse?* [online, accessed 2 March 2007] available from: http://www.nspcc.org.uk/helpandadvice/whatchildabuse/whatischildabuse_wda 36500.html

Nochimson, G. (2006). *Legg-Calve-Perthes disease* [online, accessed 17 March 2007] available from: http://www.emedicine.com/emerg/topic294.htm

Noffsinger, M. (2004). *Sever disease* [online, accessed 23 March 2007] available from: http://www.emedicine.com/orthoped/topic622.htm

Nursing and Midwifery Council (2004). *The NMC code of professional conduct: standards for conduct, performance and ethics* [online, accessed 2 March 2007] available from: http://www.nmc-uk.org/aFrameDisplay.aspx?DocumentID = 201

Paediatric minor emergencies

Nursing and Midwifery Council (2005). *Guidelines for records and record keeping* [online, accessed 2 March 2007] available from: http://www.nmc-uk.org/aFrameDisplay.aspx?DocumentID = 1120

Office for National Statistics (2005). *Health statistics quarterly* [online, accessed 12 April 2007] available from: http://www.statistics.gov.uk/downloads/theme_health/HSQ26.pdf

Offringa, M. & Moyer, V. (2001). 'Evidence based paediatrics: evidence based management of seizures associated with fever' in *British Medical Journal*, 323, 1111–1114.

Oon, S. (2005). '"Nintendo-isation": Sedentary lifestyles, obesity and increasing health problems including type 2 diabetes in modern day children and adolescents' in *Trinity Student Medical Journal*, 5, 21–24.

Owens, D., Horrocks, J. & House, A. (2002). 'Fatal and non-fatal repetition of self-harm: Systematic review' in *British Journal of Psychiatry*, 181, 193–199.

Oxford Eye Hospital (2004). *Installation of eye drops: Benoxinate* [online, accessed 21 March 2007] available from: http://www.oxfordeyehospital.nhs.uk/documents/leaflets/eyedrops_benox.pdf

Paediatric Society of New Zealand (2005). *Wheeze and chest infection in infants under one year* [online, accessed 3 November 2007] available from http://www.paediatrics.org.nz/documents/2005 % 20documents % 20denise/guidelines/Wheezeendorsed.pdf

Painter, D., Trevillion, N. & Snape, T. (2007). 'Staphylococcal scalded skin syndrome' in *Emergency Nurse*, 14 (10), 20–21.

Pane, A. & Simcock, P. (2005). *Practical Opthalmology*. London: Elsevier.

Parmar, R., Sahu, D. & Bavdekar, S. (2001). 'Knowledge, attitude and practices of parents of children with febrile convulsion' in *Journal of Postgraduate Medicine*, 47 (1), 19–23.

Patientplus (2004).*Croup* [online, accessed 22 February 2007] available from http://www.patient.co.uk/about.asp

Pillinger, J. (2005). *Costochondritis (Tietze's syndrome)* [online, accessed 18 March 2007] available from: http://www.netdoctor.co.uk/diseases/facts/costochondritis.htm

Pollard, A. & Cronin, G. (2005). 'Compression bandaging for soft tissue injury of the ankle: A literature review' in *Emergency Nurse*, 13 (6), 20–25.

Prescott, L. (1983). 'Paracetamol overdosage: Pharmacological considerations and clinical management' in *Drugs* 25, 29–34.

Prince, I. (2000). 'Reduction in incidence of severe paracetamol poisoning' in *The Lancet* 355, 2047–2048.

Prodigy (2006a). *Prodigy guidance: Febrile convulsion* [online, accessed 17 February 2007] available from: http://cks.library.nhs.uk/febrile_convulsion/extended_information/management_issues

Prodigy (2006b). *Prodigy guidance: sore throat, acute* [online, accessed 18 January 2007] available from http://www.prodigy.nhs.uk/sore_throat_acute

Prodigy (2006c). *Prodigy guidance: otitis media* [online, accessed 18 January 2007] available from: http://www.prodigy.nhs.uk/otitis_media_acute

Prodigy (2006d). *Prodigy guidance: gastroenteritis* [online, accessed 3 March 2007] available from: http://www.prodigy.nhs.uk/gastroenteritis

Prodigy (2006e). *Prodigy guidance: urinary tract infection-children* [online, accessed 3 March 2007] available from: http://cks.library.nhs.uk/urinary_tract_infection_children

Prodigy (2006f). *Prodigy guidance: constipation* [online, accessed 14 March 2007] available from: http://cks.library.nhs.uk/constipation

Prodigy (2006g). *Prodigy guidance: impetigo* [online, accessed 13 March 2007] available from: http://www.prodigy.nhs.uk/impetigo

Prodigy (2006h). *Prodigy guidance: herpes simplex-oral* [online, accessed 15 March 2007] available from: http://www.prodigy.nhs.uk/herpes_simplex_oral

Prodigy (2006i). *Prodigy guidance: scabies* [online, accessed 16 March 2007] available from: http://www.prodigy.nhs.uk/scabies

Prodigy (2006j). *Prodigy guidance: conjunctivitis* [online, accessed 22 March 2007] available from: http://www.prodigy.nhs.uk/conjunctivitis_infective

Prodigy (2006k). *Prodigy guidance: contraception - emergency* [online, accessed 21 January 2007] available from: http://www.cks.library.nhs.uk/contraception_emergency

Raby, N., Berman, L. & de Lacey, G. (1995). *Accident and Emergency Radiology: A Survival Guide*. London: Elsevier.

Rasquin-Weber, A., Hyman, P.F. & Cucchiara, S. (1999). 'Childhood functional gastrointestinal disorders' in *Gut*, 45, 1160–1168.

Resnick, R. & Hergenroeder, E. (1975). 'Children in the emergency room' in *Children Today*, Sept-Oct, 5–8.

Resuscitation Council (2008) *Emergency Treatment of Anaphylactic reactions* [online, accessed 4th May 2008] London: Resuscitation Council. Available from: http://www.resus.org.uk/pages/reaction.pdf

Robinson, J., Spady, D., Prasad, E., McColl, D. & Artsob, H. (2005). *Bartonella seropositivity in children with Henoch-Schonlein purpura* [online, accessed 18 March 2007] available from: http://www.pubmedcentral.nih.gov/articlerender.fcgi?artid = 1274276

Rodham, K., Hawton, K., Evans, E. & Weatherall, R. (2005). 'Ethnic and gender differences in drinking, smoking and drug taking among adolescents in England:a self-report school-based survey of 15 and 16 year olds' in *Journal of Adolescence*, 28, 63–73.

Royal Children's Hospital of Melbourne (2006). *Clinical Practice Guidelines: cervical spine* [online, accessed 21 October 2007] available from: http://www.rch.org.au/clinicalguide/cpg.cfm?doc_id = 5167

Royal College of Nursing (1999). *The Recognition and Assessment of Acute Pain in Children*. London: Royal College of Nursing.

Royal College of Nursing (2006). *Transcultural healthcare practice* [online, accessed 21 July 2006] available from: http://www.rcn.org.uk/resources/transcultural

Royal College of Paediatrics and Child Health (RCPCH) (1999). *Accident and Emergency Services for Children: A Report of a Multidisciplinary Working Party*. London: RCPCH.

Paediatric minor emergencies

Royal College of Paediatrics and Child Health (RCPCH) (2002). *Children's attendance at a minor injury/illness service (MIS)* [online, accessed 2 March 2007] available from: http://www.rcpch.ac.uk/publications/recent_publications/MIS.pdf

Royal College of Paediatrics and Child Health (RCPCH) (2007). *Services for Children in Emergency Departments*. London: RCPCH.

Rupp, T. & Zwanger, M. (2006). *Testicular torsion* [online, [accessed 14 March 2007] available from: http://www.emedicine.com/emerg/topic573.htm

Sadovsky, R. (2003). *Recurrent fevers in children: differential diagnosis* [online, accessed 14 February 2007] available from: http://www.aafp.org/afp/20030215/tips/25.html

Salisbury, D. & Begg, N. (eds) (1996). *Immunisation against Infectious Disease*. London: HMSO.

Salter, R. & Harris, W. (1963). 'Injuries involving the epiphyseal plate' in *Journal of Bone and Joint Surgery*, 45, 587–632.

Samaritans (2005). *Self-harm and suicide* [online, accessed 31 March 2007] available from: http://www.samaritans.org.uk/know/information/information-sheets/selfharm/selfharm_sheet.shtm#overview

Sanderlin, B. & Raspa, R. (2003). 'Common stress fractures' in *American Family Physician*, 68 (8), 1527–1532.

Sandin, B., Chorot, P., Santed, M., Valiente, R. & Joiner, T. (1998). 'Negative life events and adolescent suicidal behavior: a critical analysis from the stress process perspective' in *Journal of Adolescence*, 21, 415–426.

Schering (2007). *What will the pharmacist ask me?* [online, accessed 13 April 2007] available from: http://www.levonelle.co.uk/output/Page1.asp

Scottish Intercollegiate Guidelines Network (2006). *Bronchiolitis in children, a national clinical guideline.* [online, accessed 3 November 2007] available from: http://www.sign.ac.uk/pdf/sign91.pdf

Sersar, S., Rizk, W., Bilal, M., El-Diasty, M., Eltantawy, T., Abdelhakam, B., Elgamal, A. & Abou Bieh, A. (2006). 'Inhaled foreign bodies: presentation, management, and value of history and plain chest radiography in delayed presentation' in Otolaryngology – *Head and Neck Surgery,* 134, 92–99.

Shaw, J. (2006). *Management of burns blisters* [online, accessed 3 November 2007] available from: http://www.bestbets.org/cgi-bin/bets.pl?record = 00435

Sheikh, A. & Hurwitz, B. (2001). 'Topical antibiotics for acute bacterial conjunctivitis: a systematic review' in *British Journal of General Practice*, 51, 473–477.

Shiel, W. (2006). *Costochondritis & Tietze syndrome* [online, accessed 18 March 2007] available from: http://www.medicinenet.com/costochondritis_and_tietze_syndrome/article.htm

Sieving, R., Perry, C. & Williams, C. (2000). 'Do friendships change behaviors, or do behaviors change friendships? Examining paths of influence in young adolescents' alcohol use' in *Journal of Adolescent Health*, 26, 27–35.

Smith, M. (2003). 'Ankle sprain: A literature search' in *Emergency Nurse*, 11 (3), 12–16.

Social Exclusion Unit (1999). *Report on teenage pregnancy* [online, accessed 12 April 2007] available from:

http://www.dfes.gov.uk/teenagepregnancy/dsp_content.cfm?pageID = 87

Solan, M., Rees, R. & Daly, K. (2002). 'Current management of Torus fractures of the distal radius' in *Injury*, 33 (6), 503–505.

Stiell, I., Greenberg, G. & McKnight, R. (1993). 'Decision rules for the use of radiography in acute ankle injuries' in *Journal of the American Medical Association*, 271, 827–832.

Strozuk, S., Golden, N., Fisher, M., Seigel, W., O'Donnell, L., Saxena, H., Suss, A. & Swedler, J. (2005). 'Pediatric residents' knowledge, attitudes and opinions about emergency contraception' in *Journal of Adolescent Health*, 36 (2), 134–135.

Stump, J. (2006). *Bites, Animal* [online, accessed 4 March 2007] available from http://www.emedicine.com/emerg/topic60.htm

Talley, N.J., Jones, M., Nuyts, G. and Dubois, D. (2003). 'Risk factors for chronic constipation based on a general practice sample' in *American Journal of Gastroenterology* 98 (5), 1107–1111.

Tapert, S., Aarons, G., Sedlar, G. & Brown, S. (2001). 'Adolescent substance use and sexual risk-taking behavior' in *Journal of Adolescent Health*, 28, 181–189.

Teasdale, G. & Jennett, B. (1974). 'Assessment of coma and impaired consciousness. A practical scale' in *The Lancet*, 13 (2), 81–84.

Tenenbein, M., Reed, M. & Black, G. (1990). 'The toddler's fracture revisited' in *American Journal of Emergency Medicine*, 8, 208–211.

Tizard, E. (1999). 'Henoch-Schonlein purpura' in *Archives of Diseases in Childhood*, 80 (4), 380–383.

Todd, K., Samaroo, N. & Hoffman, J. (1993). *Ethnicity as a risk factor for inadequate emergency department analgesia.* [online, accessed 21 July 2007] available from: http://jama.ama-assn.org/cgi/content/abstract/269/12/1537

Todd, K., Deaton, C., D'Adamo, A. & Goe, L. (2000). 'Ethnicity and analgesic practice' in *Annals of Emergency Medicine*, 35, 11–16.

Trakas, D. & Sanz, E. (1996). *Childhood and Medicine Use in a Cross-cultural Perspective: A European Concerted Action.* Luxembourg: European Commission Directorate-General XII Science, Research and Development.

Tsirigotou, S. (1993). *Acute and chronic pain resulting from burn injuries* [online, accessed 24 March 2007] available from: http://www.medbc.com/annals/review/vol_6/num_1/text/vol6n1p11.htm

Tzanakis, N., Efstathiou, S., Danulidis, K., Rallis, G., Tsioulos, D., Chatzivasiliou, A., Peros, G. & Nikiteas, N. (2005). 'A new approach to accurate diagnosis of acute appendicitis' in *World Journal of Surgery*, 29 (9), 1151–1156.

Udry, R. & Chantala, K. (2002). 'Risk assessment of adolescents with same-sex relationships' in *Journal of Adolescent Health*, 31, 84–92.

UNICEF (2007). *Child poverty in perspective: An overview of child well-being in rich countries* [online, accessed 8 April 2007] available from http://www.unicef-icdc.org/presscentre/presskit/reportcard7/rc7_eng.pdf

University of Leeds (2007). *AAP help: decision support in acute abdominal pain* [online, accessed 1 March 2007] available from: http://www.media-innovations.ltd.uk/AAP.htm

University of Michigan Health System (2003). *Functional constipation and soiling in children. Guidelines for Clinical Care.*[online, accessed 14 March 2007]

available from: http://cme.med.umich.edu

Uslu Coskun, B., Sozen, E., Unsal, O. & Dadas, B. (2006). *Ear, nose and upper gastrointestinal system foreign bodies in children.* [online, accessed 19 March 2007] available from:
http://www.turkarchotolaryngol.org/v44/v44n2e/v44n2e01p077.htm

Van Beurden, E., Zask, A., Brooks, L. & Dight, R. (2005). 'Heavy episodic drinking and sensation seeking in adolescents as predictors of harmful driving and celebrating behaviors: implications for prevention' in *Journal of Adolescent Health,* 37, 37–43.

Victoria Department of Human Services (2007) *Evidence based practice guideline for the management of croup in children* [online] Victoria, Australia, Department of Human services [accessed 5 November 2007] available from:
http://www.mihsr.monash.org/hfk/pdf/hfkcroupguideline.pdf

Warner-Smith, M., Darke, S., Lynskey, M. & Hall, W. (2001). 'Heroin overdose: causes and consequences' in *Addiction,* 96, 1113–1125.

Waruiru, C. & Appleton, R. (2004). 'Febrile seizures: an update' in *Archives of Diseases in Childhood,* 89 (3), 751–756.

Westley, C.R., Cotton, E.K. & Brooks, J.G. (1978). 'Nebulized racemic epinephrine by IPPB for the treatment of croup: a double-blind study' in *American Journal of Diseases in Childhood* 132, 484–487 in Patientplus (2004) op. cit.

Wheeless, C. (2007a). *Monteggia fractures in children* [online, accessed 7 November 2007] available from:
http://www.wheelessonline.com/ortho/monteggia_fractures_in_children

Wheeless, C. (2007b). *Galeazzi's fractures in children*
[online, accessed 7th November 2007] available from:
http://www.wheelessonline.com/ortho/galeazzis_fracture_in_children

Wong, D. & Baker, C. (1988). 'Pain in children: comparison of assessment scales' in *Pediatric Nursing,* 14, 9–17.

World Health Organisation (1993). *The Treatment of Diarrhoea: Practical Guidelines.* 3rd edn. Geneva: World Health Organisation.

World Health Organisation (2004). *Meningococcal disease* [online, accessed 16 March 2007] available from: http://www.who.int/csr/disease/meningococcal/en/

Young, S., Barnett, P. & Oakley, E. (2005a). *Bruising, abrasions and lacerations: minor injuries in children 1* [online, accessed 2 March 2007] available from:
http://www.mja.com.au/public/issues/182_11_060605/you10513_fm.html

Young, S., Barnett, P. & Oakley, E. (2005b). *Fractures and minor head injuries: minor injuries in children II* [online, accessed 2 March 2007] available from:
http://www.mja.com.au/public/issues/182_12_200605/you10261_fm.html

Zola, I. (1966). 'Culture and symptoms: an analysis of patients' presenting complaints' in *American Sociological Review,* 31, 615–630.

Zoucha, R. (1998). 'Understanding the significance of culture in emergency care and treatment' in *Topics in Emergency Medicine,* 20 (4), 40–51.

Zullig, K., Valois, R., Huebner, S., Oeltmann, J. & Drane, W. (2001). 'Relationship between perceived life satisfaction and adolescents' substance abuse' in *Journal of Adolescent Health,* 29, 279–288.

Index

abbreviations, medical 79
abdominal pain 139, 142, 175-182, 188, 195, 196, 206
abuse of children see child abuse
Access to Health Records Act 78
adolescents, care of 45-58, 71, 114
Advanced Life Support Group 81, 149
advocacy, child 26-27
airway obstruction and swelling 126, 127, 145-147, 152, 155, 172
alcohol and drug abuse in children and teenagers 45, 46, 47, 51-54
allergic reactions 50, 56, 61, 193-196, 198, 205, 210, 211, 212
amnesia 83, 87, 88
amputation 104
anaesthesia 75, 97, 99, 110, 111, 127, 131, 133, 162, 168, 172, 173, 209, 210
analgesia see pain relief
anaphylaxis 50, 157, 159, 160, 163, 193-196, 198, 211, 213
ankle injuries 109, 111-113, 118
animal bites 106-107, 109
antibiotics 61, 105, 106-107, 110, 111, 131, 135, 141, 152, 159, 164, 171, 181, 182, 183, 190, 193, 197, 198, 212
anxiety, parental 89, 92, 144, 153, 160, 168
apnoea 170
apophysis, paediatric 114, 115
appendicitis 178-179, 188
appetite, loss of 178, 179, 182
arm slings, use of 92, 93, 94, 100
arthritis, juvenile 200, 201
asthma 140, 141, 144, 155, 165-169, 211
attention deficit disorder 184
autism 184
AVPU coma scoring tool 86-87, 146
avulsion fractures 95, 112, 113, 114, 118, 121, 203

bacterial tracheitis 160, 162
Battle's sign 85
binge drinking 52
bleeding
    from the ears 90
    from the rectum 177
blood pressure, checking 149, 197

blood sampling 142, 178
bowel disorders 176, 177, 180
brachial plexus injuries 92
brain injury 84
breathing support 54
British Association for Emergency Medicine 29, 132
British Medical Association 37
British Thoracic Society 166, 167, 168
bronchiolitis 169-171
bruising 42
bullying 47, 48
burns and scalds 42, 60, 123-135

capitellum 96, 98
cellulitis 189, 191, 192
cerebral bleeding 84
cerebrospinal fluid, leakage of 85, 90
chemical burns 127, 131
child abuse 2, 27, 38-44, 47, 51, 57, 78, 88, 89, 91, 115-116, 129, 157
child protection 1, 37-44, 182
Children Act (1989) 23
children's experience of emergency care 13-16, 21-22, 26-27, 65, 168-169
circulation, assessing 146
clavicle injuries 91-93, 99, 118
clinical examination 69-79, 116, 139-140, 207
    in head injury cases 84-89
Colles fracture 91, 118
comfort, patient 32, 70
communication skills 9, 21-23, 33, 69-72, 167
confidentiality, patient 78
conjunctivitis 209, 211-213
consciousness, assessing level of 146-147, 162
consent, patient 23-24
constipation 175, 178, 184-186
contraception, emergency 55-58
costochondritis 204-205
cranial surgery 89
croup 159-163
crush injuries 104, 106, 114, 122
CT scanning 81, 83, 85
cultural needs, patients' diverse 34-35
cystic fibrosis 184

Paediatric minor emergencies

Data Protection Act 78
defining minor illnesses 139
defining minor injuries 65–67
dehydration 180–181, 184, 185
dermatological conditions 139, 142, 189–198
developmental stages in children 22, 24, 33, 40, 41, 71, 73, 81, 82, 94–95
diabetes 106, 159, 181, 182
diagnostic decision making 143–144, 177
diagnosis 69–75, 145, 160, 167, 170, 175, 177, 178–179, 187, 189, 204
diarrhoea 128, 141, 175, 178, 179–181
diphtheria 160
discharge, hospital 59–61, 103, 135, 152, 153, 162, 168
    in head injury cases 88, 89–90
distraction therapy 32–33, 102, 133
documentation as part of clinical examination 72, 75–79, 119
drink driving 52
drowsiness, abnormal 83, 90, 152
drug and alcohol abuse in children and teenagers 45, 46, 47, 51–54

ear infections 147, 151, 152, 163–165, 175
E. coli 179, 182
eczema 190, 211
elbow injuries 91, 93, 100, 101–103
electrical burns 129–130, 131
emotional abuse of children 42, 43
encephalopathy 51
ENT conditions 139, 147, 155–165, 171–173, 211
epicondyle, fractures of the internal 95
epididymitis 187
epiglottis 160, 162
epilepsy 153
epiphysis, femoral 201–202, 203, 207

Faculty of Family Planning and Reproductive Health Care 57
Family Law Reform Act (1969) 23
fears, children's 13–16, 21–22, 26–27, 33, 40, 59, 65, 75, 169
febrile convulsion 60, 141, 151–153
fever 157, 159, 160, 162, 163, 165, 170, 175, 179, 181, 182, 184, 186, 187, 198, 199, 207
fingertip injuries 104
first aid 70, 132
FLACC assessment tool 30, 31
foot injuries 109–111
forearm injuries 100, 101
foreign bodies 160, 171–173, 199, 209–210
Fowler's position 156, 159, 169
fractures 41, 42, 83, 84, 85, 88, 91–101, 112–116, 118–122, 129, 203
Fraser competence 23, 57

Galeazzi fracture-dislocation 99
gastroenteritis 151, 175, 178, 179–182
gastro-intestinal illnesses 65, 141
genito-urinary disorders 139, 151, 177, 182–184, 186–188
Glasgow Coma Score 83, 85, 87, 88, 147, 152
greenstick type fractures 99
growth plate injuries 112, 114, 117, 119, 120–122

haemotomas 84, 105
hayfever 211
head injuries 53, 60, 61, 81–90, 129, 144
headaches 89, 90
Healthcare Commission 1
hearing problems 164, 173, 197
Henoch-Schonlein Purpura 205–206
herpes simplex virus 191–192
history taking 9, 39, 53, 65, 67, 69–74, 102, 117, 118, 119, 122, 139–143, 152, 158, 160, 167, 172, 175, 176, 180, 182, 187, 190, 193, 199, 205
    in head injuries 82-83, 85, 87-88
    in lower limb injuries 109, 111, 112, 115, 209
homosexual teenagers 47, 48
humerus, fractured neck of 91
hypoglycaemia 51, 53
hypotension 51, 195, 197

ice therapy 114
infections 106–107, 131, 134, 135, 151, 155, 157–159, 163–165, 173, 175, 178, 179, 182, 190–192, 200, 203, 210, 213

inflammatory bowel disease *180, 204*

immunisation *87, 107, 131, 151, 153, 157, 175*

impetigo *190–191*

Institute for Public Policy *45*

ischaemia *93, 186*

jargon, medical *77, 78–79*

kidney problems *50, 206*

Legg-Calve-Perthe's disease *201, 202, 203, 207*

life support, paediatric *1, 3*

limping *199–203*

litigation *76, 77, 79*

liver damage *49, 50, 51, 53, 56*

location, terms of *9–10*

loss of consciousness *85, 87, 88, 90*

lower limb injuries *109–116, 118*

male adolescents, particular problems of *46, 47, 51*

malignancy *199, 200, 201, 203*

Manchester Triage Group *67, 146, 148*

media portrayals of emergency care *13*

medication, cultural perceptions of *35*

medication, pain relief *29, 31–32, 33*

meningococcal disease *70, 82, 141, 142, 151, 152, 158, 190, 197–198, 205, 206, 212*

Mental Health Foundation *48*

minor injuries, defining *65*

Monteggia fracture-dislocation *97–98*

motor function *75*

movement, terms associated with *10–11*

musculo-skeletal conditions *139, 199–207*

nail injuries *105*

National Institute for Health and Clinical Excellence *81, 83, 84, 88, 90, 147, 148, 183*

National Society for the Prevention of Cruelty to Children *38, 40, 41, 44*

neck immobilisation *84, 85, 87*

negative attitudes towards adolescent patients *46, 47, 55, 56*

neurovascular status, checking *93, 94, 97, 99, 106, 110, 111, 130*

NHS Direct *66, 89, 135, 153, 159, 168, 181*

NHS *24 66, 89, 135, 159, 168, 181*

note-taking *72, 75–79*

nursery nurses *16, 18, 33*

Nursing and Midwifery Council *37, 76, 77, 79*

oedema *189, 195, 196*

opiate poisoning *53–54*

opthalmic conditions *209–213*

orthopaedic treatment *92, 97, 101, 116*

Osgood-Schlatters disease *203, 204*

ossification of bones *94, 117, 121*

Ottawa ankle and foot rules *112–113, 119*

overdose, treatment for *49*

paediatric coma scoring tool *86*

panda's eyes *85*

pain relief *29–35, 60, 61, 70, 75–76, 84, 87, 88, 89, 92, 94, 97, 100, 104, 105, 110, 111, 114, 115, 132, 135, 144, 164, 177, 178, 182, 187, 200, 205, 212*

palpation *74, 75, 84, 146, 176*

paracetamol poisoning *48–51*

parachute reflex *73, 81*

parental anxiety *89, 90*

parental responsibility *23–26, 66, 91*

parents and carers, role of *69–70, 82, 89, 172, 173, 196, 197, 210*

parent-child relationships *45*

peritonitis *176, 178*

pharyngitis *156, 175*

physical examination *9, 15, 39, 65, 67, 75–76, 82, 117, 119, 122, 142, 152, 167, 175–176, 180, 199, 200, 205*
    in elbow injuries *102*
    in head injuries *84–89*
    in lower limb injuries *109–110, 111, 112, 115*

physical environment for young patients *33–34*

physiotherapy *204*

plasma concentration *49*

plaster casts, use of *94, 97, 99, 100, 101, 112, 116*

play areas *3*

play therapy *16, 32–33*

popular culture, influence of *52*

pneumonia *158, 175, 212*

pregnancy *45, 51*

Paediatric minor emergencies

pre-hospital care of children *17–19, 66, 87*

pre-hospital practitioners *17–19, 127*

psoriasis *190*

pyelonephritis *182*

pyrexial illnesses *65*

radiation, side effects of *117, 122*

radiation burns *128–129*

radius *97, 98, 99*

rashes, skin 1*57, 189-190, 193, 197–198, 205, 206*

reassuring children *13, 14, 18, 33, 97, 111, 159, 160, 168–169, 205*

reassuring parents *153, 159, 160, 168–169, 177, 205, 206*

registered sick children's nurses *16*

rehydration therapy *181*

respiratory function, checking *143, 145–146, 157, 160*

respiratory illnesses *65, 139, 140, 142, 147, 151, 155, 156, 165–171, 175, 178, 211*

risk management *2*

Royal Children's Hospital of Melbourne *83, 84*

Royal College of Nursing *30, 31*

Royal College of Paediatrics and Child Health *1, 2, 3, 17, 19, 46, 65, 131*

safety (of practitioners) *127*

Salter-Harris fractures *112, 118, 120–122*

scabies *192–193*

scalp lacerations *84*

scarring *60*

sedation *75*

self-harm *40, 43, 46, 47, 48, 55*

sensory innervation *75*

separate paediatric services *3*

severe illness, recognising *139, 142, 145–149*

sexual abuse of children *41, 43, 47, 48, 57, 157, 159, 175, 182, 184, 192*

sexual behaviour of teenagers *45, 52, 54–58*

sexual health clinics *57, 58*

sexually transmitted disease *157*

shingles *189*

sickle cell anaemia *175*

sinusitis *175*

skull fractures *83, 84, 85, 88*

slap marks *42*

smoking *51, 155–156, 163, 167, 170–171, 205*

Social Exclusion Unit *54*

social workers *44*

soft tissue injuries *59, 60, 65*

spinal conditions *200*

spinal cord injuries *81, 84, 87*

splinting *94, 101*

steroids *171*

stool, blood in the *180, 181, 206*

suicide in children and teenagers *47, 48*

supracondylar fractures *91, 93–97, 118, 122*

suture removal *61*

synovitis *200, 201, 202, 203*

teenage pregnancy *45, 54–58, 177*

temperature, checking a child's *147*

tendon injuries *106, 113, 115*

testicular torsion *186-188, 206*

tetanus *107, 111, 131, 160*

therapeutic relationships *14, 22, 48, 61, 135*

thermal burns *123, 124–127*

three-minute toolkit *145–147*

throat infections *147, 156, 158–159, 160*

toddler's fracture *115–116, 201*

tonsillitis *147, 151, 156, 158*

Torus facture *91, 99–101, 116, 118*

training needs for paediatric emergency care staff *4, 19, 33, 46, 48, 117*

triage nomenclature *66*

ulnar fractures *97, 98, 99*

ultrasound *179, 183, 203*

underage sex *45, 54–58*

unsafe sex *52*

UNICEF *45, 46*

upper limb injuries *91–107, 118*

urinalysis *142, 143, 152, 177, 182, 183, 187*

urinary tract infections *151, 177, 182-184*

vascular disorders *205–206*
vascular status *75*
vertigo *164, 165*
violent behaviour in children and
    teenagers *45*
Volkmann's ischaemic contracture *93*
vomiting *83, 87, 89, 90, 128, 157, 162,
    164, 165, 175, 177, 178, 181, 182,
    184, 185, 195, 196*

Wong-Baker smiley faces scale *30*
wound care *60, 61, 106–107, 110, 134*
wrist injuries *101, 118*

x-ray interpretation *95, 96, 97, 98, 100,
    109, 112, 114, 115, 116, 119–122,
    188, 207*
x-ray investigation *15, 33, 92, 93, 94,
    100, 102, 106, 110, 112–114, 118,
    143, 172, 177, 188, 201, 203, 207*
x-rays, requesting *117–119, 177, 188,
    207*